Nikon D3100

Simon Stafford

MAGIC LANTERN GUIDES®

Nikon D3100

Simon Stafford

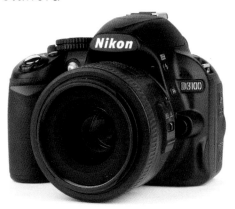

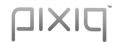

An Imprint of Sterling Publishing Co., Inc.
New York

For more information,
visit our website at www.pixiq.com

Book Design: Michael Robertson
Cover Design: Thom Gaines, Electron Graphics

Stafford, Simon.
  Nikon D3100 / Simon Stafford. -- 1st ed.
     p. cm. -- (Magic lantern guides)
  Includes index.
  ISBN 978-1-4547-0126-2
  1. Nikon digital cameras--Handbooks, manuals, etc. 2. Photography--Digital techniques--Handboo
manuals, etc. 3. Single-lens reflex cameras--Handbooks, manuals, etc. I. Title.
  TR263.N5S7343 2011
  771.3'1--dc22

10 9 8 7 6 5 4 3

Published by Lark Photography, An Imprint of
Sterling Publishing Co., Inc.
387 Park Avenue South, New York, N.Y. 10016

Text © 2011, Simon Stafford
Photography © 2011, Simon Stafford unless otherwise specified
Distributed in Canada by Sterling Publishing,
c/o Canadian Manda Group, 165 Dufferin Street
Toronto, Ontario, Canada M6K 3H6

Distributed in the United Kingdom by GMC Distribution Services,
Castle Place, 166 High Street, Lewes, East Sussex, England BN7 1XU

Distributed in Australia by Capricorn Link (Australia) Pty Ltd.,
P.O. Box 704, Windsor, NSW 2756 Australia

This book is not sponsored by Nikon.

If you have questions or comments about this book, please contact:
Lark Photography
67 Broadway
Asheville, NC 28801
(828) 253-0467

Manufactured in Canada

ISBN 13: 978-1-4547-0126-2

For information about custom editions, special sales, premium and corporate purchases, pl
Sterling Special Sales Department at 800-805-5489 or specialsales@sterlingpub.com.

For information about desk and examination copies available to college and university
requests must be submitted to academic@larkbooks.com. Our complete policy can
www.larkbooks.com.

To learn more about digital photography, go to www.pixiq.com.

Contents

Shoot and Review

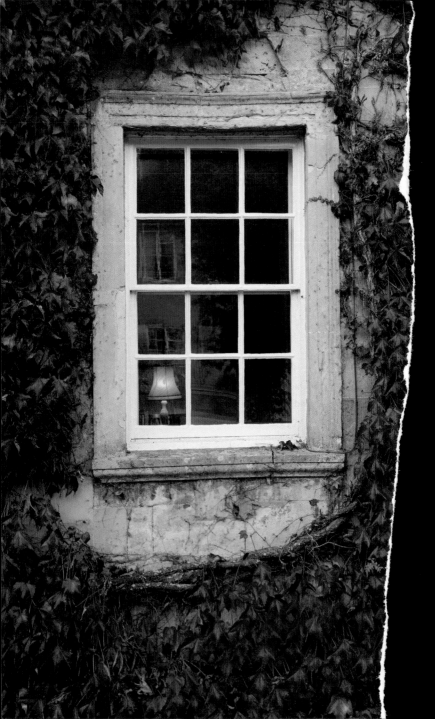

The Nikon D3100

INTRODUCTION

The Nikon Corporation has accrued many years of experience building digital cameras, beginning with a variety of hybrid cameras produced in collaboration with Kodak and Fuji respectively, but their breakthrough came in 1999 with the launch of the Nikon D1. This model represented their first fully independent digital SLR (DSLR) camera design, which not only broke new ground technically, but also made high quality digital photography financially viable for many photographers.

The long and distinguished heritage of the Nikon Corporation is rooted in its origins as an optical engineering company, which can be traced back to the early part of the twentieth century. As such, Nikon's predisposition to precision and quality has meant that they have refrained from introducing new camera models at the frequency of some well-known competitors; consequently, the development of Nikon DSLR cameras during recent years can best be described as a process of steady evolution. Nikon has unveiled a variety of models aimed at different sectors of the market, from the popular D100, launched during 2002, to the phenomenally successful D70 that arrived during 2004, and later, to the mid-range D200 and D80, together with the professionally specified D2Xs. More recently, the Lilliputian D40 provided the perfect entry point to the extensive Nikon camera system—small, well specified, and highly affordable, it held great appeal to the first time DSLR user. The groundbreaking D3 and D300 models arrived simultaneously toward the end of 2007, while the following year saw the introduction of the D60, D700, and D3x models together with the D90, the first DSLR camera to incorporate a video capability. During early 2009, the innovative D5000, with its variable-angle LCD monitor, was launched, followed closely by the D3000 that replaced the D60 to become the entry-level camera to the Nikon DSLR range, and D300s, which took over as the flagship of the Nikon DX-format DSLR camera models. Finally, during what had already been an extremely busy year for the Nikon Corporation, it announced the D3s, which was introduced to build on the huge success of the original D3, a camera that not only reversed the fortunes of the company in the professional sector of the market, but also redefined the expectations of photographers everywhere in respect of image quality at high ISO settings.

The D3100 has been launched to build on the success of the D3000, which it has replaced. The combination of the prestigious Nikon brand name, compact size, competitive pricing, and intuitive operation enabled the D3000 to become a highly popular camera; according to market research company GfK it was the best-selling DSLR camera in Europe for the first six months of 2010, which is no small feat, given the dynamic nature of this fast-moving market sector. Market research conducted by Synovate on behalf of Nikon established that their customers wanted its successor to have a higher resolution, higher ISO sensitivity, Live View, and video recording in a smaller, lighter body.

Bristling with new features and functions, such as a new 14.2 megapixel CMOS sensor, Live View with new autofocus modes, a full 1080p HD video capability, and an enhanced version of the Guide mode used in the D3000 that now offers sample photographs, the D3100 meets these requirements and raises the bar in respect to design. Yet the camera has been designed with newcomers to DSLR photography very much in mind, as it possesses a broad range of automated settings to do the heavy lifting, freeing the less experienced user from concerns about complicated functionality, while still providing full manual control for those who prefer to shoot in this style. Thus, the D3100 offers a comprehensive specification that makes it fully commensurate with its role as a camera for photographers with a wide range of experience and skill. Its key highlights include:

- DX-format (15.4 x 23.1 mm) CMOS sensor with 14.2 million pixels that provides a resolution of 4608 x 3072 pixels

- An ISO range of 100 to 3200, with the ability to be extended to an ISO equivalent of ISO 12,800

- D-Movie mode with full 1080p (1920 x 1080) HD video recording at 24 fps (frames per second)

- Live View with two new innovations: Scene Auto Selector, which selects the best mode to match the shooting situation and AF-F (Full-Time Servo) autofocus mode for continuous focusing on a moving subject

- Nikon's exclusive Expeed 2 processing regime for enhanced performance when recording video and shooting at high ISO sensitivities, plus improved image quality

- 3-inch (7.5 cm) 230,000-dot LCD monitor

- An 11-point autofocus system with a 3D Focus-Tracking feature

- A shutter unit with the ability to cycle up to 3 fps, and tested to 100,000 cycles

- Self-cleaning mechanism integrates vibration of the optical low-pass filter with the Nikon Airflow Control system that helps draw dust away from the filter

- Nikon's proprietary Scene Recognition System that enhances performance of the autofocus, metering, and Automatic White Balance functions

- Active D-Lighting

- The Picture Control System, which provides a very high degree of control over the way the camera records an image

- Six Scene Modes for improved point-and-shoot photography

- An enhanced Guide mode that leads you through settings for shooting, viewing images, and configuring the camera's controls

- An enhanced range of options in the Retouch menu, including lens distortion control, a fisheye effect, and a perspective control

- A new EN-EL14 battery and MH-24 battery charger

- Compact and lightweight body

The D3100 is a sophisticated photographic tool with the flexibility to be used for point-and-shoot style photography with complete automation, or with all of its settings under your direct control, to enable anyone from the beginner to the more experienced enthusiast photographer to cope with a wide range of subjects and shooting situations.

PRODUCTION OF THE NIKON D3100

The D3100 is assembled at Nikon's wholly owned production facility, near Ayuthaya, Thailand—the old historical capital of Siam—about 50 miles (80 Km) north of Bangkok, the present day capital. I say assembled, as a number of core parts of the camera are manufactured elsewhere, such as the camera's main printed circuit board and lens mount, which are produced at the Nikon factory in Sendai, Japan.

The Nikon Thailand plant, which produced its first Nikkor lens back in 1992, currently comprises four separate factories engaged in a wide range of activities from manufacture of specialized lens elements and camera components to the fabrication of DSLR cameras. Camera and lens production includes the D300s, D90, D7000, and D5000, together with a number of consumer grade Nikkor lenses and, of course, the D3100.

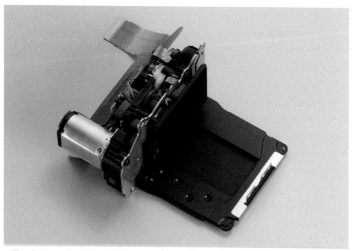

^ The shutter unit of the D3100 is tested to perform at least 100,000 actuations.

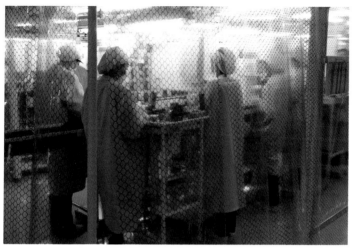

∧ The D3100 is manufactured at Nikon Thailand; clean room conditions exist at a number of points along the assembly line.

ABOUT THIS BOOK

To get the most from your D3100, it is important that you understand its features so you can make informed choices about how to use them in conjunction with your style of photography. This book is designed to help you achieve this. Besides explaining how all the basic functions work, this book also provides useful tips on operating the D3100 and maximizing its performance. The book does not have to be read from cover to cover. You can move from section to section as required, study a complete chapter, or just broaden your knowledge of the features or functions you want to use.

The key to success, regardless of your level of experience, is to practice with your camera. You do not waste money on film and processing costs with a digital camera; once you have invested in a memory card, it can be used over and over again. Therefore, you can shoot as many pictures as you like, review your results along with a detailed record of camera settings almost immediately, delete your near misses, and save your successes. This trial-and-error method is a very effective way to learn!

CONVENTIONS USED IN THIS BOOK

Unless otherwise stated, when the terms "left" and "right" are used to describe the location of a camera control, it is assumed you are holding the camera to your eye in the shooting position. In describing the operation of lenses and external flash units, it is assumed that appropriate D- or G-type Nikkor AF-S and AF-I lenses that have a built-in autofocus motor and Nikon Speedlight units compatible with the Creative Lighting System are being used to ensure full functionality. Note that lenses and flash units made by independent manufacturers may have different functionality. If you use such products, refer to the manufacturer's instruction manual to check compatibility and operation with the D3100. When referring to software, either Nikon or third-party, it is assumed that the most recent iterations of each application are used. At the time of writing, the most recent Nikon software is:

O Nikon View NX2 (version 2.0.1) incorporating Nikon Transfer 2
O Nikon Capture NX2 (version 2.2.5)

ACKNOWLEDGEMENTS

I would like to thank the following people for their assistance and support during the writing of this book. At Nikon Japan, Mr. Tetsuro Goto, Director of Laboratory Research and Development and Mr. Hideki Matsui, Manger of the Speedlight Design Section, and their staff. At Nikon Europe, Mr. Toru Iwaoka, Managing Director. At Nikon UK, Mr. Michio Miwa, Managing Director, and his staff, in particular Mr. Jeremy Gilbert, Group Marketing Director (Imaging Division), Mr. Simon Iddon, Enthusiast Product Manager, Mr. Mark Fury, Professional Channel Manager, Ms. Jenny Grace and Ms. Lily Bungay, Press & PR, and Mr. James Banfield, Nikon Professional Support.

Simon Stafford
Wiltshire, England

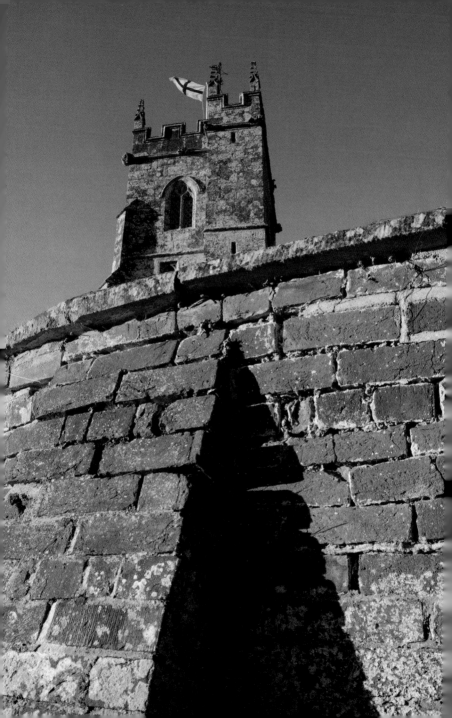

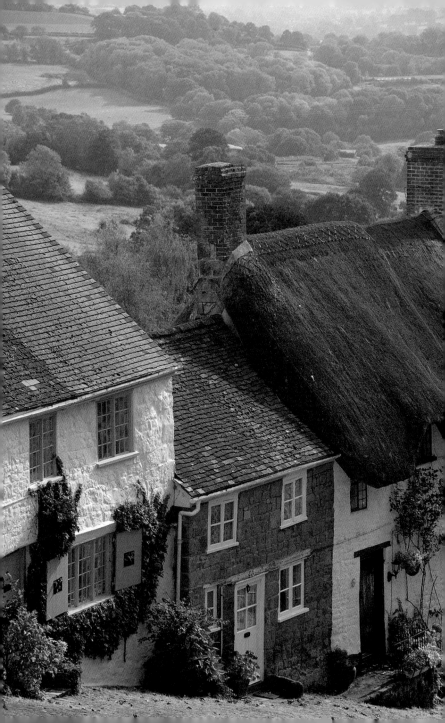

Introducing
The Nikon D3100

The D3100 has been designed to build upon the qualities of its predecessor, the D3000, and expand its capabilities by drawing on the rapidly developing technologies of digital imaging. In producing the D3100, Nikon had aimed to deliver high-end features and functions in a compact, easy-to-use, robust camera intended to provide a broad appeal to photographers ranging from the first time or less experienced DSLR user to the dedicated enthusiast. The Nikon Corporation describes the D3100 as a "Camera to guide you to beautiful pictures," by providing the ease-of-use of the D3000. Furthermore, the D3100 offers an enhanced GUIDE mode that provides intuitive, graphic-led instructions displayed on the monitor screen of the camera and a significantly higher specification than the D3000 in terms of an all-new sensor, Live View, and full HD (1080p) video.

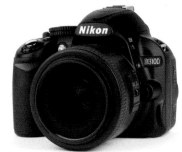

> The D3100 is pictured here with the Nikkor AF-S DX 35mm f/1.8G lens. Lenses marked with a D or a G offer the highest level of compatibility with the D3100, though you can use almost any Nikkor lens, albeit with limited compatibility.

DESIGN

At first glance, the D3100 is remarkably similar in appearance to the D3000, since the two models share a near-identical profile. The most obvious changes externally are the additional switches and buttons that have been introduced to control new functions and improve camera handling. Internally, there have been some significant changes with an all-new Nikon DX-format (APS-C size) 14.2MP CMOS sensor that supports Live View and a D-Movie mode with HD (1080p) resolution, two functions that the D3000 lacked. Also new to the D3100 is the Expeed 2 image processing regime, an extended ISO range (100 – 3200), and a continuous autofocus option when recording in its D-Movie mode. The D3100 does still share many key components and features found in the D3000, such as the same 420-segment RGB sensor for TTL metering, the built-in sensor-cleaning mechanism with the Nikon Airflow Control system, 3D-tracking autofocus, the Picture Control System, and the Multi-CAM1000 autofocus module with 11-point AF system. The TTL metering and autofocus systems work hand-in-hand with the White Balance feature to form the Scene Recognition System, which was first introduced in the D300. Furthermore, the D3000 and D3100 share the same design of built-in Speedlight flash. Improvements in the user interface introduced in the D3000 model have been enhanced further within the D3100, as has the level of in-camera image editing.

It might be said that the D3100 represents a meld of the best qualities of its highly popular predecessor, which have been enhanced and expanded to meet the requirements of an ever more demanding and competitive digital SLR camera market; this has been achieved through an uncompromising design criteria harnessed to cutting edge technology and the many years of experience accrued by Nikon in the manufacture of digital SLR cameras.

For a very compact camera, the D3100 has a nice feel in the hand. It has dimensions of: 4.9W x 3.8H x 3.0D inches (124 x 94 x 74.5 mm) and weighs approximately 16 oz (455 g) without a battery or memory card. The 3-inch (7.5 cm) LCD monitor on the rear of the D3100 is probably its most notable external feature amongst the array of buttons, dials, and switches, many of which will be familiar to users of previous Nikon DSLR cameras. The camera chassis and outer panels are made from a sturdy polycarbonate material that imparts a solid, rugged feel to the body, and

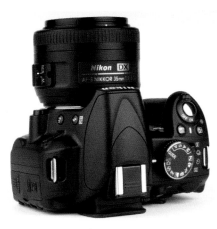

∧ Despite its diminutive size, the D3100 has a robust build quality and good handling characteristics.

the sealing around all points to prevent the ingress of moisture and dust appears to be commensurate with a camera in this class.

Nikon has long been trumpeting that image quality in the digital world rests on three pillars: optical quality of the lens, sensor technology, and internal camera processing. The D3100 epitomizes this in respect of the latter two aspects, as the sensor of the D3100 and a single ASIC (application-specific integrated circuit) that handles the image-processing system form the core of what Nikon calls their "Expeed 2" image processing system; it is at the heart of the camera's ability to record, process, and output high quality images, both still and video, at a rapid rate. This fast data processing is combined with a mechanical shutter that enables the D3100 to cycle at a maximum of 3 frames per second (fps). Furthermore, as part of the uncompromising design, the shutter unit is tested to perform at least 100,000 actuations.

The D3100 has a Nikon F lens mount with an automatic focusing (AF) coupling and electrical contacts, the design of which can be traced back to the Nikon F, introduced in 1959. The greatest level of compatibility is achieved with either AF-D or AF-G type Nikkor lenses. Other lenses can be used, but they provide a variable level of compatibility: AF and Ai-P type Nikkor lenses offer a somewhat reduced functionality, as autofocus is not supported, plus the camera's TTL metering system defaults from 3D Color Matrix metering to standard Color Matrix metering. Even manual focus Ai, Ai-s, Ai converted, and E-series Nikkor lenses can be used with the D3100, although you are restricted to Manual exposure mode only and must adjust the lens aperture manually, plus the TTL metering and autofocus system, electronic exposure display, and i-TTL flash control are not available.

THE SENSOR

The Complimentary Metal Oxide Semi-conductor (CMOS) sensor used in the D3100 is an entirely new design and unique to the camera at the time of writing. There are total of 14.8 million photo sites (pixels), of which 14.2 million are effective for the purpose of recording an image. Each photo site is just 5.0 microns (1 micron = 1/1000 mm) square and comprises the photodiode (photo-detector) and an amplifier circuit. This gives the camera a maximum resolution of 4608 x 3072 pixels, sufficient to produce a 19.2 x 12.8-inch (48 x 32-cm) print at 240ppi without interpolation (resizing). The imaging area is approximately 0.6 x 0.9 inch (15.4 x 23.1 mm), producing a 2:3 aspect ratio. Nikon calls this their DX-format, which is often referred to generically as the APS-C format. Interestingly, the linear dimensions stated for the sensor of the D3100 are somewhat shorter than those quoted for other Nikon DX-format sensors, which are typically 0.66 x 1 inch (15.8 x 23.6 mm).

The same "DX" designation is used to identify those lenses that have been optimized for use with their digital SLR cameras that have DX-format sensors. Due to the smaller size of the DX-format, the angle of view offered by any focal length is reduced compared with a lens of the same focal length used with the FX-format of the Nikon D700 and D3-series camera models or 35mm film cameras. If it helps you to estimate the angle of view for a particular focal length in comparison with the coverage offered by the same focal length on the FX-format, multiply the focal length by 1.5x (see pages 28-29 for a full explanation).

The CMOS sensor of the D3100 is actually a sandwich of several layers, each with a specific purpose; and it is known as an active-pixel sensor, as each pixel comprises a photo-detector (photodiode) and an active amplifier. CMOS sensors offer several advantages over the Charged Coupled Device (CCD) type sensor (a type of passive-pixel sensor) used in the D3000, including lower power consumption, faster operation, and lower manufacturing costs. The first layer of the CMOS sensor is the wiring layer, comprising the photodiodes and supporting electrical circuitry, which not only carries the electrical signal away from each photodiode, but also amplifies it before it is passed on to the analog-to-digital converter (ADC).

The Bayer pattern filter is a color filter layer found above the light sensitive layer of capacitors. The photodiodes on the CMOS sensor do not record color—they can only detect a level of brightness. To impart color to the image formed by the light that falls on the sensor, a series of minute red, green, and blue filters are arranged over the capacitors in a Bayer pattern, which takes its name from the Kodak engineer who invented the system.

These tiny filters are arranged in an alternating pattern of red and green on the odd-numbered rows, and green and blue on the even-numbered rows. The Bayer pattern comprises 50% green, 25% red, and 25% blue filters; the intensity of light detected by each capacitor located beneath its single, dedicated color filter according to the Bayer pattern is converted into an electrical signal before being converted to a digital value by the ADC, as described above. If the camera is set to record an NEF RAW file, the value for each sampling point on the sensor is simply saved. When you open this file in an appropriate RAW file converter, the software will interpret the digital value derived from each capacitor to produce a red-green-blue (RGB) value, which in turn, is converted into an image that can be viewed. However, if the camera is set to record JPEG files, then the value from each capacitor is processed in the camera by comparing it with the values from a block of surrounding capacitors, using a process called interpolation. The interpolation process produces a "best guess" for the RGB value for each sampling point (capacitor) on the sensor.

Immediately above the Bayer pattern filter, there is a layer of micro lenses. Since the photodiodes on the sensor are most efficient when the light falling on them is perpendicular, each one has a miniature lens located above it to channel the light into its well to help maximize its light-gathering ability; each micro-lens occupies an area larger than the capacitor well below it, and there is virtually no gap between neighboring micro-lenses. This effective ability to gather light, coupled with the relatively large, 5.0-micron pixel pitch of the camera's sensor allows it to scoop up photons very efficiently and contributes to the extremely good image quality that can be attained at high ISO settings.

Positioned in front of the CMOS sensor, but not connected to it, is an optical low-pass filter (OLPF), sometimes called an anti-aliasing filter. When the frequency of detail in an image, particularly a small, regular, repeating pattern, such as the weave pattern in a fabric, alters at or close to the pitch of the photodiodes on the sensor, there is often a side effect that produces unwanted data (often referred to as artifacts) due to the way in which the in-camera processing converts the electrical signal from the sensor to a digital value via the analog-to-digital (ADC) converter. This additional data is manifest in the final image as a color pattern known as moiré. Furthermore, the same in-camera processing can also result in a color fringing effect, known as color aliasing, which causes a halo of one or more separate color(s) to appear along the edge of fine detail in the image.

The OLPF is used to reduce the unwanted effects of color aliasing and moiré. However, the OLPF reduces the resolution of detail, so the camera designers must strike a balance between its beneficial effect and the loss of acuity in fine detail, which increases as the strength of the filter is increased. In the D3100, Nikon appears to have done well in this respect, as the JPEG files taken at the camera's default settings show plenty of crisp detail. The OLPF also incorporates a number of important coating layers to help improve image quality:

O To help prevent dust and other foreign material from adhering to the surface of the OLPF, it has an anti-static coating made from Indium Tin Oxide.

O To reduce the risk of light being reflected from the front surface of the OLPF onto the rear element of the lens, which could then result in flare effects or ghost images, the filter has an anti-reflective coating.

O The CMOS sensor is sensitive to wavelengths of light outside the spectrum visible by the human eye. This light, which can be either in the infrared (IR) or ultraviolet (UV) part of the spectrum, will pollute image files and cause unwanted color shifts and a loss of image sharpness, so the OLPF has both an IR-blocking and a UV-blocking coat. These IR and UV blocking coats are very efficient; consequently, the D3100 cannot be recommended for any form of IR or UV light photography, which was possible with some earlier Nikon DSLR cameras, such as the D1 and the D100.

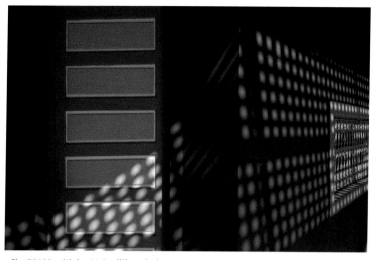

∧ The D3100, with its 14.2-million-pixel sensor, can capture more color and detail, plus a wider dynamic range, than most cameras in its price class.

SELF-CLEANING OPTICAL LOW-PASS FILTER

The D3100 has inherited the same self-cleaning feature for the OLPF as used in the D3000. It vibrates the OLPF to help reduce the presence of dust and other unwanted particles on its front surface, which is the surface closest to the rear of the lens. Dust on the OLPF is the bane of all digital photographers, because it causes dark shadow spots to appear in the final image; therefore, keeping the OLPF clean is fundamental to maintaining image quality and avoiding the necessity for time-consuming post-processing. To supplement this system, the D3100 also has Nikon's Airflow Control system, which uses small changes of air pressure inside the camera caused by the movement of the reflex mirror to draw dust and other similar unwanted particles away from the OLPF to a trap located at the bottom of the reflex mirror box (see pages 293-295 for more details on OLPF cleaning options).

DX-FORMAT

Nikon has used DX-format (APS-C) sensors in most of their digital SLR camera models, beginning with the Nikon D1, which was introduced during 1999. The only exceptions are the D700 and D3-series cameras, which have FX-format sensors that are approximately the same size as a frame of 35mm film. At 15.4 x 23.1 mm, the DX-format of the D3100 is considerably smaller than the FX-format (23.9 x 36 mm); as a consequence, regardless of the focal length of the lens mounted on the camera, the field of view covered by its sensor is narrower than the field of view produced by a lens of the same focal length on an FX-format sensor.

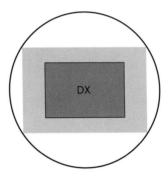

The circle represents the total area covered by the image circle projected from a lens designed to cover the FX / 35mm format. The pale grey rectangle is the image area for the FX-format sensor, while the dark grey rectangle represents the area covered by the DX-format

Through their shooting experience with DX-format Nikon cameras, many photographers have become familiar with the reduced angle of view caused by the smaller format sensor, while others still find the issue confusing. Furthermore, misconceptions persist as to what causes the altered field of view. Use of phrases such as, "it's like getting a free 1.4x teleconverter," or "the focal length is magnified by 1.5x" suggest, as if by some wizardry, that the focal length of a lens somehow increases by 1.5x when mounted on a camera that records pictures in the DX-format. This is completely false; the focal length of any lens will remain constant, and regardless of the size of the sensor or part of the sensor it projects an image onto, it is the angle of view that alters.

To clarify this concept, consider that a lens with a focal length of 200mm will produce a specific angle of view on the FX-format sensor.

However, when the same focal length is used with the DX-format, the angle of view is reduced, rendering a view equivalent to that produced on the FX-format frame when a lens with a focal length of 300mm is used. In other words, if you are accustomed to choosing a focal length based on the angle of view it produces on the FX / 35mm film frame, you will want to multiply that focal length by 1.5x (the actual factor is closer to 1.52x) in order to estimate the coverage it will provide with the DX-format. Using the example of the 200mm focal length discussed above, 200mm x 1.5 = 300mm. The following table provides an approximate effective focal length you can use to estimate the field of view with the DX-format.

FOCAL LENGTH EQUIVALENTS

Actual	12	14	17	18	20	24	28	35	50	60
Effective	18	21	25.5	27	30	36	42	52.5	75	90
Actual	70	85	105	135	180	200	300	400	500	600
Effective	105	127.5	157.5	202.5	270	300	450	600	750	900

DX-Format Pros and Cons: While this narrower field of view may be an advantage in some shooting situations because of the magnified view it offers, it has the reverse effect when you want to achieve a very wide angle of view; consequently, it is necessary to use a much shorter focal length. However, there is another beneficial side effect to the reduced angle of view of the DX-format. Since the D3100 only uses the central portion of the image circle projected by the many Nikkor lenses designed for the FX-format or 35mm film SLRs, the effects of optical aberrations and defects are kept to a minimum, as these are generally more prevalent toward the edges of the image circle. Using such as lens will often significantly reduce or eliminate some or all of the following:

- O Light fall-off (vignetting) toward the edges and corners of the image area, which can be particularly troublesome at large lens apertures
- O Appearance of chromatic aberration
- O Linear distortion—both barrel and pin-cushion
- O Effects of field curvature (i.e., center and corners of frame are not in the same plane of focus)
- O Light fall-off (vignetting) when using filters

Nikon also produces a range of Nikkor lenses designed specifically for use on their DX-format DSLR camera, known as DX lenses. These lenses only need to project an image circle that covers the DX-format sensor, enabling them to be made smaller and lighter than their counterparts designed for the FX-format or 35mm film cameras (see pages 236-237 for further information on Nikkor lens compatibility).

THE VIEWFINDER

The D3100 has a fixed, optical pentamirror, eye-level viewfinder that shows approximately 95% (vertical and horizontal) of the full-frame coverage. It is important to understand the consequence of this; reducing the viewfinder frame coverage to 95% in both linear directions actually results in a viewfinder that only displays about 90% of the image area recorded by the camera (0.95 x 0.95 – 0.90). As a result, it is not possible to frame an image in the viewfinder with complete accuracy, as there is a small but significant border area outside each edge of the viewfinder that will be included in the recorded picture. However, the monitor screen displays 100% of the recorded image, so the prudent user will make use of the Image Review and Playback options of the camera to ensure their careful compositions have not been compromised!

Another very important aspect of the viewfinder is to prevent light from entering the viewfinder eyepiece when the D3100 is used remotely (i.e., your eye is not to the viewfinder eyepiece), as it will influence the accuracy of the metering system adversely, so make sure the viewfinder eyepiece is covered with the supplied DK-5 cap when shooting this way.

> The viewfinder eyepiece is shown here covered by the DK-5; note that to fit the DK-5, the DK-20 rubber eyecup must be removed. The diopter control dial for the viewfinder eyepiece is located to its right side.

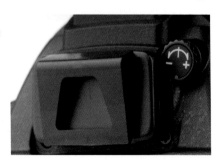

ADJUSTING VIEWFINDER FOCUS

The viewfinder has an eyepoint of 0.7 inch (18 mm). Users who wear eyeglasses may find the view of the focusing screen and viewfinder information a little restricted. However, there is a built-in diopter adjustment of -1.7 to +0.5 m^{-1} to adjust the focus of the eyepiece to an individual user's eyesight. To do this, mount a lens on the camera and leave it set to its infinity focus mark. Switch the camera on and point it at a plain surface that fills the frame. Rotate the diopter adjustment dial to the right of the viewfinder eyepiece until the AF point and focus screen markings appear sharp. It is essential to do this to ensure you see the sharpest view of the focusing screen. If the built-in diopter correction is not sufficient, optional eyepiece correction lenses, with the product code DK-20C, are available from -5 to +3 m^{-1}; these are attached by slotting them on to the eye piece frame (the standard DK-20 viewfinder eyecup must be removed first). The strength of these lenses may not match that of your prescription eyeglasses, so make sure you try them before making a purchase.

VIEWFINDER & FOCUS SCREEN DISPLAY

The viewfinder, which provides a magnification of approximately 0.8x (50mm f/1.4 lens at infinity; -1.0m^{-1}), displays all the essential information about exposure and focus. The camera is supplied with the Nikon B-type Mark VII, clear matte focusing screen, which is marked with seven pairs of square brackets that encompass the 11 autofocus points. Nikon does not offer an alternative interchangeable focusing screen for the D3100.

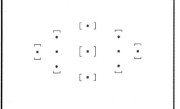

‹ The focus screen display of the D3100 is marked by 11 small squares to indicate the position of each AF point.

The focusing screen of the D3100 employs simple etched markings, so even with the battery removed from the camera they remain visible. The AF point markings and their surrounding square bracket markings are considerably fainter than the comparable marking of the D3000, and the new model does not offer the grid-line display or reference arcs for Center-Weighted metering. Also gone are the screen overlays for warning that no memory card is inserted and the battery charge status, although the latter is shown below the focusing screen in the general viewfinder information. The marked AF points are illuminated by single LEDs when they are active; however, the light from the LEDs seems to have a tendency to "bleed" into adjoining AF points, which could be confusing.

THE MULTI SELECTOR BUTTON

The Multi Selector button, located on the rear of the camera, is used to navigate the Information Display and the menu system of the D3100, plus select the AF point. Note that there is no locking switch available for this principal control, as there is on other Nikon camera models, and I have found that due to its relatively high profile that it is all too easy for the heel of my right thumb to depress the Multi Selector button inadvertently when holding the camera; in particular, I often find this causes the selection of the AF point to shift to the right side of the frame area, so be warned! Always check to see which AF point is highlighted before you shoot. The function of the Multi Selector is as shown below:

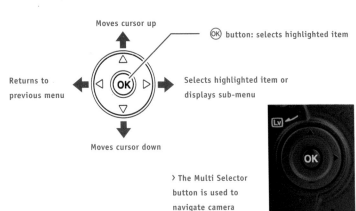

Moves cursor up

(OK) button: selects highlighted item

Returns to previous menu

Selects highlighted item or displays sub-menu

Moves cursor down

> The Multi Selector button is used to navigate camera menus, controls, and select the AF point.

The Information Display (ID) shows all the essential information about camera settings and controls on the monitor screen of the camera. Due to the size of the screen, the display is large and clear. The format of the display can be altered using the [Info Display Format] item in the Setup menu.

To open the ID, press the info button once. To change a setting for an item shown in the display, press the ⬛ button, which highlights the item selected most recently in yellow. To shift the yellow cursor, use the Multi Selector button. Once the required item is highlighted, press the ⊛ button to show the options available for that item.

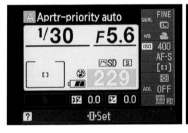

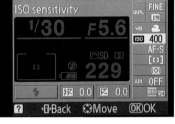

∧ The Information Display provides a comprehensive view of current camera settings.

∧ Pressing the ⬛ button displays the most recently selected item; here the ISO value is shown highlighted.

To clear the ID from the monitor, press the info button or press the shutter release button down halfway. The length of time the ID is shown is selected via the [Auto off timers] item in the Setup menu; the default duration is eight seconds. The [Auto Info Display], and [Info Display Format] items in the Setup menu can be used to further customize how and when the ID operates.

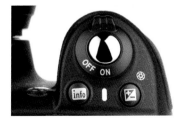

> The info button is used to open and close the Information Display.

PREPARING THE D3100 FOR SHOOTING

In line with the stated aim of Nikon to make the D3100 appeal to a very broad range of users of various skill levels, the D3100 includes the simple point-and-shoot $\overset{AUTO}{\Box}$ mode, the ⓩ Auto Flash Off mode, a further six fully automated subject- or scene-oriented, point-and-shoot exposure modes, plus four dedicated exposure modes for the more experienced photographer. Additionally, the new Guide mode introduced for the first time on the D3000 is designed to simplify camera operation and, at the same time, educate the user about camera settings and the effect they have.

The section below is intended to assist those less experienced users eager to take some pictures with their new D3100, but either unable or reluctant to spend the time, at this point, to learn how to take control of the camera.

QUICK START GUIDE

O Charge the EN-EL14 battery in the MH-24 charger until the charge lamp stops blinking. Switch off the charger, remove the battery, and open the battery chamber door on the base of the D3100. Insert the battery as per the diagram on the inside of the chamber door, and then close it.

O When the camera is switched on for the first time, it will display a language-selection menu. Use ▲ and ▼ to select the required language and then press ⓞ.

O Next, a time zone display will be shown. Use ◀ and ▶ to select your time zone, and then press ⓞ. Use ▲ and ▼ to select the required date format, then press ⓞ. A Daylight Saving time option will be displayed; if Daylight Saving is in effect in the current time zone, press ▲ to select [On], then press ⓞ. Now set the date and time. Use ◀ and ▶ to select an item, and use ▲ and ▼ to change it. Finally, press ⓞ to set the camera clock.

O Attach a lens to the D3100. If the lens has a focus mode switch with options for either A-M, or M/A-M, set the focus mode to either A (autofocus), or M/A (autofocus with manual override).

O Adjust the viewfinder focus by turning the diopter control dial (located beside the viewfinder eyepiece) until the viewfinder display and AF points appear sharp.

O Open the memory card port on the right side of the camera and insert a memory card, ensuring that the main label of the card is facing toward the back of the camera.

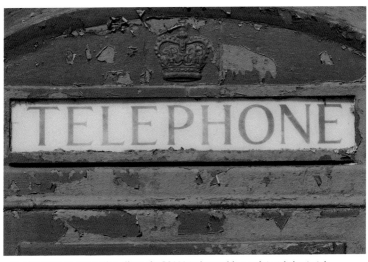

^ Its high level of automation allows the D3100 to be used in a point and shoot style. However, your photography will be more rewarding if you spend some time learning how to take control of the camera.

O Format the memory card by pressing the MENU button and selecting the [Format memory card] item from the Setup menu. Next press ▶, then highlight the [Yes] option, and finally press the ⊛ button to complete the formatting process

O To set the camera to its ᴬᵁᵀᴼ mode—a fully automated "point-and-shoot" mode that controls virtually all camera settings automatically—select ᴬᵁᵀᴼ using the Mode dial on the top of the camera. The built-in flash of the camera will fire automatically if the camera determines the light level is low. If you don't want the flash to fire automatically, select ⊕ Auto Flash Off mode.

O Compose a picture, ensuring that an AF point covers an area of the subject required to be in focus. Press lightly on the shutter release button to activate the focusing system. If the camera can acquire focus, the focus indicator ● will appear in the viewfinder. If ● is shown blinking, the camera has not been able to acquire focus; re-compose the picture, place the selected AF point over an alternative part of the subject, and press lightly on the shutter release button again.

O The shutter button has a two-stage release mechanism; pressing it down halfway activates the AF and TTL metering systems, while pressing it down all the way operates the shutter. Avoid stabbing you index finger down on the shutter release button, as this will increase the risk of camera shake. Simply roll the tip of your index finger smoothly over the edge of the shutter release button to take the picture. The green access

lamp on the back of the camera will illuminate as soon as an exposure
has been made, indicating that the camera is saving the image.

O To review a picture, press the ▶ button. Use ◀ and ▶ to review
other pictures stored on the memory card. To view additional shooting
information about the displayed picture, press either ▲ or ▼. To
return to the Shooting mode, press the shutter release button lightly.

O To delete a picture, press the ▶ button to display it on the monitor,
then press the 🗑 button. A confirmation dialog will be displayed. Press
the 🗑 button again to complete the process.

POWERING THE D3100

The D3100 can be powered either by a dedicated battery or an AC supply;
the battery supplied with the camera is the rechargeable lithium-ion EN-
EL-14 (7.4V, 1030mAh) that weighs approximately 1.7 oz (48 g).

> The EN-EL14 battery powers
the D3100; it is charged with
the dedicated MH-24 AC charger.

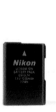
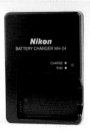

The profile of the EN-EL14 battery ensures that it can only be inserted
the correct way into the camera. It is charged with the dedicated MH-24
Quick Charger, also supplied with the camera. A fully discharged EN-
EL14 can be completely recharged in approximately 90 minutes. Unlike
some other types of rechargeable batteries, the EN-EL14 supplied with
the D3100 does not require conditioning prior to first use (it is supplied
partially charged). However, it is advisable to ensure that the initial
charge cycle for a new battery is continued until the battery cools down
in the charger before removing it. Do not be tempted to remove it as
soon as the charging / charged indicator lamp on the MH-24 stops
flashing to indicate charging is complete, as the battery is unlikely to
have reached a full 100% charge.

USING THE EN-EL14 BATTERY

Whenever you insert or remove an EN-EL14, it is essential that you set the power switch of the D3100 to the off position.

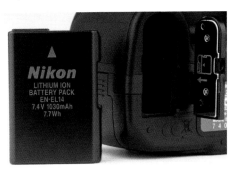

‹ The EN-EL14 battery is shown here next to the empty battery chamber of the D3100; note the diagram on the inside of the chamber cover.

To insert an EN-EL14 into the D3100:

1. Turn the camera upside down and push the small button on the battery chamber lid toward the tripod socket. Turn the camera over and the battery chamber lid should swing open.

2. Open the lid fully and slide the battery into the camera observing the diagram on the inside of the chamber lid.

3. Press the lid down (you will feel a slight resistance) until it locks (you will hear a click as the latch closes).

To remove an EN-EL14 from the D3100:

1. Repeat step 1 (above).

2. Hold the lid open, turn the camera upright, and allow the battery to slide out taking care that it does not drop.

3. Close the battery chamber lid.

NOTE: If you are in the process of making any changes to the camera settings and the battery is removed or the power supply from the EH-5a AC adapter is interrupted while the power switch is still set to the on position, the camera may not retain the new settings. Likewise, if the camera is still in the process of transferring data from the buffer memory to the storage media when the battery is removed, image files are likely to be corrupted or data lost.

To charge an EN-EL14:

1. Connect the MH-24 to an AC power supply.

NOTE: The MH-24 can be used worldwide, connected to any AC supply, at any voltage from 100v to 250v, via an appropriate power adapter.

---

2. Align the battery so its contacts are facing down and the small arrowhead printed on the opposite side of the battery casing from the contacts is pointing toward the MH-24. Slot the battery into the MH-24, and then slide it toward the indicator lamp until it locks in place. The charge lamp should begin to flash immediately, indicating that charging has commenced.

Lithium-ion batteries do not exhibit the same charge memory effects associated with certain types of rechargeable batteries, therefore a partially discharged EN-EL14 can take a top-up charge without any adverse consequences to battery life or performance. However, I do recommend that you avoid giving a battery a top-up charge when its charge level is at 90% or more, and likewise, do not repeatedly run a battery down to a charge level of 10% or less before recharging it. In the former case, there is a risk of reducing overall battery capacity; and in the latter, successive charging of a battery from near exhaustion to full charge will likely reduce its life expectancy. The battery charge status is shown in the Information Display, while a warning to indicate either a low battery charge or exhausted battery is displayed in the viewfinder.

D3100 BATTERY STATUS

MONITOR	VIEWFINDER	BATTERY STATUS
	—	Fully charged
	—	Partially discharged
	—	Low – charge battery
	—	Discharged – charge battery; shutter disabled

EXTERNAL POWER SUPPLY

The Nikon EH-5a AC adapter, which is an optional accessory, can also power the D3100 via the EP-5a DC power connector. The AC adapter is rated for an input of 100–240v, AC 50–60Hz and is particularly useful for extended periods of shooting, image playback, or data transfer directly from the camera to a computer.

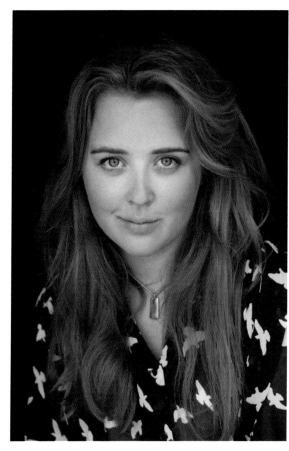

> Battery performance is influenced by a wide variety of camera and lens functions: using the monitor screen, video recording, and lens stabilization represent the largest drains on battery power.

The EH-5a cannot be connected directly to the D3100; it requires the EP-5A DC power connector to be inserted in the camera's main battery chamber, substituting for the EN-EL14 battery (ensure the + and − terminals of the EP-5A are in the correct orientation). The cord from the EP-5A should be laid in the small notch in the edge of the battery chamber (this requires the rubber grommet set in to the edge of the battery chamber to be swung outward) before closing the chamber cover. Connect the DC plug of the EH-5a to the DC terminal of the EP-5A. Finally, connect the EH-5a AC plug of the AC cord to the EH-5a AC terminal, and connect the other end to the AC supply. When powered from an AC supply, the AC indicator of the D3100 will show in the Information Display.

NOTE: Always ensure that the power switch on the D3100 is set to off before connecting / disconnecting the EH-5a and EP-5A. There is a risk that the camera's circuitry could be damaged if you plug / unplug the EH-5a and EP-5A while the power switch is set to on.

EFFECTS OF ELECTROSTATIC CHARGE

Operation of the D3100 is totally dependent on electrical power. Occasionally, the camera may stop functioning properly, or display unusual characters or unexpected messages in the viewfinder and monitor displays. Such behavior is generally due to the effects of a strong external electrostatic charge. If this occurs, try switching the camera off, disconnecting it from its power supply (remove the installed EN-EL14 or unplug the EH-5a AC adapter / EP-5A power connector), then reconnecting the power, and switching the camera back on. If the symptoms persist, the camera will require inspection by an authorized technician.

INTERNAL CLOCK/CALENDAR BATTERY

The D3100 has an internal clock / calendar that is powered by a fixed, internal, rechargeable battery; fully charged, it will power the clock / calendar for approximately one month. This battery requires charging for approximately 72 hours by the camera's power supply: This can be either an EN-EL14 inserted into the camera body or an EH-5a adapter and the EP-5A power connector. Should the clock battery become exhausted, a message that the clock is not set will be displayed on the monitor when the camera is turned on. The clock will display a date and time of 2010.01.01 00:00:00. If this occurs, the clock / calendar will need to be reset to the correct time via the **[Time Zone and Date]** item in the Setup menu.

NOTE: Should the internal clock / calendar battery fail and not retain a charge, the camera must be returned to a Nikon-approved service center for a replacement battery to be fitted.

BATTERY PERFORMANCE

Operation of the D3100 is totally dependent on an adequate electrical power supply. Obviously, the more functions the camera has to perform, the greater the demand on its battery, so reducing the number of functions and the duration for which they are active is fundamental to reducing power consumption. This can be an important consideration, especially if you are traveling with your camera or expect to spend any extended period away from an AC electrical supply. I have set out below some of the principal causes of battery power drain together with a few suggestions as to how you can conserve battery power.

Using the camera's color LCD monitor increases power consumption significantly. Unless you need it, turn the monitor off. Consider setting the **[Image review]** item in the Playback menu to **[Off]**; the default setting is **[On]**. If **[On]** is selected and you want to leave it that way, you may instead simply press the shutter release button lightly as soon as you have finished assessing the picture, since this returns the camera to its Shooting mode, switching the monitor off immediately. To help reduce time spent scrolling through the camera's menu system for any items you use frequently, consider consulting the ▤ Recent Settings menu, which lists the 20 most recently used menu items, so you only need to consult a single menu list. When using the Live View and / or the D-Movie mode functions, the battery drain will be significant compared with just shooting still pictures, so I recommend very strongly that if you intend to make regular use of either, that you carry at least one spare EN-EL14 battery.

Recording NEF RAW draws far more power compared with recording JPEG, although the power management of the D3100 appears to have been enhanced in this respect compared with previous camera models. While driving the autofocus mechanism of lenses draws relatively little power, the Vibration Reduction (VR) feature available with some Nikkor lenses is another matter. The VR function of all Nikkor lenses draws power from the camera battery and it tends to be active for far longer periods compared with AF operation. Consequently, VR can reduce battery life by approximately 10–15% when active.

Using the built-in Speedlight flash unit will place a significant demand on the battery and shorten the duration of any shooting session considerably, so turn it off if you don't absolutely need it. If you do need flash, consider using an accessory Speedlight.

If the Nikon GP-1 GPS device is connected to the D3100, it draws its power from the camera battery, so it will also reduce the battery charge level. In order to reduce this power drain, you can set the camera to shut off the GPS unit when the camera's meter shuts off after the amount of time specified using **[Auto off timers]** in the Setup menu (page 196). See pages 203-204 for information on how to set the GPS to turn off with the camera's meter.

Lithium-ion batteries are fairly resilient to cold conditions. However, to ensure you can keep shooting, particularly in freezing conditions (i.e., below 0°C/32°F), keep at least one spare battery in a warm place such as an inside pocket, and as the performance of the battery in the camera dwindles, exchange it with the warm one. Allow the used battery time to warm up again and keep rotating between the batteries to maximize the shooting capacity.

Despite my warnings above, in my experience, shooting in an average ambient temperature range of 60° to 75°F (16° to 24°C) using autofocus with Vibration Reduction (VR) switched on, moderate use of the monitor for picture assessment, I have found that a single EN-EL14 battery will still deliver sufficient power for approximately 500 exposures.

BATTERY STORAGE

A fully charged Nikon Lithium-ion EN-EL14 battery in good condition will retain its full capacity over a short period of non-use. However, if the battery is left dormant for a month or more, regardless of whether it is installed in a camera or not, expect it to suffer a perceptible loss of charge, so ensure it is recharged fully before use (see comments concerning top-up charging on page 38). If you expect to store a camera battery for a protracted period, avoid leaving it fully charged or heavily discharged. Storing a fully charged battery can have a long-term effect on its overall capacity, while storing a heavily discharged battery can risk it shifting to a deeply discharged state, which can damage it. The optimum charge level for a battery that will be stored for four weeks or more is 20–80%. Always store your camera and batteries in a well-ventilated, cool, dry place, and ensure the protective terminal cover is in place.

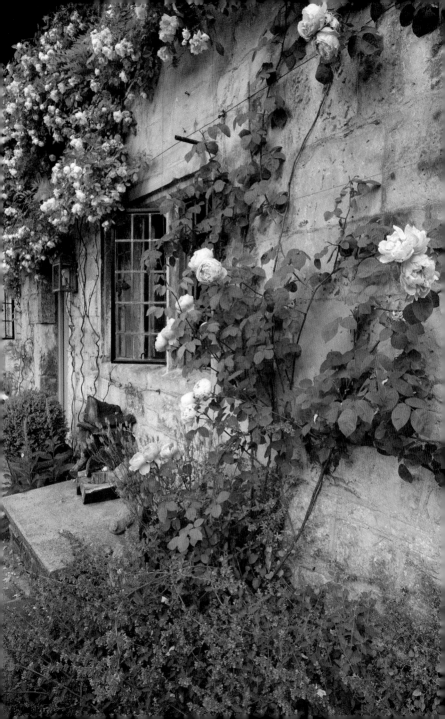

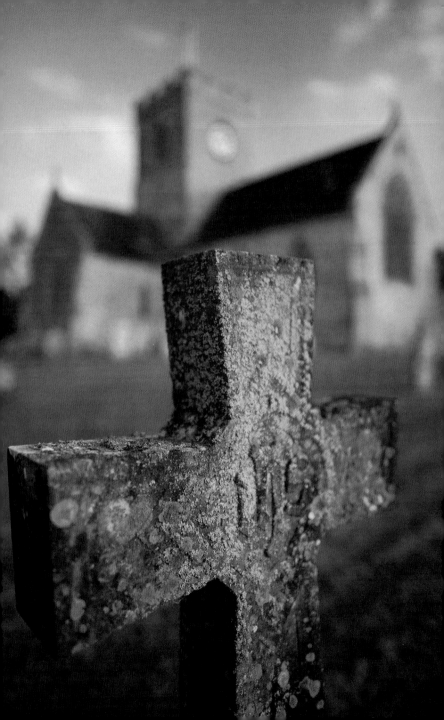

The Exposure and Focusing Systems

Regardless of whether you are content to let the D3100 make decisions about exposure settings or you prefer to take control of the camera and make them for yourself, it is essential to understand how the camera reads, evaluates, and records light.

ISO SENSITIVITY

Shooting with film requires you to make a decision about which ISO (sensitivity) rating to choose in order to cope with the prevailing or expected lighting conditions, and the entire roll must be exposed at the same ISO value. One of the great advantages of digital photography is that digital cameras allow you to adjust the ISO sensitivity from picture to picture. The ISO sensitivity rating used by Nikon DSLR cameras follows the guidelines laid down by the International Organization for Standardization for rating film speed (sensitivity) using the ISO scale; therefore, where the sensitivity setting on a camera complies with these guidelines, it is referred to as being ISO equivalent.

The D3100 offers ISO equivalent sensitivity settings from 200 to 3200 that can be adjusted in steps of 1.0 EV, plus the option to increase it by up to 2 EV above ISO 3200 in single steps of 1.0 EV (offering an extended ISO range equivalent to 100 – 12,800). The option to shift the sensitivity outside the normal range is referred to as Hi 1 (ISO 6400) and Hi 2 (ISO 12,800).

> The list of ISO values is displayed in the Information Display when you select the ISO item and press ⊗.

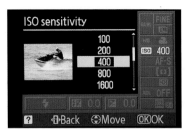

The base level ISO sensitivity of ISO 100 is where the sensor of the D3100 delivers its optimal performance, with the broadest dynamic range and lowest signal to noise ratio, so use this to derive the maximum potential image quality. To adjust the ISO sensitivity, press **Info** button to open the Information Display, and then press the **⊞** button, place the highlighted cursor on the current ISO value and press ⊗. Use ▼ and ▲ to select the required value and then press ⊗. The Hi 1 / Hi 2 options are at the bottom of the list of sensitivity values. Alternatively, the ISO sensitivity can be adjusted via the [ISO sensitivity settings] item in the Shooting menu. The camera also has the ability to adjust the ISO sensitivity automatically according to the light conditions; this feature is also set via the same item in the Shooting menu.

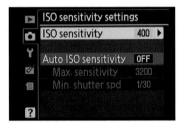
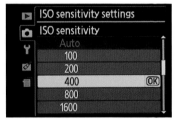

∧ The screen shots above show the main [ISO sensitivity settings] menu and the list of ISO values within the menu.

HIGH ISO PERFORMANCE

The analogy with film ISO continues insomuch as, at higher ISO sensitivity settings, a digital image will show an increasing amount of electronic noise. Generally, as the ISO sensitivity value is hiked higher and higher, other unwanted effects appear increasingly: Dynamic range is reduced (by about one stop of dynamic range for each full stop increase in ISO), plus the saturation of color and the tonal separation are reduced, leading to a flatter and duller appearance to the image.

When exposure settings are accurate, the high ISO performance of the D3100 is remarkably good. For the absolute optimum image quality, keep ISO sensitivity set to 100, where the D3100 is easily capable of producing a dynamic range of no less than nine stops. That said, unless you really ramp up the level of contrast and sharpening in-camera or photograph a scene with excessively high contrast, separating shots taken at an ISO 100, 200, or 400 is an exercise in splitting hairs; the ISO performance of the D3100 is still very good up to ISO 800, making it possible to shoot at just about any combination of camera settings (e.g., compression, contrast, color saturation, sharpening) with virtually no detrimental effect on image quality. That said, you can still expect to see noise in any image if you shoot using a long exposure (i.e., one second or longer) and forget to use the Noise Reduction feature in the Shooting menu.

Dynamic range, color saturation, resolution of detail, and noise levels, remain remarkably good at ISO 800 and 1600—practical solutions, provided that contrast and saturation are set appropriately (i.e., do not set these too high, as it is far better to adjust them at a later stage in post processing). Furthermore, the noise at ISO 1600 can be used for creative purposes, and is particularly effective with the black-and-white options available on the D3100, emulating the qualities of high-speed, grainy black-and-white film. Push the ISO to the top end of its normal range, ISO 3200, and the effects seen at ISO 1600 appear stronger with an increase in blurring of detail and noise grain pattern, but the latter is still tight and the results are very acceptable. Move beyond the normal ISO range to the Hi 1 (ISO 6400) setting, and there is a noticeable change in ISO performance, where there is a perceptible loss in dynamic range, a further increase in noise and contrast, noticeably stronger blurring of detail and some yellow / purple blotchiness in dark-tone areas of the image. I would consider the highest ISOs as last resort options, particularly the ISO 12,800 Hi2 setting. To help reduce the effects of noise at higher ISO sensitivity settings, select the [Noise reduction] feature available via the Shooting menu. While this can be quite effective, it will result in some loss of definition in very fine detail. Unless you have good reason to try and deal with ISO noise in-camera, it is preferable to use either the noise reduction feature of an NEF (RAW) file converter, or a dedicated noise reduction application, such as Dfine (www.niksoftware.com), Noise Ninja (www.picturecode.com) or Neat Image (www.neatimage.com).

ISO SENSITIVITY AUTO CONTROL

It is important to understand how this feature works, as it may not be quite what you expect. In the Programmed-Auto (P) and Aperture-Priority (A) autoexposure modes, the ISO sensitivity will not be altered unless underexposure would occur at the value specified for [Min. shutter spd] option under the [Auto ISO sensitivity] item, which is a sub-heading item under the [ISO sensitivity settings] item in the Shooting menu. The range of shutter speeds for [Min. shutter spd] extends from 1 second to 1/2000. However, if the camera cannot achieve a proper exposure at the ISO sensitivity specified as the [Max. sensitivity] value, which covers the range from ISO 200 to Hi 2 (ISO 12,800), the D3100 will then begin to select slower shutter speeds.

In Shutter-Priority (S) autoexposure mode, the ISO sensitivity is shifted when the exposure reaches the maximum aperture available on the lens. The automated control of ISO is probably most useful with this exposure mode because it will raise the sensitivity setting and thus maintain the pre-selected shutter speed, which is usually critical to the success of the picture when shooting fast paced action. Again, the [Max. sensitivity] option for the ISO sensitivity can be specified under the [Auto ISO sensitivity] item. In Manual exposure mode, the sensitivity is shifted if the selected shutter speed and aperture cannot attain a correct exposure (as indicated by the analog exposure scale displayed in the viewfinder). When the [Auto ISO sensitivity] feature is active, ISO-AUTO is displayed in the viewfinder and ISO-A is shown in the Information Display; these warnings will blink if the ISO sensitivity is altered from the value set by the user.

> The screen shot at right shows the Auto ISO Sensitivity option has been activated, together with values for the [Max. sensitivity], set to ISO 3200 and [Min. shutter spd], set to 1/30 second.

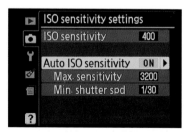

TTL METERING

The D3100 has three metering pattern options that will be familiar if you have used a Nikon AF camera before: Matrix, Center-Weighted, and Spot, which are available in P, A, S, and M shooting modes only. In all other exposure modes, the camera selects the Matrix metering pattern automatically. To select a metering pattern, press the [info] button to open the Information Display, and then press the ⏺ button, place the highlighted cursor on the current metering option and press ⊛. Use ▼ and ▲ to select the required option and then press ⊛. The appropriate icon will be displayed in the Information Display.

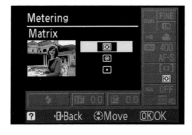

▣ *MATRIX METERING*

The metering pattern for this mode covers virtually the entire frame area with each of its 420 segments. The 420-segment RGB metering sensor is located in the viewfinder head of the camera just above the eyepiece and acts as a sampling point.

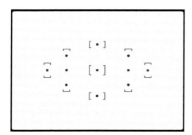

‹ The coverage of the Matrix metering pattern extends virtually to the edge of the full frame area.

There is a small diffraction grating located immediately in front of this sensor, and together, the two elements form the core of Nikon's innovative Scene Recognition System. The purpose of the diffraction grating is to separate the light falling on the sensor into its component colors and thus improve the efficiency and accuracy with which the camera assesses both the color and contrast of the light from the scene being photographed. The D3100 uses this enhanced information to improve metering accuracy, especially for skin tones.

To derive the most from the Matrix metering capabilities of the D3100, it is necessary to use a D- or G-type Nikkor lens, since these provide additional focus distance information, which assists the camera in estimating how far away the subject is located. The metering system also knows which AF point is selected and uses this information to estimate the position of the subject within the frame. Nikon calls the system 3D Color Matrix Metering II. If an AF Nikkor lens that does not communicate distance information to the camera is used, the system defaults to standard color Matrix metering II (i.e., the distance information is not integrated in the exposure computations).

In Matrix metering (and i-TTL flash control) the D3100 benefits from the enhanced analysis of highlights within the frame achieved by the Scene Recognition System feature, which is combined with its assessment of color, as well as brightness and contrast, and then compared against a database containing a total of over 30,000 brightness distribution patterns derived from actual sample images that cover an enormous range of lighting conditions. The result is Nikon's most advanced TTL metering available to date in a camera of this class. Matrix metering uses four principal factors when calculating an exposure value:

O The overall brightness level in a scene
O The ratio of brightness between the 420 segments
O The focused distance, provided by the lens (D- or G-type only)
O The location of the active AF point

When shooting an evenly illuminated scene with moderate contrast, where the active AF point covers a mid-tone value, the D3100 produces consistently good exposures via its Matrix metering. Furthermore, when shooting a scene filled with very light tones, for example snow or white sand, the Matrix metering system of the D3100 will usually cope very

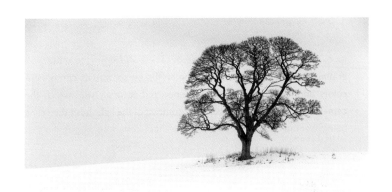

∧ Matrix metering is the most sophisticated TTL metering method on the D3100 and can be relied upon in most shooting situations, even challenging ones like this snowy scene.

well and not require anywhere near as much Exposure Compensation as applied, compared with previous Nikon camera models in this class.

However, the Matrix metering does appear to produce greater variability in results when using Single-Point AF Area mode and the active AF point covers a very light or very dark tone (i.e., the camera's metering seems to pay more attention to the tone under the active AF point compared with some Nikon camera models). In these situations, it is advisable to check the histogram display to monitor both highlight and shadow levels.

⓪ CENTER-WEIGHTED METERING

Available in P, A, S, and M exposure modes only, the Center-Weighted metering pattern harkens back to the TTL metering systems used by early Nikon SLR film cameras. In these cameras, the frame area was usually divided in a 60:40 ratio, with the bias placed on the central portion of the frame. The D3100 uses a higher ratio of 75:25, with 75% of the exposure reading based on the central area of the frame and the remaining 25% based on the outer area. For an unknown reason, Nikon has decided to dispense with marking the focusing screen that indicates the area covered by the 8-mm-diameter circle at the center of the viewfinder image, so use the position of the inner nine AF points as an approximate guide instead. Unlike Matrix metering, no color information is assessed when the Center-Weighted pattern is selected, so metering is performed using a grayscale.

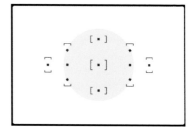

> The coverage of the Center-Weighted metering pattern places its emphasis within an 8-mm-diameter circle at the frame's center, though this area is not marked specifically on the focusing screen of the D3100.

HINT: Center-Weighted metering offers nowhere near the level of sophistication of Matrix metering, but for some subjects, its simplicity can be an advantage for photographers who like to control exposure and understand how it works.

⊡ SPOT METERING

Available in P, A, S, and M exposure modes only, Spot metering is extremely useful for metering from a highly specific area of a scene. For example, when faced with a subject against a virtually black background, Matrix metering system may overexpose the subject. The Spot meter, on the other hand, allows a reading to be taken from the subject only, without it being influenced by the background. The sensing area for the Spot-metering pattern is a circle approximately 0.14 inch (3.5 mm) in diameter, which represents about 2.5% of the total frame area. This circle is centered on the active AF point, unless Auto-Area AF is selected for AF-Area mode when shooting still pictures, in which case, the central AF point is the only area to perform metering. Again, as with the Center-Weighted pattern, no color information is assessed when the Spot-metering pattern is selected, so metering is performed using a grayscale.

HINT: It is essential to remember that in Center-Weighted and Spot metering, the TTL metering system measures reflected light, and is calibrated to give a correct exposure for a mid-tone (middle grey). When using either of these two metering patterns, you must make sure that the part of the scene you meter from represents such a mid-tone. Otherwise, you may need to compensate the exposure value. Remember, it is the tone (degree of reflectivity) that is important, not color.

HINT: In Dynamic-Area AF, the D3100 will attempt to follow a moving subject by shifting focus control between different AF points. If this occurs, the Spot metering also shifts, following the active AF point.

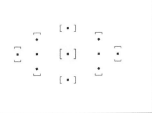

‹ The coverage of the Spot metering pattern covers a circle centered on the active AF point that represents about 2.5% of the total frame area.

AUTO AND SCENE MODES

The Auto mode, Auto Flash Off mode, and six dedicated Scene modes represent the most automated level of control available on the D3100 (note the same range of automated exposure modes is used when operating the D3100 in its GUIDE mode—see the GUIDE mode section on pages 58-65 for full details). The camera manages many key controls and features in an attempt to select a combination of shutter speed and aperture that will be appropriate for the current scene. It does this by using information from the through-the-lens (TTL) metering system, which assesses the overall level of illumination, contrast, and color quality of the prevailing light, together with information from the autofocus system used to estimate the location of the subject in the frame area and its distance from the camera, plus additional information from the camera's sensor to control automated White Balance. This leaves you with limited ability to intervene and override settings—for example, the metering pattern, Exposure Compensation, White Balance, and Picture Controls cannot be adjusted from their default settings. This is unlikely to be of any concern to the novice who is content to let the D3100 make decisions on their behalf, but the for more seasoned user, I would recommend avoiding these modes and suggest working in either Aperture-Priority, Shutter-Priority, or Manual exposure modes.

> The Information Display for the AUTO mode; notice how the White Balance, metering, Exposure Compensation, and Flash Output Compensation items are grayed out, as they cannot be altered from default settings in the auto modes.

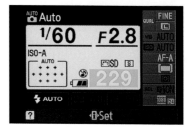

If the [Graphic] option is selected under the [Info display format] item in the Setup menu, the relationship between the shutter speed and aperture is shown by way of a diagram in the Information Display, which shows how the aperture changes to a large value (low f/number) as, the duration of the shutter speed decreases, and conversely, how the aperture changes to a small value (high f/number) as, the duration of the shutter speed increases.

AUTO AND THE SCENE MODE OPTIONS

When using the AUTO and Scene modes, the level of user control is restricted, but the following controls can be adjusted from their default settings in most cases: Image Quality, Image Size (JPEG only), ISO, AF mode, AF-Area mode, flash mode, and D-Movie settings. If you alter any default setting, it is only retained while the camera remains in the current shooting mode. If you turn the Mode dial to another shooting mode, the default setting is restored.

- The following controls cannot be adjusted from their default settings: White Balance, metering, and the Picture Controls (contrast and sharpening are applied automatically).
- The following functions are not available: Exposure Compensation, Flash Compensation.

AUTO Auto: The AUTO mode is designed as a universal point-and-shoot mode and is most effective for general-purpose snapshot photography, such as family events or vacations.

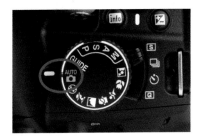

🚫 Auto Flash Off: This mode is essentially the same as the AUTO mode, with the exception that the built-in flash is turned off and will not operate, regardless of the ambient illumination (even if it is very dark). It is useful in situations where the use of flash is undesirable—for example, when shooting in a museum where flash is prohibited, or in natural low-light conditions where you do not want to spoil the atmosphere by using flash. Although the operation of the built-in flash is cancelled, the AF-Assist Illuminator lamp will still function to assist autofocus operation in poor lighting conditions.

> **HINT:** Since the camera can set slow shutter speeds in this mode, always check the viewfinder information to ensure that the selected shutter speed will allow the camera to be held without risk of camera shake affecting the picture. At slow shutter speeds, consider using a camera support, such as a tripod

🏃 Portrait: The 🏃 mode is designed to select a wide aperture (low f/number) in order to produce a picture with a shallow depth of field. Generally, this renders the background out-of-focus so it does not detract from the subject, although the effect is also dependent on the distance between the subject and the background, and the focal length of the lens used, both of which influence subject magnification. This mode is most effective with focal lengths of 100mm or more and when the subject is relatively far away from the background.

⛰ **Landscape:** The ⛰ mode is designed to select a small aperture in order to produce a picture with an extended depth of field. Generally, this renders everything from the foreground to the horizon in focus, although this will depend to some degree how close the lens is to the nearest subject. This mode is most effective with wide-angle or wide-angle zoom lenses, and when the scene is well lit.

HINT: When using a short focal length (i.e., less than 35mm), try to include an element of interest in the foreground of the scene, as well as the middle distance, to help produce a balanced composition and a way of leading the viewer's eye into the picture.

👶 **Child:** The parameters are similar to the 🧑 mode, except the Picture Control is Standard to give a more vibrant rendition of color.

HINT: One of the simplest ways to improve pictures of children is to lower the camera to your subject's eye level.

🏃 **Sports:** The 🏃 mode is designed to select a wide aperture in order to maintain the highest possible shutter speed to "freeze" motion in fast–paced action. It also has a beneficial side effect: This combination produces a picture with a very shallow depth of field that helps to isolate the subject from the background. This mode is most effective with telephoto or telephoto-zoom lenses, and when there are no obstructions between the camera and the subject that may cause the autofocus function to focus on something other than the subject.

HINT: There is always a slight delay between pressing the shutter release button and the shutter opening; therefore, it is important to anticipate the peak moment of the action and press the shutter just before it occurs. The decisive moment will be missed if you wait to see it in the viewfinder before pressing the shutter release

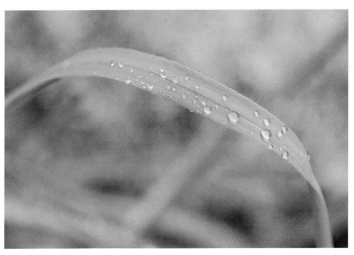

∧ The dedicated Scene modes can be helpful to the less experienced user, but they do impose limitations on some aspects of camera control.

🌷 Close-Up: The 🌷 mode is for taking pictures at short shooting distances of subjects such as flowers, insects, and other small objects. It is designed to select a small aperture (high f/number) in order to produce a picture with an extended depth-of-field. Generally, depth of field is limited when working at very short focus distances, even when using small apertures, so this program tries to render as much of the subject in focus as possible. The final effect will also be dependent on how close the camera is to the subject and the focal length of the lens used.

🌃 Night Portrait: The 🌃 mode is designed to capture properly exposed pictures of people against a background that is dimly lit. It is useful when you want to include background detail, such as a cityscape or sunset, in the photo and is most effective when the background is in low light, as opposed to near dark, or totally dark conditions. The built-in Speedlight will activate automatically in low light; alternatively, an external Speedlight such as the SB-400 or SB-600 can be used to supplement the ambient light.

THE EXPOSURE AND FOCUSING SYSTEMS

58

MODE / CONTROL	WHITE BALANCE	PICTURE CONTROL	FLASH SYNC MODE	ACTIVE D-LIGHTING	AF-AREA MODE
AUTO	Auto	Standard	Auto	Auto	Auto area
FLASH OFF	Auto	Standard	Flash off	Auto	Auto area
PORTRAIT	Auto	Portrait	TTL	Auto	Auto area
LANDSCAPE	Auto	Standard	Flash off	Auto	Single point
CHILD	Auto	Portrait	TTL	Auto	Auto area
SPORT	Auto	Standard	Flash off	Auto	Dynamic-area
CLOSE-UP	Auto	Standard	Auto	Auto	Single point
NIGHT PORTRAIT	Auto	Portrait	Auto slow	Auto	Auto area

GUIDE *MODE*

In line with the design ethos of the D3100 to provide simple, intuitive operation, even for the complete novice photographer, Nikon has endeavored to enhance the GUIDE mode of the D3100, a feature that was first introduced on its predecessor, the D3000. It can best be described as an alternative way of using the ᴬᵁᵀᴼ Auto mode, ⚡ Auto Flash Off mode, and six dedicated Scene modes, where the user is supported by a highly descriptive interface, which is peppered with graphics and example images to assist them in understanding how to achieve successful pictures of certain types of subjects. The GUIDE mode interface also embraces a number of the camera controls that can be accessed from the normal Information Display, and items from the camera's menu system. Camera settings made within the GUIDE mode are only retained while the camera remains in this mode; if you change to the ᴬᵁᵀᴼ Auto mode, ⚡ Auto Flash Off mode, any of the six dedicated Scene modes, or the P, A, S, and M exposure modes, the settings you made in GUIDE mode will no longer be effective, and the camera will revert back to whatever settings had been made previously. To enter GUIDE mode, turn the Mode dial to GUIDE; the GUIDE mode is structured around three main strands, **[Shoot]**, **[View/delete]**, and **[Set up]**, which are displayed as soon as the GUIDE mode display opens. Within each strand, you'll be led through a sequence of pages displayed on the LCD monitor that set out clearly what, how, and why certain settings are selected. Some examples of the GUIDE mode are on the pages that follow:

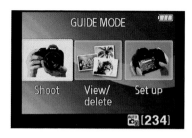

< This is the GUIDE mode main menu. Here, you select from three submenus: [Shoot], [View/delete], and [Set up].

GUIDE *MODE: SHOOT (EASY OPERATION)*

The Easy operation options allow you to select a specific subject / scene type. For example, [Sleeping faces] uses the settings for the Child scene mode, except it is modified so the flash will not fire, while [Distant subjects] and [Moving subjects] uses the Sports scene mode settings. After selecting the required item, press ▶ to open the next page that provides a description of the scene mode that will be used with hints on camera settings, as well as options for [Start shooting] or [More settings]. The icon for the scene mode in use is displayed at the bottom of the LCD monitor. If you select [Start shooting] and press ▶, the next menu page displays three options: [Use the viewfinder], [Use Live View], and [Shoot movies]. Highlight the required option and press ⊛ to enter the selected mode directly.

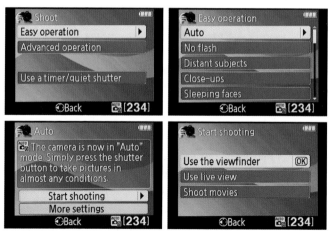

Select [Easy operation] from the [Shoot] strand. You then have the choice to select from a number of different specific camera-operation / subject / scene types. Here, [Auto] has been selected and the camera provides a description of the option, followed by access to three shooting options from the [Start shooting] item.

If you select [More settings] and press ▶, the next menu page displays options for three additional shooting parameters: [Flash mode], [Release mode], and [ISO sensitivity], as well as the [Start shooting] item. Depending on the item selected (e.g., [Distant subjects]), the option to adjust settings for the flash mode may be grayed out, as flash operation is not possible. Once the additional settings have been made, highlight the [Start shooting] item and press ▶ to display the following options: [Use the viewfinder], [Use Live View], and [Shoot movies]. Highlight the required option and press ⓞⓚ to enter the selected mode directly.

GUIDE MODE: SHOOT (ADVANCED OPERATION)

The [Advanced operation] mode does not offer the same range of specific subject / scene types as the [Easy operation]; however, there are additional options to refine control of the shutter speed and aperture for pictorial effect. The following sequence of screen shots, which is shown in chronological order, depicts the path through the [Advanced operation] > [Soften backgrounds] option to select a large aperture (low f/number) to achieve a shallow depth of field, so the background appears blurred. Note that on the second page the camera displays advice about using a "small value" for the aperture number, and shows an example picture on the third page to illustrate the effect of different aperture values on background sharpness:

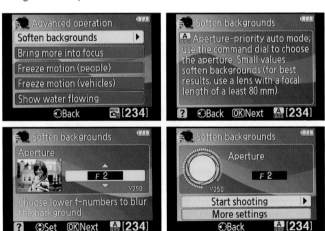

The other four options, [Bring more into focus], [Freeze motion (people)], [Freeze motion (vehicles)], and [Show water flowing] do just what the names say, and the enhanced GUIDE mode displays advice and example pictures to help you decide. Once you have established the required setting for the aperture or shutter speed according to the shooting technique you selected under [Advanced operation] you can choose to begin shooting or select [More settings] to further refine camera control. Working from the top of each list of items, the following sequence of screen shots shows the path through the [Advanced operation] > [Soften backgrounds] > [More settings] options, showing each menu item and its subsequent menu page that displays the available options (the submenus are the same for [Bring more into focus], [Freeze motion (people)], [Freeze motion (vehicles)], and [Show water flowing]).

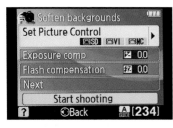

∧ The list of options on the first page of the [Soften backgrounds] screen; note that [Set Picture Control] is selected by default.

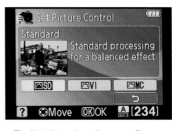

∧ The [Set Picture Control] screen allows you to select one of the following options: [Standard], [Vivid], or [Monochrome] (see pages 156-165 for more on Picture Controls).

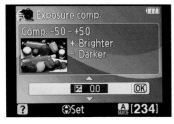

∧ The [Exposure comp.] option allows you to darken or brighten the final images by small increments (see pages 72-73 for more on Exposure Compensation).

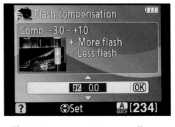

∧ The [Flash compensation] screen allows you to adjust the flash output level (see pages 249-250 for more on Flash Output Compensation).

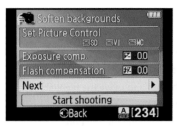

^ Selecting the [Next] option brings you to the next page of the [Soften backgrounds] menu.

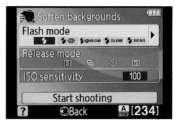

^ [Flash mode] will be selected by default in the second page of the [Soften backgrounds] screen.

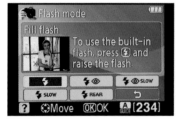

^ The [Flash mode] screen allows you to select the mode for the built-in flash (see pages 238-240 for more on flash mode).

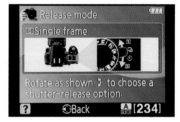

^ The [Release mode] screen allows you to select a shutter release mode (see pages 95-98 for more on release mode).

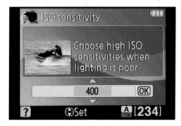

^ The [ISO sensitivity] screen allows you to adjust the ISO level (see pages 45-49 for more on ISO sensitivity).

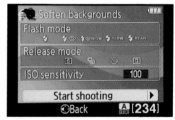

^ Select [Start shooting] to select the method of shooting: [Use the viewfinder], [use live view], or [Shoot movies].

> You will always know when you are in GUIDE mode, as the word GUIDE is displayed beneath the exposure mode icon in the top left corner of the monitor and in the menu bar at the bottom of the screen.

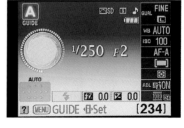

When you're finished making all of the above settings, select [Start shooting] and press ▶ to display the following options: [Use the viewfinder], [Use Live View], and [Shoot movies]. Highlight the required option and press ⊛ to enter the selected mode directly. Regardless of the mode you enter you can press the ⊞ button and move the highlighted cursor to the relevant item using the multi selector button to select any of the camera controls, or settings displayed in the Information Display. To open the item press the ⊛ button. Select the required option by highlighting it and press the ⊛ button. To return to Information Display, Live View, or D-Movie mode respectively, press the ⊞ button again.

GUIDE *MODE: VIEW/DELETE*

The items available in this menu replicate those of the main Playback menu; however, the range of items and options is restricted to help simplify camera operation. The menu contains just five items, as follows:

[View single photos]: Highlight this item and press ⊛ to display the most recent picture full-frame on the monitor. To view other pictures, press ◀ or ▶. To enlarge an image, press the ⊕ button, and use the Multi Selector to scroll around the image using the navigation window shown in the display as a guide. To return to the normal full-frame view, press the ⊖ button until the navigation window is no longer displayed.

[View multiple photos]: Highlight this item and press ⊛ to display up to four images at a time on the monitor. The currently selected image is shown with a yellow border around it. To select a different image, use the Multi Selector to shift the yellow border. To enlarge an image, press the ⊕ button, and use the Multi Selector to scroll around the image using the navigation window shown in the display as a guide. To return to the normal full-frame view, press the ⊖ button until the navigation window is no longer displayed.

[Choose a date]: Highlight this item and press ⊛ to display a calendar; a thumbnail of the first image taken on each date will be shown. A yellow border highlights the currently selected date; use the Multi Selector to highlight a different date. A thumbnail image of all the pictures taken on the selected date is shown in a column down the right side of the screen. Press the ◷ button to highlight an image in the column viewer, and then press the Multi Selector up or down to scroll through the images. To see an enlarged view of the highlighted image, press and hold the ◷ button. To return to the calendar view, press the ◷ button.

[View a slide show]: Highlight this item and press ▶ to display two options: [Start] and [Frame interval]. [Start] is highlighted by default and pressing ⊛ will begin a slide show of all the images saved in the current folder on the installed memory card. To pause the slide show, press ⊛ again; three options will be displayed: [Restart], [Frame interval], and [Exit]. Highlight the required option and press ⊛. To set the display duration for each image, highlight [Frame interval] and press ▶ to display the following options: [2 s], [3 s], [5 s], and [10 s]. Highlight the required duration and press the ⊛ button.

[Delete photos]: Highlight this item and press ▶ to display to following options: [Delete multiple photos], [Delete photos by date], and [Delete all photos].

○ Highlight [Delete multiple photos] and press ▶ to display up to six thumbnail images. The currently selected image is shown with a yellow border. To select it for deletion, press the ◷ button and the 🗑 icon will be displayed in the top right corner of the image. To select another image, press the Multi Selector to highlight it with the yellow border and press the ◷ button. Repeat the process until all the images to be deleted have been marked with the 🗑 icon. Press and hold the ◷ button to view an enlarged image. To complete the process, press ⊛ to display a confirmation dialog box, highlight [Yes], and press ⊛ again.

○ Highlight [Delete photos by date] and press ▶ to display a list of dates on which pictures have been recorded. Highlight the required date and press ▶ to place a check mark in the box next to the selected date. To view thumbnails of the images on the selected date, press the ◷ button. The currently selected image is shown with a yellow border; use the Multi Selector to highlight a different image. Press and hold the ◷ button to see an enlarged view of the highlighted image. Press the ⊖ button to return to the date list display. Once you have selected the required date(s), press ⊛ to display a confirmation dialog box, highlight **[Yes]**, and press ⊛ again.

○ Highlight **[Delete all photos]** and press ▶ to display a confirmation dialog box, highlight **[Yes]**, and press ⊛ again to delete all the pictures on the current memory card.

GUIDE *MODE: SET UP*

The items available in this menu replicate those of the main Setup menu; however, the range of items and options is restricted to help simplify camera operation.

The options in the GUIDE mode Set Up menu operate in exactly the same way as the same options in the main Set Up menu. For full details see the relevant sections as follows:

○ **[Image quality]**: See pages 121-131.
○ **[Image size]**: See pages 129-131.
○ **[Playback folder]**: See page 176.
○ **[Print set (dpof)]**: See pages 284-288.
○ **[Format memory card]**: See pages 120-122.
○ **[LCD brightness]**: See page 188.
○ **[Info background color]**: See pages 188-189.
○ **[Auto info display]**: See page 189.
○ **[Video mode]**: See page 189.
○ **[Time zone and date]**: See page 191.
○ **[Language]**: See page 192.
○ **[Auto off timers]**: See page 196.
○ **[Beep]**: See page 197.
○ **[Date imprint]**: See page 201.
○ **[Slot empty release]**: See page 201.
○ **[Movie settings]**: See page 142.
○ **[HDMI]**: See pages 189-190.
○ **[Flicker reduction]**: See page 190.

P, S, A, AND M EXPOSURE MODES

The D3100 offers four further exposure modes, which are also set via the Mode dial.

P PROGRAMMED AUTO

Programmed-Auto mode, also referred to as Program mode, adjusts both the shutter speed and lens aperture automatically to produce what the camera considers to be a properly exposed image, as determined by the selected metering mode. If you decide that a particular combination of the shutter speed and aperture chosen by the camera is not suitable, you can override the P mode settings by turning the command dial while the camera's TTL metering is active. This is called Flexible Program mode and P* appears in the Information Display and the viewfinder to indicate that you have overridden the exposure from the shutter speed and aperture values selected initially by the camera. The two values change in tandem, so the overall exposure level remains the same (i.e., setting a longer shutter speed results in the size of the lens aperture being reduced); rotating the Command dial to the right sets a larger aperture (smaller f/number) and a faster shutter speed, while rotating the Command dial to the left sets a smaller aperture (larger f/number) and a slower shutter speed.

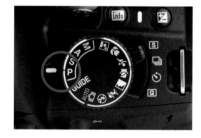

> The Mode dial set to P mode

NOTE: If you override the Program mode, it will remain locked to its new settings for shutter speed and aperture even if the meter auto-powers off and is then switched on again by pressing the shutter release halfway. To cancel the override, you must do one of the following: rotate the command dial until the asterisk * next to the P is no longer displayed, change the exposure mode, or turn the power off.

In my opinion, Program mode is little better than the point-and-shoot exposure control options of the 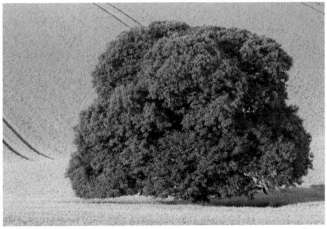AUTO and Scene shooting modes, as you effectively relinquish control of exposure to the camera. If you want to make informed decisions about shutter speed and aperture to achieve the most accurate exposure, regardless of the shooting conditions, or to impart your own creativity to your photography, do not use P mode!

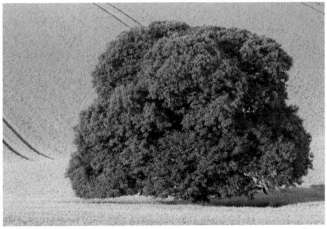

∧ In many shooting situations, control of the lens aperture is a priority, since it will determine the depth of field in the final image.

A *APERTURE-PRIORITY AUTO*

In this mode, the photographer selects an aperture value (f/number) and the D3100 will choose a shutter speed to produce an appropriate exposure, as determined by the camera using the selected metering mode. The aperture is controlled by the Command dial and is changed in steps of 0.3 EV. The shutter speed the D3100 selects will also change in steps of 0.3 EV.

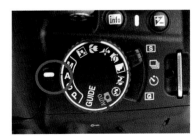

‹ The Mode dial set to A mode

S *SHUTTER-PRIORITY AUTO*

In this mode, the photographer selects a shutter speed between 30 seconds and 1/4000 second and the D3100 will choose an aperture value to produce an appropriate exposure, as determined by the camera using the selected metering mode. The shutter speed is controlled by the command dial and is changed in steps of 0.3 EV. The aperture value the D3100 selects will also change in steps of 0.3 EV.

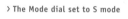

> The Mode dial set to S mode

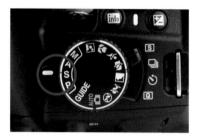

NOTE: In P, A, and S modes, the D3100 will display 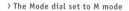 as a warning in the viewfinder if the subject or scene is too dark; and conversely, the camera will display the 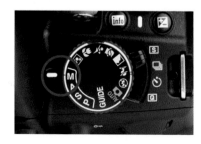 warning if the subject or scene is too bright.

M *MANUAL*

Manual mode offers the photographer total control over exposure, and is probably the most useful if you want to learn more about the relationship between shutter speed and aperture and how they affect the final appearance of your pictures. You control both the shutter speed, via the Command dial, and lens aperture, via the Command dial plus the 🔲 button.

> The Mode dial set to M mode

An analog exposure scale displayed in the Information Display and viewfinder indicates the level of exposure your settings would produce. If the camera determines the exposure values are set for a proper exposure, a single indent mark appears below the central 0 point of the scale. If the camera determines that the settings would produce an underexposed result, the degree of underexposure is indicated by the number of indent marks that appear to the right (minus) side of the central 0. Conversely, if the chosen settings would create an overexposed result, the degree of overexposure is indicated by the number of indent marks to the left (plus) side of the central 0. The more indent marks that appear, the greater the degree of deviance from the "correct" exposure, as calculated by the camera (see the illustration below).

Suggested Optimal Exposure	Underexposed by 0.3EV	Overexposed by more than 2EV
+. . 0 . .−	+. . 0 . .−	+. . 0 . .−

If the [Graphic] option under the [Info display format] in the Setup menu is selected for P, A, S, and M modes, the relationship between the shutter speed and aperture is shown by way of a diagram in the Information Display, as described previously, under "AUTO and Scene modes."

LONG EXPOSURES

To shoot at exposure durations of more than 30 seconds, the D3100 has the [Bulb] setting, which is only available in the M exposure mode. It can be useful when shooting in very low-light conditions, or for creating special effects, such as photographing fireworks or light-trails of moving traffic at night. Using a tripod or some other form of stable camera support is essential for this type of shooting if details in the scene being photographed are to be rendered with good definition. You may also want to consider using the [Noise reduction] feature, which can be found in the Shooting menu, as electronic noise in the image tends to be more prevalent when shooting at long shutter speed durations.

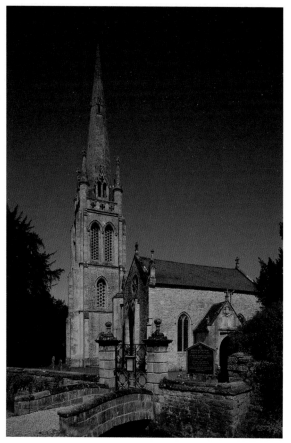

Select M on the Mode dial and rotate the Command dial until the shutter speed is displayed as **[Bulb]** in the viewfinder and Information Display, focus the camera, and then press and hold the shutter release button down all the way; to end the exposure, let go of the shutter release button. To prevent jarring the camera while holding down the shutter release button, use of the Nikon MC-DC2 remote release cable, an optional accessory, is recommended. The maximum duration of any single exposure is 30 minutes.

HINT: If you use the D3100 remotely when you make an exposure (i.e., your eye is not to the viewfinder eyepiece) you must ensure the viewfinder eyepiece is covered (the DK-5 cap is supplied for this purpose). The 420-segment RGB metering sensor of the D3100 is located within the viewfinder-head; therefore, light entering via the viewfinder eyepiece will influence exposure calculations made in P, A, and S exposure modes.

AUTOEXPOSURE (AE) LOCK

If you take a meter reading in any of the three automated exposure modes (P, A, or S) and recompose the picture after taking a reading, it is likely, particularly with Spot metering, that the metered area will now fall on a different part of the scene and probably produce a different exposure value. The D3100 allows you to lock the initial exposure reading in Center-Weighted or Spot metering before you reframe and shoot (note this feature is less effective for Matrix metering, because Matrix metering assesses the entire frame area and the range of contrast within it, as well as the level of overall scene brightness to produce the most balanced exposure). Start by positioning the part of the scene you want to meter within the appropriate metering area. Next, press the shutter release halfway to acquire focus and an exposure reading, then press and hold the **AE-L/AF-L** button to lock the exposure (and focus, except in Manual focus mode). You can now recompose and take the picture at the metered value. An **AE-L** icon will appear in the viewfinder display while this function is active. When using AE Lock, it is possible, although it requires some dexterity, to alter the shutter speed and / or aperture value in P, A, and S modes without changing the overall exposure level. A better option would be to assign the **[AE Lock hold]** option to the **AE-L/AF-L** button using the **[Buttons]** item in the Setup menu, so that once the **AE-L/AF-L** button is pressed, the initial exposure settings are locked until the button is pressed again.

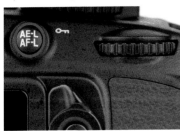

‹ The AE-L/AF-L button is located on the rear of the camera to the left of the Command dial.

HINT: It is possible to use the shutter release button to perform the Autoexposure Lock function; select **[On]** at the **[AE lock]** option under the **[Buttons]** item in the Setup menu.

EXPOSURE COMPENSATION

Exposure Compensation can be applied regardless of the TTL metering option in use, but the most consistent results are achieved with either Center-Weighted or Spot metering. As mentioned previously, in these latter two metering options, the D3100 uses simple grayscale metering with no color information or influence of the Scene Recognition System to affect the metered reading. Working on the assumption that the camera is pointed at a scene with a reflectivity that averages out to that of a mid-tone, it appears Nikon has calibrated the TTL metering against a reference that has a reflectivity value of approximately 12% to 13%. Hence, if you use an 18% gray photographic card to estimate exposure, you will find your results will be approximately 1/3 – 1/2 stop underexposed.

Many scenes you encounter will not reflect 12% to 13% of the light falling on them. For example, a landscape under a blanket of fresh snowfall is going to reflect far more light, while an animal with a coat of very dark brown or black fur will reflect far less than an average mid-tone. Unless you compensate your exposure accordingly for these extremes, the camera will attempt to render them as mid-tones, causing a light tone to appear underexposed and a dark tone to be overexposed.

To set an Exposure Compensation factor in P, A, and S exposure modes (it is disabled in AUTO and Scene shooting modes, as well as their equivalents in the GUIDE mode), hold down the ⊠ button, located to the rear and right of the shutter release button, and turn the Command dial until the required value is shown in the Information Display and viewfinder. Compensation can be set to values between -5 EV and +5 EV in steps of 0.3EV. The value is also displayed in the viewfinder while the button is held down. Exposure Compensation can also be set via the Information Display, where the level of any compensation applied will be shown. The ⊠ icon remains visible in the viewfinder, as a reminder that you have an Exposure Compensation value applied. Once you have set a compensation factor, it will remain locked until you hold down the ⊠ button and reset the compensation value to 0.0.

In M exposure mode, the exposure is set according to the values selected by the user for the shutter speed and aperture; if the analog display shows no deviance to either side of the 0 midpoint, the TTL metering system is suggesting the settings will produce a proper exposure level. This may not be the case, or the "correct" exposure may not be to your liking, so to compensate the exposure level in M mode, adjust either the shutter speed and / or the aperture value, so the display shows one or more indent marks on the analog scale, either to the right (positive compensation), or left (negative compensation) of the 0 midpoint, according to the amount of adjustment that is applied.

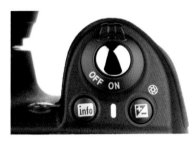

‹ The 🔲 (Exposure Compensation) button is located just behind the shutter release button.

EXPOSURE CONSIDERATIONS

If the D3100 is your first digital SLR camera, and your previous photography has been done shooting color negative film, you may find controlling exposure with the camera rather more demanding. Color negative (print) film is very tolerant to exposure errors, particularly overexposure, and the automated processing machines used to produce your prints are capable of correcting exposure errors over a range of –2 to +3 EV while adjusting color balance at the same time. Chances are that you will never have noticed your exposure errors when looking at the finished prints!

Controlling exposure with a digital SLR is analogous to shooting on transparency (slide) film—there is virtually no margin for error. Even moderate overexposure will "blow out" highlight detail, leaving no usable image data in these areas. Underexposure is no better, since it gives rise to electronic noise, which will degrade image quality, particularly in areas of dark tone, by producing a grainy texture and possibly some blotchiness in colors. To help assess the accuracy of an exposure, make sure you check the histogram display and pay attention to all three color channels, not just the luminance histogram, which is displayed in white.

There are other aspects to the selection of shutter speed and lens aperture that should be kept in mind beyond just the control of exposure level, such as attaining acceptable image sharpness when shooting with a handheld camera or photographing a moving subject, and the effect of aperture settings on depth of field.

DIGITAL INFRARED AND UV PHOTOGRAPHY

Many digital cameras have the ability to record light beyond the limits of the spectrum visible to the human eye, particularly in the region of near-infrared (IR), around a wavelength of 780nm (one nanometer = one millionth of a millimeter). Designers of digital cameras work hard to exclude IR light from digital cameras because it adversely affects apparent sharpness, reduces contrast in skies, and can reveal unappealing features of skin that would otherwise not be visible. Similar adverse effects occur due to ultra-violet (UV) light. The low-pass filter array in front of the CMOS sensor in the D3100 includes a layer designed to reduce the transmission of IR and UV light. It is very effective, and therefore, the D3100 cannot be recommended for either digital IR or UV light photography.

THE AUTOFOCUS SYSTEM

The autofocus (AF) system of the D3100 includes a 3D-Tracking capability made possible by the innovative Scene Recognition System (SRS) that has won wide acclaim in other recent Nikon DSLR camera models. However, the implementation of the 3D-Tracking in the D3100 is a little different from most of those models, with the exception of the Nikon D5000, since the camera has only eleven AF points. Therefore, less of the autofocus area (the total area of the frame covered by the AF points) provides focus information. The D3100 has fewer focus sampling points with its Multi-CAM1000 AF module compared with higher-specified Nikon models that have up to 3.5 times as many. And finally, the processing power of the D3100 is considerably lower compared with these other models. Hence,

Nikon promotes the abilities of the 3D-Tracking in the D3100 as being best-suited to rapid changes of composition where the camera to subject distance does not alter significantly between consecutive exposures, rather than trying to keep pace with a subject that is moving rapidly toward or away from the camera, particularly if that movement is erratic in both its speed and direction.

THE AUTOFOCUS SENSOR

The Multi-CAM 1000 AF module has—as its name implies—a total of 1000 photodiodes distributed between the 11 AF points. The 11 points are subdivided into one cross-type sensor at the center of the frame and ten line-type sensors; the latter are oriented in a variety of directions (see diagram on the next page).

When autofocus operation is initiated, the D3100 uses a phase-detection focusing method; the system uses a beam splitter comprising two optical prisms in a small semi-transparent area of the main-reflex mirror that capture the light rays coming from the opposite sides of the lens. They are coupled with a small secondary mirror located behind the main mirror that directs the light from these prisms to the Multi-Cam 1000 module, which is located in the base of the mirror box at the bottom of the camera. The double image projected onto the AF module is then analyzed for the patterns of light intensity and the phase difference between them and calculated to determine whether the subject is in front of or behind the current plane of focus. This not only informs the AF system which way the focus must be adjusted, but also by how much. The focus point is adjusted immediately and the phase difference checked; provided it is within the tolerances of the AF system, focus will not be altered again, as the camera has determined that focus has been acquired.

The central AF point is a cross-type, meaning it is sensitive to detail in both horizontal and vertical orientations; therefore, it is the most reliable. The remaining ten AF points are line-types; these are generally only sensitive to detail in a direction that is perpendicular to their orientation, for example, with the camera held horizontally, the two AF points farthest to the left and right of the frame generally only detect detail aligned with the long edge of the viewfinder frame. A new innovation in the D3100 is the diagonal alignment of some of the AF points; in previous cameras, the line-type sensors are aligned with either the long or short edges of the frame. In some shooting situations, where the line-type sensor aligns with a straight edge in the scene being photographed like a horizon line or the side of a building, the AF system can have difficulty in acquiring focus, whereas a diagonally aligned AF sensor is more likely to detect such an edge. It is also important to understand that the coverage of the AF point extends some way beyond the area covered by the markings for each shown on the focusing screen.

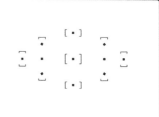

> The distribution of the 11 AF points is centered in the viewfinder frame.

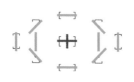

< The approximate coverage of the 11 AF points. In each case, the coverage extends farther than the area defined by the square brackets and small squares shown on the focusing screen. The central sensor (red) is a cross-type sensor, while the remaining ten (green) are line-type sensors (the colors are purely for illustrative purposes).

HINT: Sometimes when using one of the line-type sensing areas, the autofocus system of the D3100 will "hunt" (i.e., the camera will drive the focus of the lens back and forth, but is unable to attain focus). This indicates that the detail in the subject is aligned in the same orientation as the focus sensing area of the active AF point, and thus, there is insufficient contrast in the subject for the AF system to acquire focus. If this occurs, try twisting the camera slightly (10 – 15°). This slight adjustment is often enough to allow the camera to acquire focus, as the focus sensing area can detect more contrast in the detail of the subject. Once focus is confirmed, lock it and recompose the picture before releasing the shutter.

The AF point you select in either Single-Point AF or Dynamic-Area AF can have a profound effect on the camera's ability to achieve autofocus, depending on whether it is a cross- or a line-type. For example, the single cross-type sensor at the center of the frame is far more reliable in low-light or low-contrast conditions compared with the line-type sensors, which can often take longer (or even fail) to acquire focus in such conditions.

HINT: The AF system is designed to work with any Nikkor AF lens that has a maximum aperture of f/5.6 or larger. If an accessory such as a teleconverter or extension tube is used with a lens and reduces its effective maximum aperture to less than f/5.6, autofocus operation is likely to become slow and unreliable.

SCENE RECOGNITION SYSTEM

The autofocus system of the D3100 also benefits from the capabilities of Nikon's Scene Recognition System (SRS). This has enhanced the abilities of the 420-pixel, RGB-metering sensor, as described in the exposure section above. It enables the 420-pixel sensor to recognize a subject by its shape, size, and color. To employ the benefits of the SRS, it is necessary to use a D- or G-type Nikkor lens. The SRS requires the focus distance information these lenses provide to perform the necessary calculations in order for its two principal features, subject identification and subject tracking, to function. The system brings significant benefits to the performance of the autofocus system, as well as improving the autoexposure and Auto White Balance functions.

The SRS is optimized to recognize skin tones, particularly in any area on the 420-segment RGB sensor that relates to the average size of a human face; this is why the focus data from a D- or G-type lens is essential, as the camera calculates the size of the area on the 420-segment RGB sensor based on the distance information supplied by the lens. To the human eye, the range of skin tones can look noticeably different; however, a metering system that uses a red-green-blue sensor does not "see" in the same way, and skin tones all appear very similar to such a system. An example of how this improves the autofocus can be seen in how this subject identification information is used in the Auto-Area AF mode to assist the D3100 in focusing on people in a scene. The subject identification is also used in the 3D-Tracking (11 points) mode to enhance tracking a subject moving laterally across the frame. In very simple terms, once the camera has acquired focus initially, it monitors the location of the pattern of pixels on the 420-segment RGB sensor created by the shape and color distribution of the subject (i.e., the subject identification information based on subject color and contrast) to determine the position of the subject in the frame. This mapping of the subject by the 420-segment RGB sensor is combined with the focus tracking information from the Multi-CAM 1000 autofocus sensor module, enabling the AF system to predict with speed and precision which AF point(s) to use to maintain focus.

Remarkably, the 420-segment RGB sensor's subject mapping, which covers virtually the entire frame area, continues to operate if the subject moves momentarily outside the area covered by the 11 AF points; as soon as the subject returns to the area within the AF points, autofocus resumes, even if the subject is at a different location within the area covered by the 11 AF points from the one it occupied immediately before it left the area (note that if the subject moves completely outside the frame area, so it is no longer visible in the viewfinder / monitor screen, it will be necessary to re-acquire focus). This combined tracking of the subject by the AF sensor and the 420-segment RGB metering sensor is only used in the Auto-Area and 3D-Tracking AF-Area modes, and although far from foolproof (the Auto-Area tends to be more reliable than 3D-Tracking), they can produce quite amazing results and certainly offer a very advanced form of focus tracking.

The 3D-tracking (11-point) mode differs from the Dynamic-Area AF mode because the camera automatically selects the active focus point as soon as focus is acquired even if the camera and / or subject move relative to one another. This enables focus to be maintained while rapid and significant changes in composition are made, because it is no longer necessary to maintain tracking by keeping the selected AF-point over the subject, which is necessary except for brief lapses in the Dynamic-Area AF mode.

However, when Dynamic-Area AF is selected, the D3100 only uses its Multi-CAM 1000 AF sensor to perform normal focus tracking (i.e., following a subject as it travels toward or away from the camera). Essentially, the camera reverts to the established AF system used by earlier Nikon DSLR cameras. In some situations, this can be an advantage, since the camera has far fewer computations to perform compared with the 3D-Tracking option; therefore, the AF response is faster. This option will be more reliable when shooting some types of moving subjects under artificial light, where the light source is non-white (e.g., some types of fluorescent and mercury-vapor lighting), as this affects the ability of the 420-segment RGB sensor to detect skin tones, which renders the SRS less effective, which in turn will impinge on the performance of the Auto-Area AF and 3D-Tracking (11-point) AF.

FOCUS MODES

The D3100 has three principal methods of focusing when you shoot still pictures (the focusing options when recording video are dealt with on pages 133-135), known as focusing modes: AF-S (Single-Servo AF), AF-C (Continuous-Servo AF), and Manual focus (M). A fourth option AF-A (Auto Select), which is the default setting, leaves the camera to automatically select either AF-S, if it determines the subject is stationary, or AF-C if the camera detects the subject is moving. To set the AF mode, press the [info] button to open the Information Display, and then press the button. Place the highlighted cursor on the current AF mode and press ⊛. Use ▼ and ▲ to selected the required option and then press ⊛. The autofocus mode can also be selected via the [Focus mode] item in the Shooting menu.

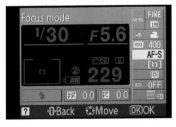

^ The focus mode in use is highlighted in the Information Display.

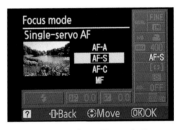

^ Once you press ⊛, you'll see the four focus mode options.

AF-A Auto Select (default setting): In an attempt to remove the burden of choosing which of the two principal autofocus modes (AF-S and AF-C) you should use, Nikon developed this option. In AF-A mode, the D3100 assesses the focus information and selects either AF-S or AF-C mode, depending on whether the camera determines that the subject is stationary or moving. More often than not, the AF-A option will select the appropriate AF mode, but if it makes the wrong choice, the result can spell disaster for your photos! In my opinion, the fully automated nature of the AF-A option simply does not provide sufficient reliability for correct autofocus-mode selection. I recommend you select the specific AF mode you require, based on the nature of the subject being photographed.

AF-S Single-Servo AF: As soon as the shutter release button is pressed down halfway, the D3100 focuses the lens. The shutter can only be released once focus has been acquired and the In-Focus indicator ● is displayed in the viewfinder. Focus will remain locked while the shutter release button is depressed halfway. No form of focus tracking is performed when the camera is set to AF-S; therefore, this mode should be used when the camera-to-subject distance will remain constant (i.e., the subject is not moving).

AF-C Continuous-Servo AF: The D3100 focuses the lens continuously while the shutter release button is pressed down halfway. If the camera-to-subject distance changes (i.e., the subject begins to move), the camera will initiate Predictive Focus Tracking in order to shift focus as it follows the subject. This mode monitors focus constantly, so it does not matter whether the subject continues to move or stops and starts periodically; the camera will continue to focus until either the shutter is released or you remove your finger from the shutter release button.

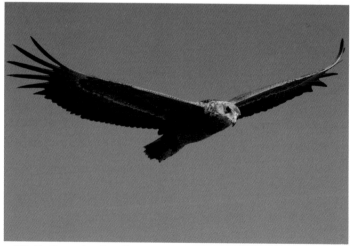

∧ AF-C (Continuous-Servo) enables the D3100 to track a moving subject using its Predictive Focus Tracking system.

M Manual focus: You must rotate the focusing ring of the lens to achieve focus. There is no restriction on when the shutter can be released. When using a lens with a maximum aperture of f/5.6 or larger, the electronic rangefinder feature will display the In-Focus confirmation signal ● when focus is achieved. This confirmation can be particularly useful in low-light or low-contrast conditions.

NOTE: If the lens you are using has a switch that allows you to select an M/A (manual/autofocus) mode on the lens, you need only to touch the focusing ring to disengage AF, and the lens can then be focused manually. As soon as you release the focusing ring and press the shutter release button down halfway, the camera will resume autofocus operation.

SINGLE-SERVO VS. CONTINUOUS-SERVO

It is important that you appreciate the fundamental difference between the Single-Servo AF (AF-S) and Continuous-Servo AF (AF-C) modes. In Single-Servo AF (AF-S), the shutter cannot be released until focus has been acquired; Nikon refers to this mode as having "focus priority." Once focus is acquired in this mode, the focus distance is locked as long as the shutter release button is pressed down halfway. In most shooting conditions, particularly in good light, the delay in acquiring focus is so brief that it is not perceptible and it is has no practical consequence. However, under certain conditions, such as low light or low contrast, there can be a discernable lag between pressing the shutter release button and the shutter opening. This is because it generally takes longer for the camera to establish focus in these circumstances, particularly if one of the outer, line-type AF sensing areas is used. Conversely, in Continuous-Servo AF (AF-C), the camera monitors focus constantly even after focus is acquired—as long as the shutter release button is held down halfway or the **AE-L/AF-L** button is pressed when it is set is perform the **[AF-ON]** role (selected via the **[Buttons]** item in the Setup menu)—and will shift the point of focus accordingly if the camera-to-subject distance alters. The shutter will operate immediately when you press the shutter release button all the way down, regardless of whether focus has been achieved; Nikon refers to this mode as having "release priority."

Some photographers mistakenly assume that if the shutter is released before the camera has attained focus in the AF-C mode, the picture will always be out of focus. In fact, the combination of constant focus monitoring and Predictive Focus Tracking in this mode (engaged when the camera detects a moving subject; see details below), is normally successful in causing the focus point to be shifted within the split-second delay between the reflex mirror lifting and the shutter opening, resulting in a sharp picture. Even if the camera's calculations are slightly off, the depth of field of the image often masks minor focusing errors. That said, to maximize AF performance while using Continuous-Servo AF (AF-C) mode to photograph a moving subject, it is imperative that the camera is given sufficient time to assimilate information to perform the focusing action. To achieve this, press and hold the shutter release button halfway down as long as possible before releasing the shutter to make the exposure. You may prefer to use the **AE-L/AF-L** button in its **[AF-ON]** role, as you can then use it to activate autofocus and concentrate on timing the exposure by pressing the shutter release when required.

PREDICTIVE FOCUS TRACKING

Whenever the shutter release is pressed all the way down to activate the shutter mechanism, there is a very short delay between the reflex mirror lifting out of the light path to the camera's sensor and the shutter actually opening. If a subject is moving toward or away from the camera, the camera-to-subject distance will change during this delay. In Continuous-Servo AF-C mode, the D3100 uses its Predictive Tracking system to shift the point of focus on the lens to compensate for this change in camera-to-subject distance; regardless of whether the subject is moving at a constant speed, is accelerating or decelerating. Predictive Focus Tracking is always initiated when the camera detects the camera-to-subject distance is changing (i.e., the subject is moving toward or away from the camera) while the shutter release is held down halfway or the **AE-L/AF-L** button is pressed when it is set is perform the **[AF-ON]** role, regardless of whether this occurs while the camera is establishing focus, or if it detects that the subject moves after focus is first acquired.

USING TRAP FOCUS

It is possible to use the functionality of the focus system in the D3100 to perform the "trap focus" technique. Trap focus allows the camera to be pre-focused at a specific point and have the shutter released automatically as soon as a subject passes through the area. If you can accurately predict the path of the subject, this technique can be very effective.

The following steps will enable you to set up the D3100 for trap focusing:

1. Set [AF ON] for [AE-L/AF-L] in the [Buttons] item in the Setup menu, so that focusing is only performed when the AE-L/AF-L button is pressed, not when the shutter release button is pressed down halfway.
2. Select AF-S (Single-Servo AF) focus mode.
3. Select Single-Point as the autofocus area mode (see below). If the lens you are using has a focus mode switch on it, set it to A or M/A.

Pre-focus the lens on a point that is the same distance from the camera as the point the subject will pass through by aligning it with the selected autofocus sensing area and pushing the AE-L/AF-L button. Once focus is acquired, release the AE-L/AF-L button (focus is now locked at that distance). Re-compose the picture so the selected AF point covers the point you expect the subject to pass through. Now, fully depress and hold the shutter release button down (this is necessary to keep the camera activated and enable the shutter to be released as soon as focus is detected—remember the camera is set to AF-S focus mode). Using the locking shutter release button of the optional MC-DC2 remote release cable makes this task much easier than holding down the camera's shutter release button. When the subject enters the space covered by the selected AF point, the camera will detect focus and the shutter will automatically be released.

AUTOFOCUS AREA MODES

The D3100 has four Autofocus-Area modes (not to be confused with the three autofocus modes described above) that determine how the 11 AF points will be used: Single-Point AF, Dynamic-Area AF, Auto-Area AF, and 3D-Tracking (11 points); the 3D-Tracking (11 points) is only available when the AF mode is set to AF-C or AF-A.

To select the AF-Area mode, press the ![info] button to open the Information Display, and then press the ![AF] button. Place the highlighted cursor on the current AF-Area mode and press ⓸. Use ▼ and ▲ to selected the desired option and then press ⓸. The autofocus area mode can also be selected via the **[AF-area mode]** item in the Shooting menu.

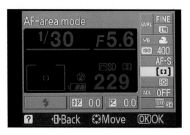

[ɿ] **Single-Point AF:** The D3100 uses only the single AF point that you selected with the Multi Selector button. The camera takes no part in choosing which AF point is used. The selected AF point is shown in the Information Display. The selected AF point is highlighted for approximately 1 second.

[ɿ] **Dynamic-Area AF:** In AF-A and AF-C, the D3100 uses the user-selected AF point for focusing. However, if the subject leaves the area covered by this AF point briefly, the camera immediately evaluates information from the other surrounding AF points and will attempt to maintain focus using these AF points as needed until the originally selected AF point covers the subject. The area selected initially is highlighted in the viewfinder and Information Display where it remains highlighted, even if another AF point is used to momentarily maintain focus. In AF-S mode, the camera only uses the single AF point that you selected for autofocus; therefore there is no benefit in selecting this AF-Area mode when the camera is set to AF-S autofocus mode. The selected AF point is highlighted for approximately 1 second.

[▣] **Auto-Area AF:** The D3100 selects the AF point(s) automatically using information from the Multi-CAM 1000 autofocus module. If a D- or G-type Nikkor lens is used, the subject identification information based on the color and contrast pattern of the subject as established by the Scene Recognition System, will also be used to map the position of the subject within the frame. Generally, the camera will set focus on what it determines to be the subject closest to it. This system is particularly adept at identifying skin tones and is, therefore, very useful when photographing people. The active AF point(s) is / are highlighted for approximately 1 second.

[3D] **3D-Tracking (11 points):** In AF-A and AF-C, the D3100 uses the user-selected AF point for focusing. Operation is similar to the Auto-Area AF mode insomuch as, when shooting with a D- or G-type Nikkor lens, the subject identification information based on the color and contrast pattern of the subject as determined by the Scene Recognition System, will be used to map and track the position of the subject as its position shifts within the frame. In this AF-Area mode, the highlighting of the AF point changes according to which AF point is active as the focusing system follows the subject, even if there is a significant change from the original composition. You will always know which AF point the camera is using because the active AF point blinks. If the subject moves outside of the frame area while the AF system attempts to follow it, the 3D-Tracking will not resume when the subject reappears inside the frame area, so it is necessary to lift your finger off the shutter release button, recompose the picture and use the AF point selected originally.

> **NOTE:** I recommend that the 3D-Tracking (11 points) AF-Area mode is most appropriate for subjects that remain at or close to a constant distance from the camera.

SELECTING AN AUTOFOCUS POINT

In Single-Point AF, Dynamic-Area AF, or 3D-Tracking (11 points) AF, the AF point that the D3100 will initially use to acquire focus must be selected manually by pressing the Multi Selector button. In the viewfinder and in the Information Display, the selected AF point will be shown highlighted in red for approximately 1 second. The center AF point can be selected by pressing the ⊛ button at the center of the Multi Selector.

The D3100 lacks a locking mechanism on the Multi Selector to prevent unintentional selection of an alternative AF point; I have found this to be a weak point in its design, as all too often while holding the camera, the heel of my right thumb will press the Multi Selector and shift the AF point selection. Make sure you check the position of the selected AF point before you shoot!

FOCUS MODE AND AF-AREA MODE OVERVIEW

If you are new to Nikon's AF system it will probably take a while to get used to the functionality of the Focus Mode and Focus Area Mode options of the D3100. Therefore, you may wish to re-read the sections above and refer to the following table that summarizes the various autofocus operations.

AF MODE	AF-AREA MODE	SELECTION OF FOCUS AREA
Manual	Single-Point AF	User
AF-S (Single-Servo)	Single-Point AF	User
AF-S (Single-Servo)	Dynamic-Area AF	User [1]
AF-S (Single-Servo)	Auto-Area AF	Camera
AF-C (Continuous-Servo)	Single-Point AF	User
AF-C (Continuous-Servo)	Dynamic-Area AF	User [3, 4]
AF-C (Continuous-Servo)	Auto-Area AF	Camera [2, 3]
AF-C (Continuous-Servo)	3D-Tracking (11 point)	User [4]

1. Only the selected AF point is used; camera makes no reference to other AF points
2. Active focus point(s) is not displayed.
3. Camera will use an alternative AF point if the subject momentarily leaves the selected AF point.
4. Camera will shift focus to an alternative AF point if the composition is altered; the subject is tracked automatically, based on color and contrast pattern information.

As you change from Single-Point to Dynamic-Area to Auto-Area to 3D-Tracking (11 points), you relinquish more control to the camera in the selection of the AF point; therefore, consider the most appropriate option based on the nature of the subject you are photographing and whether or not it is moving. For static subjects, use AF-S (Single-Servo) with Single-Point AF-Area mode. For subjects that move in a predictable direction, use AF-C (Continuous-Servo) with Dynamic-Area AF. And, when photographing a subject that moves in an unpredictable manner, or when you need to recompose the picture rapidly while maintaining focus, use AF-C (Continuous-Servo) with 3D-tracking (11 points). Finally, for point-and-shoot style photography, especially with people in the scene, consider using AF-C (Continuous-Servo) with Auto-Area AF. Remember, a D- or G-type Nikkor lens is necessary to make the most of the 3D-Tracking (11 points) and Auto-Area options.

FOCUS LOCK

Once the D3100 has acquired focus, it is possible to lock the autofocus system so the shot can be recomposed and the original focus distance will be retained, even if an AF point no longer covers the subject.

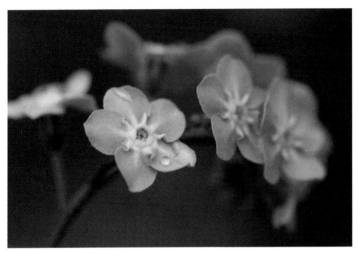

∧ When shooting close-up pictures, it is advisable to use Manual focus, as the depth of field is extremely shallow, so placement of the plane of focus is critical.

In Single-Servo AF, pressing the shutter release button halfway will activate autofocus. As soon as focus is acquired, the In-Focus indicator ● is displayed in the viewfinder and focus is locked and will remain locked while the shutter release button is held halfway down. Alternatively, press and hold the **AE-L/AF-L** button to lock focus.

NOTE: If [Buttons] > [AE-L/AF-L] in the Setup menu is set to its default, [AE/AF lock], pressing the **AE-L/AF-L** button will lock both focus and exposure. You may consider selecting the [AF lock only] option, if you want to use the **AE-L/AF-L** to lock focus only.

In Continuous-Servo AF, the autofocus system remains active while the shutter release button is held down halfway, constantly adjusting focus as necessary; therefore, if you recompose the picture so that the selected AF point no longer covers the subject, the focus will shift to the point now covered by the selected AF point. To lock focus in Continuous-Servo AF, press and hold the **AE-L/AF-L** button (consider the options available at the **[AE-L/AF-L]** option under the **[Buttons]** item in the Setup menu, as described in the note below). Alternatively, in AF-C mode, which is most useful for photographing a moving subject, it is possible to lock focus by assigning activation of the AF system to the **AE-L/AF-L** button instead of the shutter button, using the **[AF-ON]** option at the **[AE-L/AF-L]** option under the **[Buttons]** item in the Setup menu. Press and hold the button down until focus is achieved, and then release the button to lock focus. Now the picture can be recomposed and the shutter release button can be pressed to make the exposure without having any effect on the focus.

NOTE: If the **[AE-L/AF-L]** option under the **[Buttons]** item in the Setup menu is set to **[AF-ON]**, the Vibration Reduction (VR) feature available on some Nikkor lenses will not operate when the **AE-L/AF-L** button is pressed; VR is only activated by pressing the shutter release button. If you are controlling autofocus operation via the **AE-L/AF-L** button and want to use VR, when you decide to take a picture, press the shutter release button and pause briefly at the point it is depressed halfway (even though you are not using that button to focus) to allow the VR system to activate and settle before pressing it all the way down to operate the shutter

Once focus has been locked in either AF-S or AF-C focus mode, ensure the camera-to-subject distance does not alter. If it does, reactivate autofocus and refocus the lens at the new distance before using the Autofocus Lock options.

AF ASSIST ILLUMINATOR

The D3100 has a small, built-in AF-Assist Illuminator, which is designed to facilitate autofocus in low-light conditions; it is located on the front of the camera between the finger grip and the viewfinder head. Whatever the intentions of the camera's design team were, I consider this feature largely superfluous! Here are a few reasons why I suggest setting the [AF-assist] item in the Shooting menu to [Off].

○ The lamp only works if you have an autofocus lens attached to the camera, the focus area mode is set to either Single-Point AF or Dynamic-Area AF with the center focus point selected, or if Auto-Area AF is active.

○ It is only usable with focal lengths of 18mm – 200mm.

○ The operating range is restricted to 1.6 – 9.8 feet (0.5 – 3.0m).

○ Due to its location, many lenses obstruct its output, particularly if they have a lens hood attached.

○ The lamp overheats quite quickly (6 to 8 exposures in rapid succession is usually sufficient) and will automatically shut down to allow it to cool. Plus, at this level of use, it also drains battery power fairly quickly.

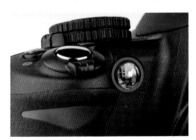

< The AF-Assist lamp of the D3100 may help the camera acquire focus in low-light conditions, but its value is questionable.

The D3100 can also use the built-in AF-Assist Illuminator lamp of either the SB-900, SB-800, SB-700, or SB-600 Speedlight, or that of the SU-800 Speedlight commander unit (operation of the camera's lamp is disabled in these circumstances). The wider coverage provided by the AF-Assist Illuminator of the external units is particularly useful with cameras such as the D3100, with its relatively wide array of 11 AF points, plus the AF-Assist Illuminator is located farther off the lens axis, reducing the risk that its light will be obstructed by the lens. The AF-Assist function can be used in isolation on the SB-900 and SB-800 by canceling flash firing via the Custom Settings menu of the Speedlight.

When used with AF lenses with focal lengths of 17–135mm, the SB-900 provides AF-Assist for autofocus with the following AF points:

17–105 mm		106–135 mm	

When used with AF lenses and focal lengths of 24-105mm, the SB-800, SB-600, and SU-800 provide AF-Assist for autofocus with the following AF points (on the next page):

24–34 mm		35–105 mm	

If you want to use either the SB-600, SB-800, or SB-900 off-camera, the SC-29 TTL flash lead has a built-in AF-Assist lamp that attaches to the camera's accessory shoe.

LIMITATIONS OF THE AF SYSTEM

Although the autofocus system of the D3100 is quite capable, there are some circumstances or conditions that can impair or limit its performance:

- Low light
- Low contrast
- Highly reflective surfaces
- Subject too small within the autofocus sensing area; this often occurs with wide-angle lenses
- The AF point covers a subject comprising fine detail
- The AF point covers a regular geometric pattern
- The AF point covers a region of high contrast
- The AF point covers objects at different distances from the camera

If any of these conditions prevent the camera from acquiring focus, either switch to Manual focus mode or focus on another object at the same distance from the camera as the subject, then use the AF Lock feature to lock focus before recomposing the picture.

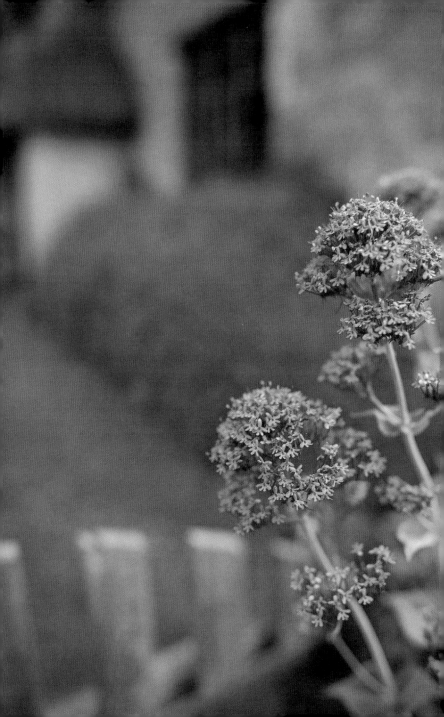

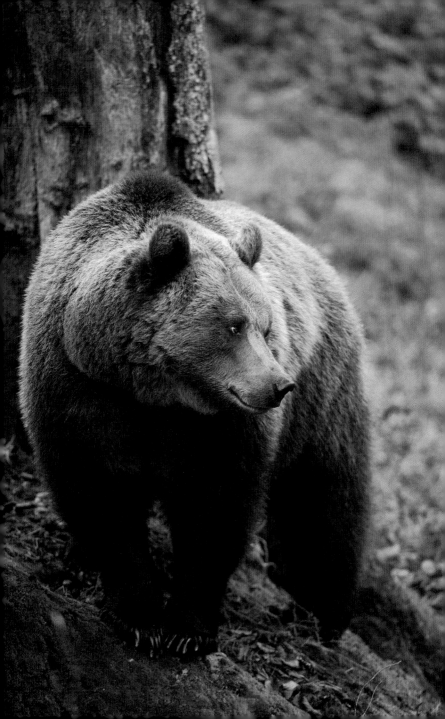

Shoot and Review

THE SHUTTER

The electronically timed, mechanical shutter used in the D3100 is impressive for a camera in its class. The shutter blades are constructed from a durable composite of Kevlar ™ and carbon-fiber material, which provides great strength with low mass to ensure both durability and accuracy; the unit is proven to perform at least 100,000 cycles.

The shutter speed range of the D3100 runs from 30 seconds to 1/4000 second and can be set in steps of 1/3EV. There is also an option for exposures beyond 30 seconds to a maximum duration of 30 minutes by using the buLb setting. The D3100 has a Noise Reduction feature, which should be used in such circumstances (see pages 183-185 for more details). The maximum flash synchronization shutter speed is 1/200 second.

SHUTTER RELEASE

The main shutter release button of the D3100 is located, conventionally, on the right top of the camera, surrounded by the power switch collar. When the camera is switched to [ON], a light pressure on the shutter release button, which depresses it halfway, will activate the metering system and initiate autofocus, if it is selected. If pressure is no longer applied to the shutter release button, the camera will remain active for a fixed period of time, the duration of which depends on the selection made under the [Auto-off timers] item in the Setup menu; eight seconds is the default setting.

If you fully depress the shutter release button, the shutter mechanism will operate and an exposure will be made. There is a very short delay between pressing the button all the way down and the shutter opening; this delay is known as shutter "lag."

The capacity of the buffer memory is probably the most common cause of shutter delay. It does not matter if you shoot in Single or Continuous release mode (read on for descriptions); once the buffer memory is full, the camera must write data to the memory card before any more exposures can be made. As soon as sufficient space for another image is available in the buffer memory, the shutter can once again be released. For this reason, using memory cards with a fast data write speed is recommended. The D3100 supports a maximum data write speed of approximately 15MB/second, so using any card that can sustain a write speed of 20MB/s (x133) will ensure the maximum performance as far as clearing the buffer memory is concerned (in this respect a card with an even faster write speed will deliver no additional benefit, since the camera imposes the limiting factor). Other factors that may contribute to shutter delay include the following:

O When the camera is set to Single-Servo autofocus mode, the shutter is disabled until the D3100 has acquired focus. In low-light or low-contrast scenes the autofocus system will often take longer to achieve focus, particularly if one of the outer single-line sensor type AF points is used.

O In low-light conditions, the D3100 can activate its AF-assist lamp, or that of an external Speedlight, or the SC-29 TTL flash control cable, which can introduce a short delay while the lamp illuminates and focus is acquired.

O The Red-Eye Reduction function (one of the flash modes available on the camera) introduces an additional, and significant, one-second delay between pressing the shutter release button and the exposure being made (see page 208 for details on Red-Eye Reduction with the D3100).

RELEASE MODES

Unlike a 35mm film camera, the D3100 does not have to transport film between each exposure using a motor drive, but the shutter mechanism still has to be cycled. The camera offers a range of release modes, which are set via the Release-Mode selector located along the right side of the Mode dial. Choose one of the following options:

S *SINGLE FRAME*

A single image is recorded each time the shutter release button is pressed. To make another exposure, the button must be released and pressed again. You can continue to do so until the buffer memory is full, in which case you must wait for data to be written to the memory card. The shutter release button will also lock if the memory card is full.

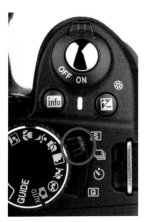

‹ The Release Mode selector switch set around the Mode dial helps to improve the handling of the D3100.

HINT: You do not have to remove your finger from the shutter release button completely between frames; by raising it slightly after each exposure, but maintaining a slight downward pressure on the shutter release button, you can keep the camera active and be ready for the next shot. If you want to take a rapid sequence of pictures in Single-Frame mode, avoid "stabbing" your finger down on the shutter release button in quick succession. Keep a light pressure on the button and roll your finger over the top of the button in a smooth, repeating action. This will reduce the risk of camera shake spoiling your pictures.

⊒ CONTINUOUS

In this mode, if you press and hold down the shutter release button, the D3100 will continue to record images up to a maximum rate of 3 frames per second (fps). The Continuous release mode can be particularly helpful in situations where your subject is moving quickly, or there is only a fleeting moment in which to capture the image.

> **NOTE:** The quoted frame rates for the D3100 are based on the camera being set to manual exposure (M), or Shutter-Priority autoexposure mode (S), and a minimum shutter speed of 1/250 second. It is important to remember that the selected shutter speed, use of the Vibration Reduction (VR) feature available on some Nikkor lenses, the buffer capacity, other autoexposure modes, and autofocus (particularly in low light) can, and often will, reduce the maximum frame rate significantly.

⏱ SELF-TIMER

The Self-Timer releases the shutter after a predetermined delay. The default delay is 10 seconds, but can be changed to 2 seconds via the [Self-Timer] item in the ⚊ Setup menu. One exposure is taken by the D3100 each time the Self-Timer feature is used.

Once the required delay for the Self-Timer has been selected, position the Release-Mode selector to ⏱ and place the camera on a tripod or other stable support. Frame the picture and press the shutter release button down halfway to achieve focus (the shutter release will be disabled unless focus is acquired in Single-Servo AF mode). When the shutter release button is fully depressed, the Self-Timer lamp will begin to blink (a beep will accompany the blinking light if [Beep] has been selected via the ⚊ menu). Approximately 2 seconds before the exposure will be made, the lamp will stop blinking and remain on (the beep will become more rapid) until the shutter is released. To cancel the Self-Timer release at any time during the delay, turn the camera off.

Traditionally, the Self-Timer has been used to enable the photographer to be included in the picture, but there is another very useful function for this feature. The Self-Timer allows the photographer to release the shutter without directly touching the camera, thus reducing the chance of camera shake. This is particularly useful for long exposures when the subject is static and precise timing of the shutter release is less critical.

HINT: Make sure nothing passes in front of the lens when pressing the shutter release button down halfway, as autofocus operation may shift the point of focus. You may find Manual focus (MF) mode easier and more reliable when using the Self-Timer feature.

HINT: Because the camera is not held to the eye while utilizing the Self-Timer feature, it is essential to cover the viewfinder eyepiece to keep extraneous light from entering the viewfinder and influencing the camera's TTL metering sensor. Nikon provides a DK-5 eyepiece blind with the camera for this purpose. However, fitting the DK-5 requires removal of the DK-20 rubber eyecup; this is a nuisance and increases the risk of losing the eyecup. I find it far quicker and more convenient to keep a small square of thick felt material in my camera bag to drape over the viewfinder eyepiece when using the self-timer mode.

Q *QUIET SHUTTER*

In this release mode, the camera exposes a single image just like in Single-Frame release, but the shutter does not make any sound after the exposure is made and the camera does not beep when focus is achieved. If you press and hold the shutter release button down all the way, the exposure will be made, but the reflex mirror will remain in the raised

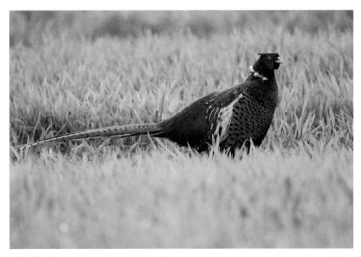

∧ The **Q** Quiet shutter release mode is ideal in situations where camera noise needs to be kept to a minimum.

position until you lift your finger off the button, or lift off the release button of the MC-DC2 remote release (see below). This makes the operation of the camera noticeably quieter compared with the Single-Frame release mode. An extra damping mechanism has been added to the D3100 to slow the movement of the reflex mirror down on its return. The **Q** release mode is ideal for shooting discreetly in any environment where the noise may be intrusive.

◼◖))) *REMOTE RELEASE*

The benefit of mounting a camera on a tripod or other type of rigid camera support to increase image sharpness will be compromised by manually depressing the shutter release button. To eliminate or reduce camera vibration, it is advisable to use a remote release to operate the shutter. The MC-DC2 remote release cord can be used with the D3100 in any of its release modes. It connects to the accessory terminal located under the large rubber cover on the left side of the camera.

NOTE: The D3100 does not support the Nikon ML-L3 wireless infrared (IR) remote release that is common to several other Nikon DSLR cameras.

THE LCD MONITOR

On the rear of the D3000 is a 3-inch (7.62 cm), 230,000-dot, color TFT LCD monitor. Unlike the viewfinder, the LCD monitor screen shows virtually 100% of the image file when used for review. Pictures can be displayed either as a single image or in multiples. When used to display a single image, the review function has a zoom facility that enables it to be enlarged by up to 27x (for [Large] size images only—lower magnifications are available for [Medium]–20x and [Small]–14x).

The maximum magnification of a [Large] size image is equivalent to a 400% view, so to examine the image at a 100% (i.e., actual pixel level), press the ⊕ button until the maximum magnification is reached, and then press the ⊕▦ button twice to reduce the image to a 100% view.

Use the Multi Selector to scroll through a range of pages containing shooting information, which are superimposed on any image reviewed in single-image Playback (see pages 101-108 for more details). Pictures can be edited in the camera by reviewing them on the LCD monitor, with the options to delete them, protect them from being deleted unintentionally (see page 111 for more details), or make adjustments using the items in the Retouch menu. In addition to the display of images and image information, the LCD monitor is used to display the various camera menus.

IMAGE REVIEW OPTIONS

One of the most useful features of a digital camera is the ability to get near-instant feedback on photographs as you shoot. Using the Playback functions on the D3100 will allow you to view not only the images you have taken but also a range of useful information about them. As mentioned above, the monitor screen of the D3100 provides virtually a 100% view of the image file when it is reviewed / played back. Pictures can be displayed either as a single image or in multiples.

Assuming [On] is selected for [Image review] in the Playback menu, the most recently taken image in Single-Frame and Self-Timer shooting modes will be displayed in the monitor screen almost instantaneously. In the Continuous shooting mode, the camera must write the image data from the buffer memory to the memory card for each image taken before they can be viewed. This causes a short delay that becomes cumulative as more images are recorded; the camera displays each image chronologically, as soon as it has been saved. If [Off] is selected for [Image review] in the ▶ Playback menu, no image is displayed after an exposure is made. In this case, use single-image Playback to evaluate images by pressing the ▶ button.

FULL-FRAME PLAYBACK

To view the last image recorded by the camera, press the ▶ button. If you wish to view other images saved on the memory card, press ◀ and ▶ to scroll through them. To display the information pages for a still image, use ▲ and ▼ (see below for full details). To return to the Shooting mode, press the ▶ button again—although the quicker method, if you are in the midst of shooting, is to press the shutter release button down halfway.

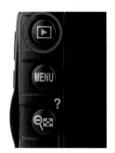

> The Playback button is located on the back of the camera, near the LCD screen's upper left-hand corner.

To display images shot in an upright (vertical) format in the correct orientation, select [On] for the [Auto Image Rotation] item in the Setup menu, and select [On] for the [Rotate tall] item in the Playback menu. Although this may seem a convenient method to display an image, the size of the displayed picture is reduced in order to fit the long edge of the image within the short edge of the monitor screen.

The preview image, including those for NEF files, is derived from a JPEG file to which in-camera processing (White Balance, Contrast, Saturation, etc.) has been applied. The actual NEF file will contain more data and have a wider range of tonal values and colors; therefore, an overexposed highlight in the JPEG preview may not be an overexposed highlight when the NEF file is examined in a RAW file converter such as Nikon Capture NX2. Because they are derived from an 8-bit JPEG preview image, you should treat the highlights warning and histograms that the camera displays with a degree of latitude, and not as an absolute definitive that over- or underexposure has occurred.

INFORMATION PAGES

A very useful feature of the Image Playback function on the D3100 is the wealth of information that can be accessed while viewing the image on the monitor screen. This information can help ensure that you have achieved a good exposure, as well as give you detailed information about how, when, and where the exposure was made. Depending on the selections made in the **[Display Mode]** item in the Playback menu, there are up to seven different pages of information that can be displayed for each image file viewed on the monitor screen.

To access these information displays, press ▼ to scroll through each page in the following order: File Information, RGB and Composite Histograms, Highlights (warning), Shooting Data (1), Shooting Data (2), Shooting Data (3), GPS, and Overview data. Press ▲ to scroll through in the reverse order.

File Information: This page displays an unobstructed view of the image while providing the following additional information:

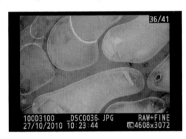

‹ The File Information page provides the date and time the image was created as well as other useful information, such as the file name.

- O Protect status
- O Retouch indicator
- O Frame number / total number of frames
- O File name
- O Image Quality
- O Image Size
- O Time of recording
- O Date of recording
- O Folder name

RGB Histogram: The RGB Histogram page provides an individual histogram for each the red, green, and blue channels, together with an RGB composite (luminance) histogram and a thumbnail of the image file. The horizontal axis indicates the pixel brightness with black at the extreme left end and white at the extreme right end. The vertical axis indicates the number of pixels. To magnify a part of the image, press the ⊕ button and use the Multi Selector to scroll around the full image (a smaller thumbnail image is displayed to assist navigation within the full frame area). The histogram will represent only the enlarged section of the image displayed on the monitor screen. This page is only displayed if **[RGB histogram]** is selected under the **[Display mode]** item in the Playback menu. The following information is displayed on this page:

- O Protect status
- O Retouch indicator
- O White Balance / White Balance Fine-Tuning / Preset Manual
- O Camera name
- O Histogram – RGB (Luminance)
- O Histogram – red channel
- O Histogram – green channel
- O Histogram – blue channel
- O Frame number / total number of frames

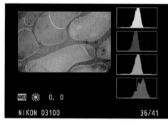

∧ The histogram display shows a luminance histogram (white) and the three individual color channel histograms.

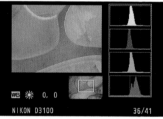

∧ To display a histogram for a specific section of an image, press the ⊕ button to magnify the image. A yellow frame indicates the selected section; use the Multi Selector button to shift the position of the yellow frame. The histogram applies only to the area within the yellow frame.

Highlights: The Highlights page shows an unobstructed view of the entire image. Any area of the image that may be overexposed is shown with a flashing border. This page is only displayed if **[Highlights]** is selected under the **[Display mode]** item in the Playback menu, and provides the following information:

- O Protect status
- O Retouch indicator
- O Image highlights
- O Camera name
- O Frame number / total number of frames

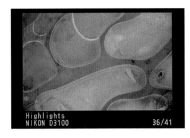

NOTE: When recording NEF (RAW) files, the highlights warning is taken from an embedded 8-bit JPEG file, which may suggest an area of the image is overexposed when in fact this is often not the case. The histogram display is generally more reliable at indicating whether a JPEG image has areas that are overexposed.

Shooting Data Page 1: A block of information will be superimposed over the center portion of the screen, obstructing the view of the image. This page is only displayed if **[Data]** is selected under the **[Display mode]** item in the ▶ Playback menu and displays the following information:

- O Protect status
- O Retouch indicator
- O Metering method
- O Shutter speed
- O Aperture
- O Shooting mode
- O ISO sensitivity[1]
- O Exposure Compensation
- O Focal length
- O Lens data
- O Focus mode
- O VR lens[2]
- O Flash mode
- O Flash Control / Compensation
- O Camera name
- O Frame number / total number of frames

[1]Displayed in red if ISO Auto Control was on
[2]Displayed only if a VR lens is attached

> **The first shooting information page**

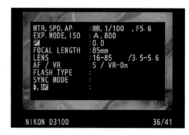

NOTE: This screen can be particularly useful if you are trying to achieve similar results in a similar environment, learn about your shooting style, and learn what settings produce particular results.

Shooting Data Page 2: A block of information will be superimposed over the center portion of the screen, obstructing the view of the image. This page is only displayed if **[Data]** is selected under the **[Display mode]** item in the ▶ Playback menu and displays the following information:

O Protect status

O Retouch indicator

O White Balance / color temperature / WB Fine-Tuning / Preset Manual

O Color space

O Picture Control

O Quick Adjust[1]

O Original Picture Control[2]

O Sharpening

O Contrast

O Brightness

O Saturation[3]

O Filter effects[4]

O Hue[3]

O Toning[4]

O Camera name

O Frame number / total number of frames

[1] **[Standard]**, **[Vivid]**, **[Portrait]**, and **[Landscape]** Picture Controls only
[2] **[Neutral]**, **[Monochrome]**, and custom Picture Controls
[3] Not displayed with Monochrome Picture Controls
[4] Monochrome Picture Controls only

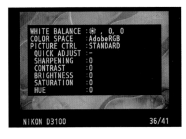

‹ The second shooting information page

NOTE: This screen can help you understand the effects of image settings and adjustments on the appearance of your picture.

Shooting Data Page 3: A block of information will be superimposed over the center portion of the screen, obstructing the view of the image. This page is only displayed if **[Data]** is selected under the **[Display mode]** item in the ▶ Playback menu and contains the following information:

○ Protect status
○ Retouch indicator
○ Noise Reduction
○ Active D-Lighting
○ Retouch history
○ Image comment
○ Camera name
○ Frame number / total number of frames

> The third shooting
information page

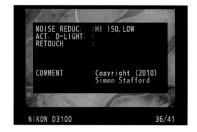

GPS Data: A block of information will be superimposed over the center portion of the screen, obstructing the view of the image. This page is only displayed if the optional Nikon GP-1 GPS device was connected to the D3100 and active when the picture was recorded (when recording in D-Movie mode the GPS data applies to the position of the camera at the start of recording). This screen displays the following information:

> The GPS data page

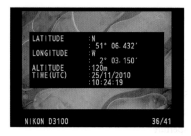

- O Protect status
- O Retouch indicator
- O Latitude
- O Longitude
- O Altitude
- O Coordinated universal time (UTC)
- O Camera name
- O Frame number / total number of frames

Overview Data: This page provides a thumbnail view of the image file with two panels containing the following information:

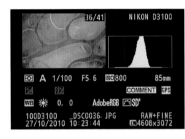

< The overview data
page

- O Frame number / total number of frames
- O Protect status
- O Camera name
- O Retouch indicator
- O Histogram (composite only)
- O ISO sensitivity[1]
- O Focal length
- O GPS data indicator
- O Image comment indicator
- O Flash mode
- O Flash Compensation
- O Exposure Compensation
- O Metering method
- O Shooting mode
- O Shutter speed
- O Aperture
- O Picture Control

O Active D-Lighting

O File name

O Image Quality

O Image Size

O Time of recording

O Date of recording

O Folder number

O White Balance / color temperature / WB Fine-Tuning / Preset Manual

O Color space

'Displayed in red if ISO Auto Control was on during shooting

VIEWING MULTIPLE IMAGES

If you wish to view multiple thumbnails of images on the monitor screen, press the ⊞ button to change from Single-Frame, to four, nine, or seventy-two images, and finally to the Calendar Playback, which displays pictures based on the date they were taken. To return to a single image view from multiple image display, press the ⊕ button repeatedly until a single image is displayed.

In a multiple thumbnail display, a yellow border surrounds the currently highlighted image file. To highlight an alternative thumbnail image, scroll with the Multi Selector. To view the highlighted image in full-frame view, press ⊛; to return to the thumbnail view, press the ⊞ button. The highlighted thumbnail image can be protected by pressing the ⊡ (**AE-L/AF-L** button) and deleted by pressing the 🗑 button. To return to the Shooting mode at any time, press the ▶ button, or press the shutter release button down halfway.

CALENDAR PLAYBACK

To view an image file taken on a specific date, press the ⊝⊞ button until 72 thumbnail images are displayed, and then press it once more. Once the Calendar Playback display is shown, any date on which one or more images was recorded will be indicated by a thumbnail image on that date; use the ⊝⊞ button to switch back and forth between the calendar of dates **[Date list]** and the list of thumbnails **[Thumbnail list]** displayed to the right of the calendar. To highlight a specific date or image in the thumbnail image list, use the Multi Selector button.

In the **[Date list]** use ⊕ to exit to the 72-thumbnail display, ⊛ to view the first picture taken on the selected date, ⊕ to highlight a date, or ⊞ to delete all the pictures taken on the selected date. In the **[Thumbnail list]** press and hold ⊕ to enlarge the highlighted picture, ⊛ to view the highlighted picture, ⊕ to highlight a picture, or ⊞ to delete the highlighted picture; to return to the Shooting mode, press the ▶ button, or press the shutter release button down halfway.

PLAYBACK ZOOM

The image displayed on the monitor screen is usually too small to check its sharpness with any certainty. The Playback Zoom will allow you to enlarge a **[Large]** size image by up to 27x (equivalent to approximately a 400% view on a computer screen), a **[Medium]** size image up to 20x, and a **[Small]** size image up to 14x. To see a 100% view (i.e., an actual pixel view) of a **[Large]** image, enlarge to full magnification and press the ⊝⊞ button twice. At this magnification it is possible to make a general assessment of the sharpness and noise level in the image, although the resolution of the monitor screen (230,000-dot) is relatively low, so any critical analysis of sharpness, as well as color and contrast, should be left until the image is displayed on a computer monitor screen.

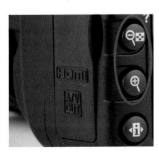

‹ ThePlayback Zoom buttons are located on the rear of the D3100 to the left side of the monitor.

To zoom into the image displayed on the monitor screen, press the ⊕ button. The enlarged image will be displayed with a yellow frame border inside a navigation window. To increase the degree of magnification, keep pressing ⊕ button; the size of the yellow frame will reduce to indicate the area of the image that will be enlarged. The selected area, as defined by the yellow frame, is shown in the monitor screen. To view an alternative part of the image at the same magnification, use the Multi Selector to scroll through the image. The same area of another image at the same magnification can be viewed by rotating the Main Command dial to scroll through the images. This is a useful feature if there are a number of similar images of the same subject on your memory card and you want to check a specific detail, such as a certain person's eyes in a group portrait. To return to the Shooting mode, press the ▶ button, or press the shutter release button down halfway.

> The ability to enlarge an image while it is displayed on the monitor screen is a helpful for a number of reasons, including to assess sharpness.

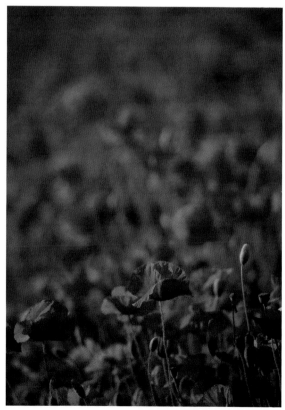

PROTECTING IMAGES

To protect an image file against inadvertent deletion, display the image or video file on the monitor screen in full-frame single-image Playback or highlight it in multiple-thumbnail Playback, and then press the 🔒 (**AE-L/AF-L** button). A small key 🔒 icon will appear in the upper left corner, superimposed over the image. To remove the protection, open or highlight the image or video file and press 🔒 again. Check to make sure the 🔒 is no longer displayed. A protected image will still be "deleted" if the memory card is formatted; however, the protect status is preserved when the file is transferred to another storage device or computer. To remove the protection from all images in a folder or folders currently selected in the **[Playback folder]** menu, press and hold 🔒 and 🗑 simultaneously for approximately 2 seconds.

DELETING IMAGES

Images can be deleted using one of two methods. The quickest and easiest way to delete a single image file is to press the 🗑 button when the image to be deleted is displayed on the monitor screen. The first press of the button opens a warning dialog box that asks for confirmation of the delete command. To complete the process, simply press the 🗑 button again. To cancel the delete process, press the ▶ button.

Images can also be deleted in multiples via the **[Delete]** item in the Playback menu. There are three options: **[Selected]** only those image files selected for deletion will be deleted, **[Selected date]** to delete all image files taken on a selected date, or **[All]** to delete all image files in the folder currently selected for Playback.

HINT: Never be in too much of a hurry to delete pictures unless they are obvious failures. I always recommend that it is better to leave the editing process to a later stage—your opinions about a particular picture can, and often do, change. These days, memory cards are remarkably cheap and come in much larger capacities than only a few years ago, so there is no excuse to skimp on image storage!

The histogram is a graphical display of the tonal values recorded by the camera. The shape and position of the histogram curve indicates the range of tones that have been captured in the picture. The horizontal axis represents 256 different tonal values from pure black at the extreme left end to pure white at the extreme right end; darker tones will be distributed to the left of the histogram graph and lighter tones to the right. The vertical axis represents the number of pixels that have that specific tonal value.

In a well-exposed picture of a scene containing an average distribution of tones that includes a few very dark shadows, a sizable number of mid-tones, and a few bright highlights, where no clipping of shadow or highlights has occurred, the curve will extend across much of the horizontal axis; in this case all tones in the scene will have been recorded. Obviously, not all scenes contain an even spread of tones; many have a natural predominance of light or dark areas. In these cases the histogram curve will be biased to the right with scenes containing mainly light tones, or to the left when the scene contains mainly dark tones; this is not an indication of over- or underexposure, respectively, but an indication of the limited range of tones in the scene. Hence, there is no single, perfect, or ideal histogram curve for all scenes and subjects; the shape of the histogram curve will vary widely depending on the nature of the scene recorded. Provided the histogram curve stops on the bottom axis before it reaches either end of the graph, the image will contain the fullest range of tones from the darkest to the lightest in the scene being photographed.

However, if the curve begins at a point part way up the left or right vertical axis of the histogram display (i.e., it does not end on the horizontal axis, but the histogram curve looks as though it has been cut off abruptly), the camera will not have recorded some tones. This is often referred to as "clipping." If the curve is stacked up against the left axis, or there is a peak in the histogram against the left axis, some of the darker tones (i.e., shadows areas in the image) will likely be compromised due to underexposure. In contrast, if the curve is stacked up against the right axis, or there is a peak in the histogram against the right axis, some of the lighter tones (i.e., highlight areas in the image) will likely be compromised due to overexposure. The exception would be in a scene with very bright specular highlights, such as the sun reflecting off water, or streetlights in a nighttime cityscape—these small areas will almost invariably be much brighter than most of the other light tones in the scene, and therefore it is of little consequence if they are overexposed. Significant under- or overexposure is to be avoided if possible; but especially overexposure, as it is unlikely that highlight areas that have been overexposed will be able to render any detail, and nothing can be done to rectify this in post-processing. It is often possible to recover shadow detail lost due to underexposure; however, there is likely to be a penalty of reduced image quality in these areas due to the effects of an increased level in noise.

Many photographers adopt a technique known as "expose to the right," in which they adjust the exposure to the point that the histogram curve is as far to the right as possible without clipping, to ensure they capture as wide a tonal range as possible and with as many levels to describe those tones. While this is a valid technique, for best results, do not base your exposure on just the composite RGB histogram; look carefully at the histograms for the three individual channels. It is often possible to encounter a situation where one of the color channel histograms begins to show clipping not apparent in the composite RGB histogram. A common example occurs when photographing a sunrise or sunset, when it is likely the red channel will begin to clip first due to the higher level of red / orange / yellow light in the scene.

As previously mentioned, the "clipping" of the histogram curve is usually an indication of under- or overexposure, but do remember that the preview image, including those for NEF (RAW) files, is always derived from an 8-bit JPEG file to which the camera settings (White Balance, Contrast and Saturation, etc.) have been applied, and it is the tonal distribution of this JPEG file that the histogram describes. An NEF file will contain more data and have a wider range of tonal values; therefore, an overexposed highlight in the JPEG preview may not be an overexposed highlight when the NEF (RAW) file is examined in a RAW file converter such as Nikon Capture NX2. Even if an NEF file has been incorrectly exposed, it is possible to apply retrospective Exposure Compensation using software such as Nikon View NX2 or Nikon Capture NX2, between about -1.0 EV to +1.5 EV; no such flexibility is possible with a JPEG file.

Scenes that are low in contrast will have a rather narrow curve that ends before reaching either the left- or right-hand extremities of the bottom axis. You have two choices for how to deal with this situation: (1) Use the Picture Control system to increase the contrast level, or (2) adjust the contrast level at a later stage using an image-processing software application. I would recommend the latter approach, as it offers a far greater degree of control.

HINT: It is always preferable to err on the side of lower image contrast because it is easier to boost contrast than it is to try to reduce it at any stage subsequent to the original exposure.

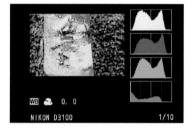

∧ The histogram indicates that a full range of tones has been recorded in the image. The curve extends to the right side representing the very light tones in the subject without bisecting the right side vertical axis, which would indicate possible overexposure.

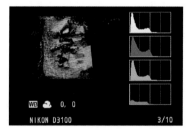

∧ Here, the exposure was reduced by 2 EV; notice how the histogram curve has shifted to the left to represent the range of darker (denser) tones that have been recorded. The reduction in the exposure level has caused the curve of the composite RGB and individual color channel histogram curves to become stacked against the left side vertical axis, indicating that shadow detail is likely to have been compromised in this picture.

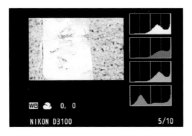

NIKON D3100   5/10

⌃ Here, the exposure was increased by 2 EV; notice how the histogram curve has shifted to the right to represent the range of lighter (brighter) tones that have been recorded. The increase in exposure has caused the curve of the composite RGB and individual color channel histograms to become stacked against the right side vertical axis, indicating that highlight detail has been compromised in this picture, and it is highly unlikely that it can be recovered in post-processing.

IMAGE STORAGE WITH SD CARDS

SD (Secure Digital) memory cards are small, solid-state cards that measure 1.3 x 0.9 x 0.08 inches (34 x 22 x 2 mm), have a capacity of up to 2GB, and are structured rather like the hard drive disk of your computer in that they have a file directory, a file allocation table, folders, and individual files. They are capable of retaining data even when they are not powered, and since they have no moving parts they are reasonably robust, so a minor impact from the card being dropped 8 to 10 feet (2.7 – 3 m) or exposure to the natural elements should not cause any problems. But total immersion in water should be avoided! Obviously, you should treat any memory card with the same care you would all your camera equipment, and it is advisable to keep them in the small plastic case supplied with each card.

Typically, SD cards have a temperature-operating range of -4F° to 167F° (-20°C to 75°C), and no altitude limit. They also have a small, sliding write-protect switch on one edge that, when set to the locked position, prevents any data being written or deleted (if you insert a locked SD card into the D3100, the camera will emit a beep sound as a warning if you try to release the shutter). Finally, unlike photographic film, they are not affected by ionizing radiation from X-ray security equipment that is widely used these days.

SDHC & SDXC CARDS

As camera development led to larger file sizes there was soon a requirement for SD cards with a capacity greater than 2GB. Secure Digital High Capacity (SDHC) cards were introduced as a new standard to meet this demand. They have the same physical dimensions and write-protect feature of SD cards, comply with the SD specification version 2.0 (which supports a card capacity of 4GB and over), and come in three speed classes of performance capability and minimum requirements. Full details on the SD 2.0 specification can be viewed at: www.sdcard.org.

The D3100 is fully compatible with memory cards that comply with the SDHC standard and, at the time of writing, most manufacturers already offer card capacities up to 16GB with some producing 32GB cards. While such capacious storage may sound tempting, I believe it is important to consider the potential risks of placing all your proverbial "eggs in one basket," and suggest it would be prudent to disperse the risk of loss or corruption of image data by using multiple cards with smaller capacities.

More recently SDXC memory cards, which represent the next generation of flash memory card, have been introduced and in time will be the natural successor to the popular SDHC card format. Based on the latest SD 3.0 specification, capacities of the new SDXC cards are planned to range between 32GB and 2TB, and SanDisk has already released a 64GB SDXC card. The file structure of the SDXC format cards enables long duration HD video recording at a high data transfer rate; widespread adoption of the new format is expected as many cameras, such as the D3100, incorporate an HD video capability.

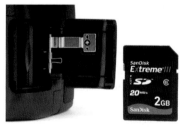

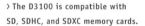

> The D3100 is compatible with SD, SDHC, and SDXC memory cards.

NOTE: Some older devices, including cameras, only support the SD standard and do not support the newer SDHC and SDXC cards. It is important to check that whatever external device you use supports the appropriate SD standard for the memory card you use. For example, an SDHC-compliant card reader supports both SD and SDHC cards but will not support the SDXC format.

APPROVED MEMORY CARDS

There is a plethora of memory cards on the market, but Nikon has only tested and approved those listed in the table below for use with the D3100. SD, SDHC, and SDXC card technology is well established, so although Nikon will not guarantee operation with other makes of cards, you should not experience any problems or have any concerns if you use an alternative brand. In the chart below are the Nikon Approved Memory Cards for use with the D3100; all cards of the make and capacity listed here can be used regardless of their read / write speed.

MANUFACTURER / CAPACITY	SD	SDHC	SDXC
Lexar Media	512MB, 1GB, 2GB	4GB, 8GB	N/A
Panasonic	512MB, 1GB, 2GB	4GB, 6GB, 8GB, 12GB, 16GB, 32GB	48GB, 64GB
SanDisk	512MB, 1GB, 2GB	4GB, 8GB, 16GB	64GB
Toshiba	512MB, 1GB, 2GB	4GB, 8GB, 16GB, 32GB	64GB

Nikon states that other brands and capacities of cards have not been tested with the D3100; therefore, operation cannot be guaranteed. If you intend to use a memory card not listed in the table above, it is advisable to check with the manufacturer in relation to its compatibility with the D3100. If you purchase a new memory card, always test it a few times before using it for any important photography. Should you experience any problems related to the memory card, use one of the approved cards for the purposes of troubleshooting.

MEMORY CARD CAPACITY

When considering the capacity of the memory cards you will use, bear in mind that the 14.2MP resolution of the D3100 will result in larger file sizes compared with the 12.3MP D3000 camera model or earlier 6MP Nikon camera models such as the D40. So, if you have been in the habit of using 1GB or 2GB memory cards regularly with your 6MP to 8MP DSLR, you may want to think about stepping up to 4GB or 8GB. On average, I find that when shooting NEF (RAW) files, I can expect to record about 450 images on an 8GB card. This provides plenty of scope, especially if you shoot for techniques such as high dynamic range (HDR) or panoramic, requiring multiple shots per final image. I find an 8GB card offers a good compromise between storage capacity and the risks (card failure or loss) inherent with saving all your shots to a single, high-capacity 16GB or 32GB card. However, if you expect to use the HD video capability of the D3100, such high capacity cards will be more convenient.

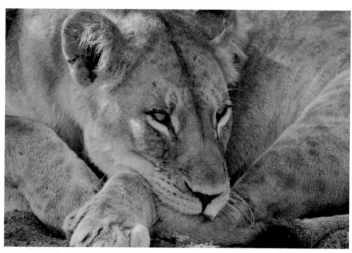

∧ Memory cards are relatively inexpensive, small, and very light, so it is worth carrying several whenever you are out shooting, particularly if you will not have access to stores where you can purchase them.

The table below provides information on the approximate number of images that can be stored on a typical 4GB SD memory card at the various image quality and size settings available on the D3100. All memory cards use a small proportion of their memory capacity to store data required for the card to operate. Therefore, the amount of memory available for storing image files will be slightly less than the quoted maximum capacity of the card. Likewise, capacities may vary slightly if a different brand of memory card is used.

QUALITY	IMAGE SIZE	FILE SIZE[1]	NO. IMAGES[1]	BUFFER CAPACITY[2]
NEF (RAW)	n/a	12.9	226	13
NEF (RAW) + JPEG Fine[3]	L	19.8	151	9
JPEG Fine	L	6.8	460	100
	M	3.9	815	100
	S	1.8	1700	100
JPEG Normal	L	3.4	914	100
	M	2.0	1500	100
	S	0.9	3300	100
JPEG Basic	L	1.7	1700	100
	M	1.0	3000	100
	S	0.5	6000	100

[1] File size will vary according to the scene photographed and the make of memory card used; therefore, all figures are approximate.
[2] This is the maximum number of image files that can be stored in the buffer memory. Capacity of the buffer will be reduced by the following: ISO sensitivity set to Hi 1.0, Noise Reduction turned on, Active D-Lighting turned on.
[3] File size is the combined total for the NEF (RAW) and JPEG files. The size of an NEF file cannot be altered, so the image size applies to JPEG files only.

INSERTING AND REMOVING MEMORY CARDS

Switch the power off before inserting a memory card into the D3100. Open the memory card slot cover by sliding it toward the back of the camera; the door will spring open to reveal the memory card slot. Insert the card with its contact terminals pointing toward the front of the camera and main (top) label of the card facing toward the back of the camera (i.e., toward yourself with the camera in shooting position). The beveled corner of the card will be to the upper left as it enters the camera. It will slide in a short distance and then you will feel a slight resistance—keep pushing the card until it locks into place (the green memory card access lamp illuminates briefly as confirmation that the card is installed properly).

To remove the card, switch the camera off, open the memory card slot cover, and press the exposed edge of the card toward the camera; then release it. The card will pop partially out of its port; then slide it free from the camera. Memory cards can become warm during use; this is normal and not an indication of a problem.

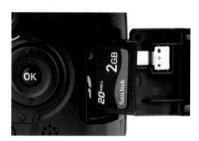

> The memory card will only fit into the camera one way, so it is virtually impossible to insert it incorrectly.

If the memory card is removed when a charged battery is installed in the camera, or it is connected to an AC power supply, (-E-) appears within the exposure counter brackets in both the viewfinder (blinking) and shooting Information Displays, plus the 🄳 icon blinks in the lower left corner of the viewfinder frame area as a warning.

If [Release locked] is selected under the [Slot empty release lock] item in the ⚐ Setup menu, the shutter release is disabled when no memory card is installed in the camera. If the [Enable release] option is selected, it is possible to take a picture and it will be displayed on the monitor screen but marked with the warning "Demo," and the image is not recorded.

FORMATTING A MEMORY CARD

The memory of an SD, SDHC, and SDXC card has a similar structure to that of a hard disk drive: a file directory, file allocation table, folders, and files. As data is written to and deleted from the card, small areas of its memory can become corrupted and files can become fragmented. This is particularly true if you repeatedly delete individual image files. Formatting the card in the camera will clean up the majority of the worst effects of fragmentation.

In the D3100 instruction book, Nikon states that formatting memory cards "permanently deletes any data they may contain." While this is a salutary warning, it is somewhat misleading. The formatting process actually causes the existing file directory information to be overwritten, so the indicators that direct any reading device, including the camera itself, to the image data held on the card are removed; it does not actually delete / erase all the data, as Nikon states. However, it does make it difficult, although not impossible, to recover previously written data from a card once it is formatted. If you inadvertently format a card, it is often possible to recover the image files by using appropriate recovery software, provided no further data is written to the card. Since prevention is better than a cure, always save your images to a computer or other storage device before formatting a card. Also make sure to create a backup copy of these files.

To format a card using the D3100, insert the memory card and turn the camera on. Press the MENU button to display the menu system and open the ᵧ Setup menu. Navigate to the **[Format memory card]** item, and then press ▶. Highlight **[Yes]** and press the ⊚ button. The message "Formatting memory card" is displayed during the formatting process. To leave the process without formatting the memory card, highlight **[No]** and press ⊚.

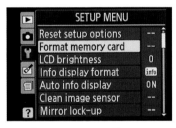

∧ The **[Format memory card]** item is the second item in the Setup menu.

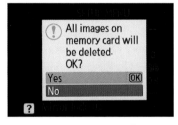

∧ A warning is displayed in the ᵧ Setup menu before the formatting process can be activated.

Once complete, the remaining exposure display shows the approximate number of photographs that can be recorded on the installed memory card at the current size and quality settings. The displayed figure is only an approximation because file size will vary due to file compression; it is often possible for the camera to record and store more images than the remaining exposure count display initially suggests after formatting.

HINT: After ensuring its contents have been saved and backed up, format the memory card each time you insert it into the camera. This is especially important if it has been used in a different camera model, or formatted by a computer or other device. Failure to follow this procedure may lead to the card not functioning properly in the camera, resulting in image files being rendered as unreadable or becoming corrupted.

NOTE: You should never switch the camera off or otherwise interrupt the power supply to the camera during the formatting process, as this results in corruption of the memory card.

IMAGE QUALITY AND FILE FORMATS

The D3100 saves still images to the memory card in two file formats: Joint Photographic Experts Group (JPEG) and Nikon Electronic File (NEF) RAW format.

EXPEED 2 IMAGE PROCESSING

Expeed 2 is the generic name given by Nikon to its latest in-camera image-processing engine; in combination with the Picture Control system (see pages 156-165), its purpose is to ensure consistency in the appearance of images in terms of color and contrast, although component parts of the system—both hardware and software—may differ from camera model to camera model. If you have experience shooting film, it might help to understand the concept by thinking about the way a specific film type can be matched with particular developer to produce consistent, repeatable results, regardless of which camera was used.

The Expeed 2 processing concept is applied to the D3100 is an enhanced version of the Expeed system used by the D5000, D90, D300-series, D700, and D3-series models. When the camera is set to record images in the JPEG file format, it uses the integrated ADC (analogue to digital converter) to convert the electrical signals generated by the capacitors (pixels) on the sensor to 12-bit RAW data before the value for each pixel is rendered via a demosaicing (conversion) process to 12-bit RGB data. Remember, the demosaicing process is necessary to render an RGB value for each pixel because each sampling point on the sensor (pixel) only records a value for red, green, or blue.

Next, the 12-bit RGB data is passed to the Expeed 2 processing engine where all further processing, such as color manipulation, contrast control, and sharpening (plus an automated reduction of the effects of lateral chromatic aberration to reduce color fringing at distinct edges in image detail) is performed in a 16-bit depth space to ensure there is no compromise of the data. The final stage of the image processing is the encoding of the data to create the JPEG file; it is only at this point that the 12-bit data is reduced to 8-bit. The result is a noticeable improvement in image quality compared with JPEG files generated by earlier Nikon DSLR camera models that lacked the Expeed system, particularly in the lower shadow tones. This is of considerable benefit when the finished 8-bit JPEG files are to be subjected to post-processing in a computer, which would otherwise compound errors generated during in-camera processing had it been performed on 8-bit data rather than the 12-bit data handled by the D3100.

When the D3100 is set to record an image in the Nikon Electronic File (NEF) format, the data saved is essentially the "raw" data generated by the ADC with no interpolation or other adjustment of the information from the sensor. The settings for the Picture Control System are not applied in-camera but recorded and appended to the RAW file as a set of instructions, to be subsequently read by the RAW converter used to open the NEF (RAW) file. This lack of processing is the reason such a file is referred to as a RAW file, and the ability to modify the instruction set to each RAW file at any subsequent point after the original image is recorded is the key to the tremendous flexibility offered by the RAW format.

However, unlike other higher-specified Nikon camera models, which offer a choice of bit depth, the D3100 can only record NEF (RAW) files at a 12-bit depth, and it always applies compression to the image data. So the ADC performs the conversion of the information from the sensor at 12 bits. The data is maintained in the selected bit depth while it is built and output; this means that at a 12-bit depth each pixel can have one of 4096 distinct values. Essentially, an NEF file uses the same structure as a TIFF file; it starts with tags that point to the EXIF (camera settings) and White Balance value information, then saves a small thumbnail image as a JPEG file, followed by the raw pixel data. However, since the D3100 can only save NEF files in a compressed form, some of the original information captured by the sensor is discarded in a process that Nikon describes as being "visually lossless."

To summarize, when comparing between the JPEG and NEF formats, the principal differences lie in how the camera deals with the data from the sensor. Using the JPEG format, the camera produces a finished image based on the sensor data and camera settings at the time of the exposure. Although it is possible to use these finished files directly from the camera to produce a print or post to a website, these files can still be post-processed after they have been imported to a computer. However, using the NEF format requires the photographer to process the image after the fact, using a computer with NEF-compatible software.

If you are beginning to form the impression that, to eek out every last ounce of quality the D3100 has to offer, you should shoot in the NEF format, you are not too far off the mark! However, while many photographers prefer the NEF format, I prefer to consider this issue in terms of the flexibility the formats offer and recommend that you use the one that is best suited to your specific requirements.

JPEG

Probably the greatest benefit of the JPEG format it that it can be read by most software and it supported by HTML, the computer language used to build web pages. This enables these files to be shared widely, regardless of the type of computer or software that may be used.

The process of saving a JPEG file involves taking 8 x 8 blocks of pixels and subjecting each block to a series of calculations that determines compression. Essentially, the numeric value of the pixels is converted into an equation that represents an average value of the pixels in that block. The compressed result for each block is then brought together as a single sequence of binary values, which is encoded using a further lossless form of compression. While the compression process varies with the range of pixel values in each block, it will ultimately result in the permanent loss of some data. As a rule of thumb, a JPEG compression ratio of 1:4 or less will produce an image in which the effects process are imperceptible.

However, the JPEG format has three properties that can potentially influence image quality in an adverse manner. The in-camera processing reduces the 12-bit data from the sensor to 8-bit values when it creates a JPEG file. The D3100 does have the advantage that it makes all in-camera adjustments to image attributes (i.e., sharpening, contrast, and saturation) at a 12-bit level before the data is reduced to 8-bits. Therefore, if you have no intention of doing any post-processing, the reduction to 8 bits is of no real consequence. However, if you make significant changes to an image using software in post-processing, then the 8-bit data of a JPEG file can limit the manipulation that can be applied. This is particularly true of color, sharpening, and contrast adjustments.

In respect to color and contrast, it appears that Nikon has maintained consistency with their current crop of camera models: The default settings on the D3100 tend to produce images that have slightly over-vivid color and boosted contrast. Consequently, JPEG files straight from the D3100 can produce JPEG images that are a little difficult to handle in post-processing. It is often preferable to have an image with a slightly flatter contrast and more neutral color, since it is much easier to increase color saturation and contrast levels than it is to reverse their effects.

So, if you expect to work on your JPEG images after the event using digital imaging software, you may wish to consider turning down the saturation / contrast levels in the Picture Control System. Likewise, you may want to reduce or remove in-camera sharpening. However, if you wish to produce images direct from the camera with no intentions of any post-processing, I suggest you leave the D3100 at its default settings for the Picture Controls.

When the camera saves an image using the JPEG format, it encodes most of the camera settings for attributes such as White Balance, sharpening, contrast, saturation, and hue into the image data. If you make an error and inadvertently select the wrong setting, you will need to try to fix your mistake in post-processing. Inevitably, this is time consuming and there is no guarantee it will be successful, particularly in respect to trying to reduce the effects of over-sharpening, reducing contrast, or correcting color because the wrong White Balance setting was used for the original image.

The development of digital imaging technology is extremely fast-paced, and the electronics used in any particular camera are only as good as the day the manufacturer decided on the specifications and finalized the design of the camera. Granted, most modern cameras can have their firmware (installed software) upgraded by the user. This helps to offset obsolescence, but it is only effective for so long. By processing images in software on a computer you can often take advantage of the very latest advances in image processing, which are unavailable in the camera.

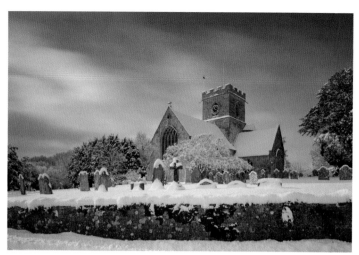

⌃ To extract the optimum image quality form the D3100, it is well worth the trouble of shooting in the NEF (RAW) format.

NEF (RAW)

Using the NEF format has only one serious disadvantage in my mind—the extra time you will need to invest in post-processing each image to produce a finished picture. However, this will be time well spent if you want to achieve the best possible image quality from your D3100, especially for any images you intend to print. The larger file size of the NEF format can also present an issue in terms of the amount of available storage in your memory card or external storage device; but modern data storage devices are relatively cheap, so this shouldn't be too much of a concern. Additionally, there can be limitations and variability with third party software's ability to read and interpret Nikon NEF files. On the other hand, the benefits of the NEF format include:

O More consistent and smoother tonal gradations
O Color that is more subtle and true to the original subject or scene
O A slight increase in the level of detail resolved, compared with JPEG

- The ability (within fairly limited parameters) to adjust exposure in post-processing to correct for slight exposure errors, or to help extend the dynamic range of an image—for example, it is often possible to gain an extra 1 stop (1Ev) in the highlights of an image to reveal more detail and tonal gradation
- Increased post-processing ability to correct and/or change image color by resetting attributes such as the White Balance value, saturation, and hue—plus improved control over image contrast and brightness

I have already alluded to the fact that unlike some of its current stable mates in the Nikon lineup, such as the D300s and D7000, the D3100 does not allow you to choose the bit depth used to record the NEF (RAW) file, nor whether or not compression should be applied to an NEF (RAW) image.

Compressed NEF (RAW): Inevitably, since you have no option but to record compressed NEF files with the D3100, the question is: what, if any, effect does this have on image quality? Nikon describes the compression applied to NEF files as "visually lossless," by which they mean it is almost impossible to differentiate visually between an image produced from an uncompressed file and one produced from a compressed file. The compression process used by Nikon is selective; it only works on certain image data while leaving other data unaffected. Nikon's use of the word "compression" in this context is rather misleading, as the process involves two distinct phases. The first phase sees certain tonal values grouped and then rounded, and the second phase is the point at which a conventional lossless compression is applied. Once the analog signal from the sensor has been converted to digital data, the first phase of the compression process separates the values that represent the very darkest tones from the rest of the data. Then the data with values that represent the remaining lighter tones is divided into groups, but this process is not linear. As the tones become lighter, the size of the group increases; so the group with the lightest tones is larger than a group containing mid-tone values. A lossless compression is then applied to each individual dark tone value and the rounded value of each group in the mid and light tones.

When an application such as Nikon Capture NX2 opens an NEF file recorded by the D3100, it reverses the lossless compression process. The individual dark tone values are unaffected (remember the compression applied here is lossless), but, and here is the twist, each of the grouped values for the mid and light tones must be expanded to fit its original range. Since the rounding error in each group becomes progressively larger as the tonal values it represents become lighter and lighter, the gaps in the data caused by the rounding process also become progressively larger at lighter tonal values.

It is important to put these data "gaps" into perspective. A single compression / decompression cycle performed on an NEF file produces an image that is, for most intents and purposes, indistinguishable from one produced from an original, uncompressed NEF file. The human eye does not respond in a linear way to increased levels of brightness; therefore, it is incapable of resolving the very minor changes that have taken place, even in the lightest tones where the rounding error is greatest and therefore the data gap is largest (remember, Nikon's phrasing is "visually lossless").

Furthermore, our eyes are generally only capable of detecting tonal variations equivalent to those produced by 8-bit data. Since even a compressed NEF file has the equivalent to more than 8-bit data, the data gaps caused by Nikon's compression process are of no consequence. Similarly, many photographers will ultimately reduce their 12-bit NEF (RAW) file to an 8-bit RGB-TIFF or JPEG file prior to printing, which can mask any loss of tonal gradation caused by compressing the original NEF file.

In spite of our eyes' inability to recognize these changes, it is important to understand that the data loss caused by compression of NEF files can affect final image quality. Thankfully, this unwanted effect is rare and likely to manifest itself only in the highlight area(s) of an image subjected to a significant level of color and / or contrast adjustment during post-processing, or where excessive sharpening is applied; the result is posterization, which creates course shifts in color and tone where there should be gentle, smooth transitions.

In considering the attributes of the JPEG and NEF formats, many photographers make an analogy with film photography; they consider the NEF file as though they have the original film negative to work from, and the JPEG file as being akin to a machine-processed print. I do not disagree, but this is where my point about the flexibility of the two formats comes back: not every photographer has the desire, ability, or time to spend post-processing NEF files. The good news is that we have a choice, so consider the points made in this section and make your decision based on which format is best suited to your purposes. If you have sufficient storage capacity on your memory card(s), you could always select the NEF + JPEG combination from the **[Image Quality]** options, as the D3100 can record a picture in both formats simultaneously.

JPEG Image Quality: The D3100 allows you to save JPEG files at one of three different levels of quality:

- O FINE: uses a low compression ratio of approximately 1:4
- O NORMAL (default): uses a moderate compression ratio of approximately 1:8
- O BASIC: uses a high compression ratio of approximately 1:16

As the processing involved in the creation of a JPEG file uses compression that discards data, to maintain the highest image quality, you should select the lowest level of compression. A file saved at the FINE setting will be visually superior to a file saved at the BASIC setting.

JPEG Image Size: Each JPEG can be saved by the D3100 at one of three different sizes:

- O L: Large (4608 x 3072 pixels)
- O M: Medium (3456 x 2304 pixels)
- O S: Small (2304 x 1536 pixels)

NOTE: Image size is not applicable to NEF files, which always have the dimensions of an image saved at the **[Large]** size option when opened in appropriate software, such as Nikon View NX2 or Nikon Capture NX2.

SETTING IMAGE QUALITY AND SIZE

To set Image Quality on the D3100, open the Information Display by pressing the 📷 button, and then press the Information Display ⊞ button to highlight the cursor. Highlight the [Image Quality] item and press the 🆗 button to open the list of options. Use 🔆 to highlight the required setting; there are five options available: NEF, JPEG Fine, JPEG Normal, JPEG Basic, and NEF + F (JPEG – Fine/Large). Finally, press the 🆗 button to confirm the selection.

To set image size for the JPEG format on the D3100, open the Information Display by pressing the 📷 button, and then press the ⊞ button to highlight the cursor. Highlight the [Image size] item and press the 🆗 button to open the list of options. Use 🔆 to highlight the required setting. There are three options available: L (Large), M (Medium), or S (Small).

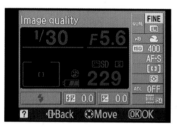 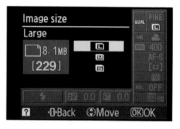

^ The [Image quality] item is shown here, highlighted in the Information Display.

^ The [Image size] option, directly below [Image quality], enables you to determine how many pixels the camera will utilize when recording an image.

Alternatively, the [Buttons] item in the ⌇ Setup menu can be used to assign selection of Image Quality and Image Size by pressing and holding the **Fn** button, and then rotating the Command dial. Although this sounds convenient, it takes somewhat longer because it is necessary to scroll through a greater number of combinations of quality and size, compared with setting each attribute separately as just described.

As if that were not enough, the [Image quality] and [Image size] items in the Shooting menu can also be used, although once again, this route is slower compared with using the method described for the ⊞ and 🔆 buttons.

NOTE: The file size displayed in the Information Display for the NEF (16MB) and NEF + JPEG Fine (24MB) settings is the full uncompressed file size. The files saved in-camera will be in a compressed form with an NEF file typically 12.9MB and the NEF +JPEG Fine files having a combined size of approximately 19.8MB.

NOTE: At the NEF + JPEG Fine setting, two images are recorded—one NEF (RAW), and the other a JPEG at the Fine Image Quality but always at an image size of [Large]. When reviewing a picture recorded using the dual format option, only the JPEG image is displayed on the D3100; however, when pictures recorded at this setting are deleted, both image files are deleted.

LIVE VIEW

Live View provides a real-time video signal from the camera's sensor to the monitor screen, which refreshes at 24 frames per second (fps), to show the view of the scene (it is the same view as the optical viewfinder). This enables pictures to be composed in situations when using the optical viewfinder is difficult or not desirable—for example, when shooting from a very low position or when the enlarged view offered by the monitor is helpful in composition or for checking focus.

One fundamental difference between the optical viewfinder and Live View, on the D3100 is the method of autofocus; in Live View, the camera uses contrast detection autofocus, which employs information from the CMOS sensor to assess contrast at the selected focus point and adjust focus based on the highest level of contrast. The advantage of this system is that the focus point can be positioned anywhere within the area of the frame and is not restricted to the 11 AF points used by the phase detection AF system in normal shooting via the optical viewfinder. However, contrast detection AF has the distinct disadvantage of being considerably slower. Plus, to acquire focus, it must focus through the plane of the intended subject so that the system can sense a lower contrast level before readjusting focus to the point of maximum contrast. In a nutshell, autofocus for Live View is very good for static subjects, especially when the most accurate focus is required, as in close-up photography, but it is of little use for moving subjects because it simply is not quick enough.

> The Live View display is shown here with the Live View Information Display turned on; note the AF point is displayed in red to indicate that focus has not yet been acquired.

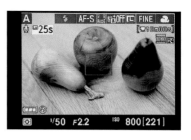

SHOOT AND REVIEW

132

One very welcome refinement of the D3100 is the single "flick" type switch used to open Live View; located on the back of the camera where it can be reached very conveniently with the right thumb, it is quick and efficient compared with previous Nikon cameras where a separate button had to be pushed, or dial positioned, before the shutter release button could be pressed down. It may be stating the obvious, but for Live View to operate the reflex mirror of the D3100 must be raised out of the light path from the lens to the camera's sensor; therefore, the optical viewfinder is always blacked out when Live View and D-Movie mode are active, plus the normal Information Display is not available. The Live View shooting Information Display shows much of the information you would see in the optical viewfinder display and the Information Display shown on the monitor screen, without impinging too much on the Live View image area. The information displayed includes: Shooting mode, AF mode, AF-Area mode, Active D-Lighting, Image Size, Image Quality, White Balance, Metering mode, Shutter speed, Aperture, ISO, Exposure Compensation, Battery status, Number of shots remaining, Time remaining (before Live View ends automatically), and Self-Timer mode. Also shown is the recording time (minutes and seconds) remaining in D-Movie mode at the current resolution and quality settings, plus an indicator for the status of the built-in microphone. There are two further Live View display options: one hides the Information Display and only shows the exposure settings, while the other overlays the screen with a grid pattern to facilitate framing and composition. However, there is no support on the D3100 for a real-time live histogram to assess exposure prior to releasing the shutter or recording a video clip.

To open Live View, rotate the ⌷ switch clockwise; the reflex mirror will lift and the view through the lens will be displayed on the LCD monitor together with the Live Information Display and the AF point, which will vary in appearance according to the option selected for Live View AF-Area mode. To scroll through the Live View Display Options, press the ⌷ button to show or hide the Live View Information Display or display a gridline pattern.

Next, choose the focus mode by pressing the ⌷ button. The Live View display will close and be replaced by the Information Display. Highlight the focus mode item and press ⊗ to display the following options:

o AF-S (Single-Servo AF): Ideal for stationary subjects, the focus will be adjusted and lock when the shutter release button is pressed down halfway. The shutter can only be released if focus is acquired.

o AF-F (Full-Time Servo AF): Intended for moving subjects, the camera focuses continuously during Live View and D-Movie mode. The shutter can only be released if focus is acquired.

o MF (Manual focus): The lens must be focused manually. The shutter can be released at any time, regardless of the focus status.

Highlight the required focus mode and press ⊗ to select it. Assuming that either AF-S or AF-F mode is selected, it is also necessary to set the AF-Area mode. AF-area mode can be selected in all Shooting modes except ⌷ and ⌷; if Live View is selected in the ⌷ and ⌷ Shooting modes, the D3100 will activate its Automatic Scene Selection mode to analyze the subject/scene and select what it considers to be the most appropriate Shooting mode when autofocus is enabled. Highlight the AF-area mode item in the Information Display and press ⊗ to display the following options:

o ⌷ Face-Priority AF: The D3100 detects the face of a person and focuses on it automatically. The subject's face usually needs to be square to the camera lens for positive detection.

o ⌷ Wide-Area AF: The AF point covers a large area of the frame making it ideal for handheld picture taking of large subjects or scenes; use the Multi Selector button to shift the AF point to the required spot in the frame area.

o ⊞ Normal-Area AF: Use this option for precision focus on a very specific area in the frame. It is best suited to shooting from a tripod and is particularly useful in close-up photography. Use the Multi Selector button to shift the AF point to the required spot in the frame area.

o ⊞ Subject-Tracking AF: In this mode, the D3100 will attempt to track a selected subject as it moves within the frame area; it is most effective and reliable when the camera-to-subject distance remains constant (i.e., the subject moves laterally across the frame).

Highlight the required AF-Area mode and press ⊛ to select it. The Live View AF-Area modes can also be selected using the **[Live view/movie]** option in the **[AF-area mode]** item of the Shooting menu. Press the ⊟ button to return to the Live View display. The nature of the AF point will depend on the AF-Area mode selected and focus status as follows:

o ⊡ Face-priority AF: A double yellow border will be displayed when the camera detects a person's face pointing toward it (if there are multiple faces, the camera, will focus on the one it considers to be closest; to focus on an alternative face, shift the AF point using the Multi Selector). Press the shutter release down halfway to focus. If the subject looks away from the lens so their face is no longer visible to the camera, the AF point borders will no longer be displayed.

o ⊟ Wide-area AF & ⊟ Normal-Area AF: Initially, this will be displayed as a red square. Use the Multi Selector to shift the AF point to the required spot in the frame area, or press the ⊛ button to position the AF point at the center of the frame. Press the shutter release down halfway to focus and the AF point will turn green if the D3100 can acquire focus on the subject or blink red if it cannot acquire focus.

o ⊞ Subject-Tracking AF: Initially, this will be displayed as a white square with four additional corner markings; position the AF point over the subject and press the ⊛ button. The focus point will change color to yellow and track the subject as it changes position within the frame area. Press the shutter release down halfway to focus and the AF point will turn green if the D3100 can acquire focus on the subject or blink red if it cannot acquire focus; the AF point will continue to track the subject. To end AF tracking press the ⊛ button.

NOTE: Except in ⚙ and ⚘ shooting modes, exposure can be locked by pressing the **AE-L/AF-L** button, and focus can be locked by pressing the shutter release button down halfway.

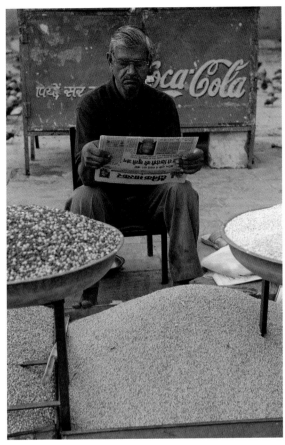

> Face-priority AF can be very helpful when shooting candid pictures of people using Live View.

NOTE: Subject-Tracking is unlikely to track a subject if it and the background are particularly bright or dark, or if the subject is particularly small in the frame area, moving quickly (especially toward or away from the camera), very similar in color to the background, leaves the frame area, or changes size significantly.

To take a picture from Live View, press the shutter release button down all the way; the LCD monitor screen will turn off. If the **[Image review]** item in the Playback menu is set to **[On]**, the picture will be displayed on the monitor screen for approximately four seconds, or until the shutter release button is pressed down halfway; if the **[Image review]** item is set to **[Off]**, the monitor screen will remain blank. The D3100 will then return to its Live View mode. Finally, to exit Live View, rotate the ⬚ switch clockwise again. There are a few general points to consider when shooting in Live View:

O Since the sensor is exposed continuously during Live View, never point the camera directly at the sun or any other high-intensity light source; this may damage the sensor.

O The monitor screen display will adjust its brightness automatically, so the final exposure may differ from the image seen on the monitor screen.

O Exposure can be adjusted in P, S, and A modes by ±5 EV in steps of 0.3 EV, although the effects of values beyond ±3 EV will not be shown in the monitor.

O It is possible to magnify the image in Live View to assist in precise focusing; press the ⬚ button to magnify the image by a maximum of approximately 6.8x, and press the ⬚ button to reduce magnification. In Wide-Area and Normal-Area AF you can use the Multi Selector to scroll to other areas of the image. However, since the camera only uses a small proportion of its pixels in Live View, the resolution of an image enlarged in this way is very low, rather defeating the purpose of this function!

O It is important to block light from entering the viewfinder eyepiece when shooting in Live View, as it may influence the TTL metering and therefore the exposure level.

O A countdown of 30 seconds will be displayed before Live View ends automatically; the timer display turns red at 5 seconds remaining. This feature is designed to prevent the sensor from overheating and protect the other electrical circuitry of the camera from thermal damage.

O Live View may end automatically in advance of the normal countdown timer in conditions of high ambient temperature if the camera has already been used for protracted periods in Live View or D-Movie mode or has been shooting in Continuous release mode for extended periods.

O You may observe banding or flickering in the Live View image displayed on the monitor screen under certain types of artificial lighting, such as fluorescent lighting. Use the **[Flicker reduction]** item in the ⬚ Setup menu to help reduce this effect.

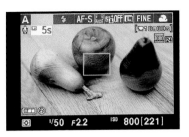

‹ In the Live View display the countdown timer, in the upper left of the screen, will turn to red when 5 seconds remain before Live View is automatically switched off.

D-MOVIE MODE

The D3100 is the first Nikon DSLR to offer a full HD 1080p resolution (previous models such as the D90 and D5000 had a maximum resolution of HD 720p), plus it is also the first Nikon DSLR camera with a full-time AF capability during video recording; although this employs a contrast-detect method, as described in the Live View section above, so it is inherently slower than the phase-detection AF used for normal autofocus shooting. The D3100 also employs a different compression regime for video, replacing the Motion JPEG used by previous models. The camera records a variety of different resolutions and frame rates using the H.264 / MPEG-4 AVC compression and stores video in a .MOV container file (the H.264 / MPEG-4 AVC compression is far more efficient in terms of file size compared with Motion JPEG). At all resolutions a frame rate of 24 fps is available, while at the lower resolution of 1280 x 720 pixels there are also frame rates for 30 and 25 fps. The monaural microphone records in 16-bit PCM audio with an apparent sampling rate of 24 kHz (Nikon has not disclosed the precise figure), regardless of the video resolution and frame rate (there is no option to use an external microphone on the D3100).

However, once you begin to peel away at exactly what the D3100 can deliver in its Movie mode, it soon becomes apparent that there are a number of significant restrictions imposed by the system. The D3100 is without doubt an extremely fine, state-of-the-art, entry-level digital SLR camera, but it is not a fully fledged video camera by any stretch of the imagination!

Once the camera is in Movie mode, you relinquish any control over shutter speed, aperture, and ISO level. In effect, the camera shifts into a fully automated point-and-shoot mode. The reason behind this is the way that Nikon has implemented the recording of video in the D3100; in essence, the camera takes the video feed that provides the real-time image displayed on the monitor in Live View and uses this for its Movie mode.

In Movie mode, the exposure settings for shutter speed and ISO used for still picture shooting are irrelevant since you cannot change them. The only parameters you can control are Manual focus, manual lens zooming, Exposure Compensation, and AE Lock.

The lens aperture, which can be set to any value between the maximum aperture and f/16 (when using a Nikkor lens with an electronic aperture control), should be selected prior to beginning video recording; it is not possible to adjust the aperture value once in Live View or Movie mode. Likewise, any of the parameters that can be set within the Picture Control system must be set beforehand. It is important to avoid setting the level of contrast and sharpening too high when recording video, as the former will cause a reduction in dynamic range, and the latter can result in a "ghost" image, in which a black edge appears to follow any moving elements. Similarly, the White Balance setting should also be selected prior to entering Live View.

Unless you intervene, the D3100 will exercise fully automatic control of the exposure. Matrix metering is used during video recording, regardless of the metering pattern selected on the camera. This raises a series of issues. First, if the level of illumination in the scene changes—for example, the camera is panned from an area that is lit brightly to an area of deep shadow—the camera will adjust shutter speed and ISO accordingly in order to maintain what the camera thinks is an appropriate exposure. As a consequence, the noise level in the image can increase perceptibly as the ISO level is increased. Furthermore, as with any automated exposure system, it is highly likely that if the scene is predominantly filled with particularly dark tones, it will be overexposed and underexposed if the tones in the scene are primarily light. Allied to this problem is the way the camera adjusts exposure changes in a distinctly stepped manner, causing a noticeable shift in the level of illumination in the recorded image.

So, how can you tame the D3100 in its Movie mode and exercise some degree of control over the exposure to obtain both greater consistency and accuracy? Well, there are two options: it is possible to use the ☒ Exposure Compensation feature or you can use the **[AE Lock (hold)]** option for the **AE-L/AF-L** button available under the **[Buttons]** item in the Setup menu. Both of these controls must be used after the camera has entered its Live View mode if they are to be effective during video recording. So the following is my suggested sequence for setting up the D3100 to achieve a consistent exposure level in Movie mode:

1. Before activating Live View, select the required lens aperture value in the camera's normal still-picture Shooting mode (remember, the minimum aperture value available in Movie mode using a Nikkor lens with electronic aperture control is f/16). Also, confirm that the **[AE Lock (hold)]** option is selected for operation of the **AE-L/AF-L** button.

2. Activate Live View by rotating the ⊡ switch. Next, set the AF mode and AF-Area mode as described previously in the Live View section.

3. Point the camera at the subject and focus using Live View autofocus; if the subject comprises tones that are significantly lighter or darker than average, middle-value tones, use the Exposure Compensation to set a positive or negative value, respectively, and then press the **AE-L/AF-L** button.

4. As an alternative to Step 3 (above), use a middle-tone reference, such as a photographic 18% gray card. Ensure it is placed in the same light as the light falling on the subject, and then point the camera at the reference, and press the **AE-L/AF-L** button. This approach ensures that the camera will record average tones accurately, which will result in lighter and darker tones also being rendered accurately, provided they are within the dynamic range of the sensor. Plus, the lens can be zoomed without risk that the camera will shift the exposure level if the tonal range in the scene changes significantly.

5. By pressing the **AE-L/AF-L** button as described in either step 3 or step 4 above, the exposure level calculated by the camera will be locked until the **AE-L/AF-L** button is pressed again—the **[AE Lock (hold)]** option can be switched on and off as required during a video recording by pressing the **AE-L/AF-L** button; when it is active "AE-L" is displayed in the lower left corner of the monitor screen next to the Matrix-metering icon (☺).

NOTE: It appears that the application of an Exposure Compensation value also influences the shutter speed that the D3100 will use during video recording. Although no definitive values are available, setting any negative Exposure Compensation seems to result in the use of a faster shutter speed, while positive Exposure Compensation values cause a slower shutter speed to be set.

ROLLING SHUTTER EFFECT

There is one other surprise that awaits the uninitiated user of the D3100 in Movie mode; it concerns the way in which the readout from the sensor is handled. The CMOS sensor does not capture each frame of video simultaneously but records it in a scanning process of horizontal lines that starts from the top edge of the sensor and works toward the bottom. The consequence of this is exhibited when the camera and / or the subject moves rapidly during recording; the subject can appear at different parts of the frame leading to vertical lines in static subjects that are skewed in a diagonal direction, or moving subjects that appear to have a cartoon-like, exaggerated lean.

A more pernicious version of this skewing effect occurs with a handheld camera that, due to a lack of stability, moves laterally left and right during recording with the result that vertical static lines in the frame, such as the edge of a building, take on a wavy appearance and look as though they are wobbling. If the lens in use offers Nikon's Vibration Reduction (VR) feature, I very strongly recommend that you switch it on for handheld video recording.

In my opinion the results produced by the D3100 in terms of the rolling shutter effect are not as well suppressed as some other recent Nikon DSLR cameras, such as the D300s. Therefore, it is a matter of anticipating them in certain situations and attempting to mitigate the worst effects by shooting appropriately—for example, panning the camera slowly, or following a moving subject accurately and accepting the inevitable distortion in the foreground and background. The single most effective step you can take is to avoid this problem is to use a tripod to support the D3100 when recording in D-Movie mode.

There are several limitations built into the D-Movie mode of the D3100:

○ Due to the high data rates at Full HD resolution, Nikon recommends the use of at least a Class 6 SD memory card for recording video clips.

○ The maximum recording duration for a single video clip is ten minutes.

○ It is important to keep the autofocus capabilities during video recording in perspective. The contrast-detect system used for Live View and D-Movie mode is slower than the phase-detection system used in normal shooting. Do not expect too much of the system and you will not be disappointed—for example, it will not keep pace with a subject involved in fast paced action or sports but will do better with far more modest levels of subject movement, especially if the subject is not too close to the camera.

○ The camera controls the maximum duration for the use of the Live View and the D-Movie mode automatically to prevent the camera from overheating and its circuitry being damaged. In high ambient temperatures, or after protracted use of Live View and / or D-Movie mode, the camera may end Live View unexpectedly.

○ The audio recording of the D3100 uses its built-in 16-bit mono channel microphone, which has a relatively low sampling rate of just 11 kHz (most dedicated video cameras provide stereo channel sound recording with a sampling rate of 48 kHz). This leaves something to be desired in sound quality—the sounds generated by camera operations, such as rotating the Command dial, adjusting the zoom position of a lens, or the AF and Manual focus actions are recorded with distressing clarity! The built-in microphone may be acceptable for casual recording, but if you want to include ambient sounds with video clips, I would recommend the use of a separate audio recorder with stereo microphones, enabling the video and audio tracks to be edited together in appropriate video-editing software.

○ As well as writing data continuously to the memory card and running Live View, it is likely the VR function of appropriate Nikkor lenses will also be active; these two latter actions are the most power-demanding functions of the D3100, so pack plenty of spare batteries if you anticipate extended use of the Live View and / or D-Movie mode.

○ The D-Movie mode is simply an extension of the Live View function, so make sure you never point the camera at the sun or any other very intense light source when Live View or D-Movie mode are active. Doing so risks damage to the sensor and/or other associated electrical circuitry.

USING MOVIE MODE

To use the D-Movie mode, the first step is to set the options under the **[Movie settings]** item in the Shooting menu:

○ Highlight **[Movie settings]** and press ▶.

○ Select **[Quality]** and press ▶ to choose a frame size from the chart below, and then press ⊛. The frame rate will depend on the "look" you want to achieve and the type of device the video clip will be displayed on, as follows: 30 fps—NTSC devices, 25 fps—PAL devices, and 24 fps to emulate the frame rate of motion pictures.

○ To set the options for the built-in microphone, highlight **[Sound]** and press ▶. Highlight the required option as follows: **[Off]** or **[On]**, and press ⊛.

OPTION	FRAME SIZE (PIXELS)	FRAME RATE (FPS)	CLIP DURATION
1920 x 1080, 24 fps	1920 x 1080	23.976	
1280 x 720, 30 fps		29.97	
1280 x 720, 25 fps	1280 x 720	25	10 minutes
1280 x 720, 24 fps		23.976	
640 x 424, 24 fps	640 x 424		

RECORDING MOVIES

Follow these steps to record a movie on the D3100:

1. Select the required lens aperture value and set **AE-L/AF-L** button to the **[AE Lock (hold)]** option.

2. Rotate the ⎘ switch to activate Live View and select the required AF mode and AF-Area mode, as described in the Live View section.

3. Compose the opening frame of your video and acquire focus, as described in the Live View section. If required, adjust the exposure level in P, S, and A modes using the Exposure Compensation feature, and / or lock the exposure level by pressing the **AE-L/AF-L** button (the exposure level will be held until the button is pressed again). Exposure lock is not available in the 🔄 and ⊕ shooting modes.

4. To start recording, press the record button at the center of the ⎘ switch. A recording indicator and the time remaining for recording will be displayed on the monitor screen.

5. If you use the built-in microphone, which is located on the front of the camera just above the D3100 badge, take care not to obstruct it. Also remember, the built-in microphone is prone to record the operation of camera controls.

6. To end the recording, press the record button again. Recording will stop automatically after 10 minutes or when the memory card is full. A countdown display for 30 seconds will be shown in red before recording in the D-Movie mode ends automatically; this may appear considerably sooner than the full 10-minute clip duration has elapsed if the camera's electronics have become warm. If this occurs, allow the camera to cool before resuming D-Movie mode recording.

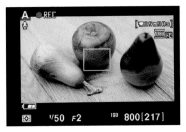

< The camera displays a recording indicator when the D-Movie mode is active; it can be seen in the top left corner of the monitor.

VIEWING MOVIES

A video file is indicated by a 🎥 icon in full-frame Playback; press the ⊗ button to begin viewing it. The following operations can be performed:

○ To pause, press ▼.
○ To resume Playback, press the ⊗ button.
○ To rewind / advance press ◄ or ►, respectively.
○ To increase the volume, press ⊕; to decrease the volume, press ⊝.
○ To edit the video clip, press the **AE-L/AF-L** button.
○ To resume shooting, press the shutter release down halfway.
○ To display menus, press the **MENU** button.
○ To exit to full-frame Playback, press ▲ or ▶.

NOTE: To edit D-Movie clips in the D3100 or capture a single frame from a video clip, see the section on the **[Edit movie]** item in the Retouch menu.

In-Camera Processing

WHITE BALANCE

We are all familiar with the way the color of sunlight changes during the course of a day from the warm orange / yellow colors immediately after sunrise, to the cooler (blue) color of light around midday, returning to the orange / yellow colors that appear as the sun sets. These changes are significant, and our eyes can see them quite clearly. However, the color of light (not to be confused with the color of the objects from which it is reflected) changes in subtle ways at other times of the day and in different climatic conditions. Furthermore, artificial light sources, such as a household light bulb or camera flash unit, emit light with a wide range of different colors. In many instances, our eyes and brain are remarkably good at adapting to these changes in the color of the light, so they are not visibly apparent to us. Think about what you see when you stand outside a building in which the interior lamps are switched on in daylight—the light the lamps emit often appears very yellow. But, if you look into the same building after dark, the light from the lamps now appears to be white. This is an example of the adaptive process that our eyes and brain apply to light, one which cameras, regardless of whether they use film or a digital sensor, cannot perform!

Film has a response limited to a specific color (for daylight-balanced film that is equivalent to direct sunlight at midday under a clear sky). Digital cameras, such as the D3100, are far more flexible; they can process the picture data to equate to a variety of specific light colors, either automatically or by selecting settings manually. This function is known as the White Balance control.

The color of light is often referred to as its color temperature, which is expressed in units called degrees Kelvin (K). It sounds counterintuitive, but warm light (red / orange colors) has a low color temperature and cool light (blue tones) has a high color temperature.

Why is this? Well, the color temperature of a light source equates to the color of something called a black body radiator—a concept used by scientists that involves a theoretical object that can re-emit 100% of the energy it absorbs. As heat is applied to this black body radiator, it becomes hotter and its color changes from black to red, orange, yellow, through to blue. The color temperature of a particular light source is said to approximate the color of a black body radiator at the same temperature. Thus, at a low temperature the color of the light emitted would contain a high proportion of red wavelengths, and at a high temperature the light would contain a high proportion of blue wavelengths.

Generally, film is balanced to either direct sunlight under a clear sky at midday (a color temperature around 5500K), or the light emitted by a tungsten photoflood lamp (a color temperature around 3400K). If the temperature of the ambient light in which you are shooting differs from these values, your photographs will take on a color cast (unnatural tint), and you will need to use color-correction filters to counter the effects.

NOTE: The color temperature of daylight will vary according to a number of factors, including time of day, time of year, latitude, altitude, and the prevailing atmospheric and climatic conditions. The color temperature of 5500K, to which daylight film is balanced, is a somewhat arbitrary value and should only be used as a rough guide.

Digital cameras are far more versatile and can either automatically adjust their response to light within a range of different color temperatures or allow you to set a specific color temperature. This feature is known as the White Balance control. Assuming the color temperature value of the chosen White Balance corresponds to the color temperature of the prevailing light in the scene, it will be rendered without any noticeable color cast (unnatural tint). You can also use the White Balance feature creatively by setting an alternative value, which does not correspond to the prevailing light, thereby inducing a deliberate color shift.

WHITE BALANCE OPTIONS

The D3100 camera offers two different methods for setting White Balance when shooting in the P, A, S, or M exposure modes (in all other exposure modes, White Balance is automatically set by the camera)—via the Shooting menu or the Information Display.

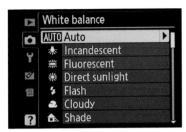

‹ Here, **AUTO** is being selected in the [White balance] item in the Shooting menu.

Open the Shooting menu and navigate to the [White Balance] option, press ▶ on the Multi Selector, and highlight the required option from the displayed list by pressing either ▲ or ▼ (you must take this route if you want to alter the color temperature value for the [Fluorescent] option). Then press ▶ to open the fine-tuning control and set any desired adjustment. Finally, press ⊛ to confirm the selection.

The alternative, and in my opinion the quicker method, is to use the Information Display. Open it by pressing the 🛈 button, and then press the ⊕ button to illuminate the cursor in the display. Use the Multi Selector to highlight the current White Balance setting, and press the ⊛ button. Select the setting you want and press the ⊛ button again. The White Balance control of the D3100 offers eight principal White Balance options. Read on for details.

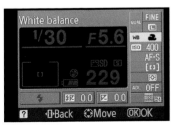

^ The White Balance option, set to 🌥 Cloudy, is shown here highlighted in the Information Display.

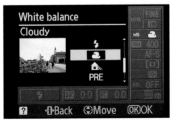

^ The White Balance options, as available via the Information Display.

AUTO Automatic (3500 – 8000K): The D3100 uses its Scene Recognition System (SRS), which enhances the abilities of its 420-pixel, RGB-metering sensor. For example, the system helps enable the D3100 to distinguish between the greens of foliage and the green wavelengths of light produced by a florescent light tube.

Nikon states that the effective color temperature range of the Automatic White Balance option on the D3100 is 3500K to 8000K. While I have found this option to be very effective and very reliable when shooting in the middle of that range (i.e., typical daylight conditions), I would suggest that the color temperature range is closer to 4000K to 6500K. For example, in lighting conditions with low color temperature values, such as typical domestic incandescent lighting, I find the D3100 consistently sets a color temperature that is too high, resulting in an overly warm (too much yellow) cast. As with all automatic features, you will need to be aware of the limitations of the **AUTO** White Balance option. This is especially true in situations such as the following: under normal household lighting when the color temperature of light sources is likely to be lower than 4000K, outdoors in bright overcast conditions, or at high altitudes where the color temperature of daylight is likely to exceed 6500K.

☀ Incandescent (3000K): Use this option when shooting under typical household incandescent lighting, as its color temperature is a better match. However, you may find that results still have a color cast and look too warm (i.e., the red content is too high), in which case you should use either the fine-tuning feature or a Preset manual measurement.

▒ Fluorescent (2700K – 7200K): The light emitted from fluorescent tubes is notorious for causing unwanted color casts. This is primarily due to the variability in the color temperature of the light they produce and the way light is emitted in a rapid series of peak and decay cycles. In an effort to increase the accuracy of color rendition under the wide variety of fluorescent bulbs, the D3100 has seven sub-options available under the [Fluorescent] White Balance option in the Shooting menu. To access these options, open the Shooting menu and navigate to the [White Balance] option, press ▶ on the Multi Selector and highlight [Fluorescent], then press ▶ again to display the seven bulb types. Highlight the required bulb type and press ⊛ to confirm. The bulb type will be displayed in the Shooting menu, as ▒ next to a number from 1 to 7 (see table on next page).

BULB TYPE	COLOR TEMPERATURE	SHOOTING MENU DISPLAY
SODIUM-VAPOR LAMPS	2700	☰ 1
WARM-WHITE FLUORESCENT	3000	☰ 2
WHITE FLUORESCENT	3700	☰ 3
COOL-WHITE FLUORESCENT	4200	☰ 4
DAY WHITE FLUORESCENT	5000	☰ 5
DAYLIGHT FLUORESCENT	6500	☰ 6
MERCURY-VAPOR	7200	☰ 7

Selecting **[Fluorescent]** from the Information Display will select the bulb type set via the **[White Balance]** option in the Shooting menu, but only ☰ is displayed. It is not possible to select the bulb type when setting the White Balance via the Information Display route.

☀ **Direct Sunlight (5200K):** This option is intended for subjects or scenes photographed in direct sunlight during the middle part of the day (i.e., from around two hours after sunrise to two hours before sunset). At other times, when the sun is low in the sky, the light tends to be warmer—using this setting at those times will produce pictures with a higher red content.

> **HINT:** White balance is a very subjective issue, but to my eye, Nikon's color temperature for the **[Direct sunlight]** option is too low. When shooting in these conditions, I often prefer to use either the **[Flash]** or **[Cloudy]** option. I recommend you experiment to find a setting that meets your requirements.

⚡ **Flash (5400K):** As its name implies, this option is intended for use whenever a flash (Nikon refers to their own flash units as Speedlights) is the main lighting source.

> **HINT:** Similar to the **[Direct Sunlight]** option, I consider the color temperature of the Flash option to be slightly too low. The color temperature of light emitted by Nikon Speedlights is generally in the range of 5500 – 6000K, so I often select the **[Cloudy]** option when working with Nikon flash units as the main lighting source.

Cloudy (6000K): This White Balance option is intended for shooting under overcast skies, when daylight has a high color temperature. It ensures the camera renders colors properly without the typical cool (blue) tone, which can impart a "cold" appearance to a photograph, particularly in pale skin tones.

Shade (8000K): This option applies a greater degree of correction than the Cloudy option and is intended for those situations when your subject or scene is in open shade beneath a clear, or nearly clear, blue sky. Under these conditions, the light will have a very high blue content, as it is principally comprised of light reflected from the blue sky above.

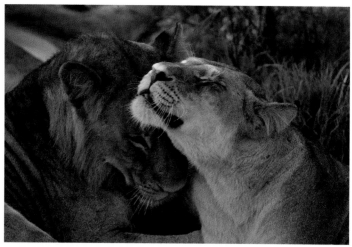

^ The White Balance feature of the D3100 allows you to exercise extensive control over the way the camera records colors. Here, the Shade option ensured a pleasing rendition of the naturally warm colors.

PRE Preset Manual: This option allows you to manually obtain a measurement of the exact color temperature of the light illuminating the subject or scene by making a test exposure of a white or neutral gray test target. Alternatively, the color temperature value from an existing image stored on the memory card can also be used as the source for obtaining a preset reading.

PRESET MANUAL WHITE BALANCE

The [Preset manual] option allows you to manually set a White Balance value measured from the lighting falling on the subject or scene being photographed. This generally provides the most accurate way of setting a White Balance value in conditions with mixed lighting sources or any type of lighting that has a strong color bias, such as artificial light sources.

There are two methods available with the D3100 for obtaining a value for a Preset Manual White Balance: direct measurement from a reference target or copying the White Balance value from a photograph stored on the memory card installed in the camera. The camera can store only one value at a time for the Preset Manual White Balance option.

HINT: The Nikon instruction manual suggests that you can use either a white or gray card as a reference target for the Preset Manual White Balance option. I strongly recommend that you use only a gray card for two reasons. First, white cards often contain pigments used to whiten them; this can cause the camera to render colors inaccurately. Second, it is more difficult to expose correctly for a pure white subject. To try to compensate for this, the D3100 will automatically increase exposure by 1 EV when measuring for the Preset Manual White Balance in P, A, or S exposure modes; but errors in exposure from a white test target can occur nonetheless and will affect the White Balance reading you obtain from the test target. If you use M mode, adjust the exposure to ±0.0 for a grey card and +1 EV for a white carda

---

HINT: In place of a test target, such as a piece of gray card, there are a number of products that can be attached directly to the lens and allow the camera to not only obtain a White Balance measurement but also take an incident reading for the ambient light, using its TTL metering system. Probably the best device I have used for this purpose is the ExpoDisc (www.expodisc. com).

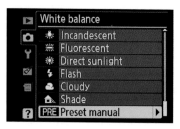

^ The [Preset manual] option shown highlighted in the [White balance] item in the Shooting menu.

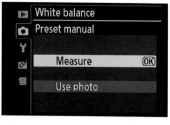

^ To use a reference test target, highlight the [Measure] option.

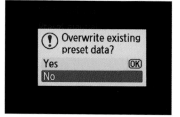

^ The following page shows this warning since the camera can only store one Preset White Balance setting at a time.

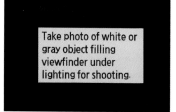

^ The final page in the sequence provides these instructions for taking the measurement.

To measure a Preset Manual White Balance value, start by placing your test target in the same light that is illuminating the subject to be photographed. The exposure mode you use is not critical, but I suggest using Aperture-Priority (A). If you use the Manual exposure mode, it is important to ensure the reference test target is not under- or overexposed (see hint above). Next, select the [Preset manual] option via the [White balance] item in the Shooting menu, as described above, and press ▶. Highlight [Measure] and press ▶, then highlight [Yes] and press the ⊛ button (the screen shots above show the sequence of menu pages). The following message will be displayed on the LCD screen: "Take a photo of a white or gray object filling the viewfinder under lighting for shooting."

You can also access the measurement phase of the Preset manual White Balance option directly from the Information Display by first selecting the **PRE** option via the Information Display, and then pressing and holding the ⊛ button for a few seconds. Alternatively, selection of the White Balance option can be assigned to the **Fn** button via the [Buttons] item in the Setup menu. If the Preset option is selected using this route, pressing and holding the **Fn** button for a few seconds will also access the preset measurement phase directly.

Whichever of these three routes you follow, as soon as the camera is ready to measure the ambient light, it will display **PRE** in the Information Display and $Pr\xi$ in the viewfinder, both icons flashing. While they continue to flash, frame the reference test target so it completely fills the viewfinder (make sure you do not cast a shadow over the test target card), and then press the shutter release down all the way (it is not necessary for the camera to focus on the reference test target). The shutter will cycle, but no image will be recorded.

If the camera is able to obtain an adequate measurement and set a White Balance value, ξd will appear, blinking, for approximately eight seconds in the viewfinder before the camera is restored to its Shooting mode. Pressing the shutter release button down halfway will return it to this mode immediately.

If the camera is unable to set a White Balance value, it probably means that the light level is either too low or too high. In this case, $no\ \xi d$ will blink in the viewfinder; press the shutter release button down halfway and $Pr\xi$ will be displayed, blinking, in the viewfinder. Repeat the process of taking a measurement from the test target, adjusting the illumination level of the test target until a measurement is achieved.

The White Balance is now set for the prevailing light falling on your subject and this value will automatically be stored and retained, replacing any previous value stored there until you take another Preset White Balance measurement. To use the new White Balance value immediately, ensure that **PRE** is selected as the White Balance option.

NOTE: The D3100 can only store one value for the Preset Manual White Balance. If no White Balance value is measured for the [Preset manual] option, the color temperature will be set to 5200K (the same as the [Direct sunlight] option).

COPYING A WHITE BALANCE VALUE

If you want to use the White Balance value of a photograph previously recorded by the D3100, open the [White Balance] option in the Shooting menu, highlight the [Preset manual] option, and then press ▶. Highlight [Use photo] and press ▶.

The next page offers two options. **[This image]** selects the last image to be used for Preset White Balance. Press ⊛ to complete the process. To use a different image, highlight **[Select image]** and press ▶ to display a list of all the picture folders. Select the folder containing the source picture and press ▶; a thumbnail view of the images stored in the folder will be displayed. Highlight the desired photograph using the Multi Selector; a narrow yellow border will surround the currently selected picture. To magnify this image on the LCD screen, press and hold the ⊕ button. To copy the White Balance value from this picture, press ⊛.

FINE-TUNING WHITE BALANCE

This feature enables the White Balance to be fine-tuned to compensate for variations in the color temperature of a particular light source or to create a deliberate color cast in a picture. The system effects change in equally spaced MIRED values (see "What is MIRED?" on page 156). You may find this system easier to use than the somewhat counterintuitive Kelvin scale, where positive and negative values create cooler and warmer results, respectively.

The fine-tuning of White Balance is achieved via the **[White Balance]** option in the Shooting menu and provides control over adjustment of both color temperature and color rendition in all White Balance options, except the Preset manual. Open the Shooting menu and navigate to the **[White Balance]** option and press ▶ to display the list of options. Highlight the desired White Balance option, then press ▶ to display a color graph; its horizontal axis is used to fine-tune for the level of amber (A) to blue (B), while the vertical axis is used to adjust the level of magenta (M) to green (G). If **[Fluorescent]** is selected, you must select a bulb type and press ▶ before the color graph is displayed.

› Here, the White Balance has been fine-tuned toward Amber (A2), so the picture will appear slightly warmer.

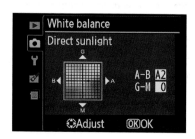

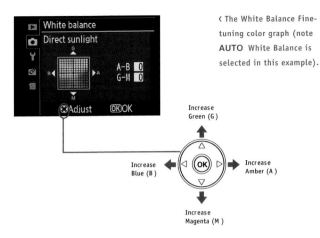

‹ The White Balance Fine-tuning color graph (note **AUTO** White Balance is selected in this example).

Increase Green (G)

Increase Blue (B)

Increase Amber (A)

Increase Magenta (M)

Using the Multi Selector, select an adjustment value between 1 and 6 along each axis of the color graph, working from the central point (see graphics above). Shifting along the amber (A) / blue (B) axis is similar to adjusting the color temperature; by increasing the B value colors become "cooler," while increasing the A value makes colors appear "warmer." Each step on the A / B axis is equivalent to about 5 MIRED; the higher the number, the greater the color shift. Shifting along the green (G) / magenta (M) axis is analogous to using color compensating filtration, as you may have done when shooting on film. A combined color temperature and color balance shift is possible by moving the cursor of the graph display into one of the four quadrants of the graph. Once you have set the fine-tuning adjustment, press ⊛ button to save the setting and return to the Shooting menu.

It is important to appreciate that the colors on the axes of the color graph are relative and not absolute. This means shifting the cursor toward A (amber) when a White Balance option with a high color temperature value, such as ☁ Cloudy, is selected will only make the picture slightly "warmer"; it will not result in a stronger color cast, as it would if you made the same shift with the ☀ Direct sunlight setting.

What is MIRED?

MIRED (Micro Reciprocity Degree) is a method of defining a shift in color in such a way that each shift in MIRED value is equivalent to the difference in color we perceive. A drawback of degrees Kelvin (K) is that a relatively small shift in Kelvin value at low color temperatures (e.g., less than 4000K) creates a much larger perceived shift in visible color than the same small shift in Kelvin value at high color temperatures (e.g., more than 6000K). The MIRED value is calculated by multiplying the reciprocal of the color temperature by ten to the power six (10^6). So, the difference of 1000K between a color temperature of 3000K and 4000K is equal to 83 MIRED, whereas the difference between 6000K and 7000K is only 24 MIRED.

CREATIVE WHITE BALANCE

Feel like getting creative? It is easy with the White Balance control on the D3100. You do not have to set the White Balance to match the color temperature of the prevailing light—try mismatching it instead! For example, rather than shooting a subject or scene lit by daylight using one of the daylight White Balance values, set the White Balance to ☀ Incandescent—now your picture will have a strong blue color cast. The great appeal of digital photography is the ability to experiment!

Remember, if the color temperature of the prevailing light is lower than the color temperature of the White Balance value set on the camera, the subject or scene will be rendered with a warmer appearance. Conversely, if the color temperature of the prevailing light is higher than the color temperature of the White Balance value set on the camera, the subject or scene will be rendered with a cooler appearance.

THE PICTURE CONTROL SYSTEM

The Picture Control System (PCS) replaces the Color Mode options and Optimize Image features that were used in previous Nikon DSLR cameras, such as the D80 and D200, to influence the appearance of pictures in terms of sharpening, contrast, brightness (gamma), color saturation, and hue. In the P, S, A, and M exposure modes, the six Picture Controls of the D3100 can be selected at will to suit the shooting conditions or create a particular effect; in all other exposure modes, the camera selects the Picture Control automatically.

The purpose of the PCS is to provide a single, all-encompassing solution for obtaining consistent results with different Nikon cameras, while also integrating Nikon software, particularly Nikon Capture NX2. Once you have adjusted settings to achieve your desired result on one camera, the result can be replicated by using the same settings on another D3100 camera. Furthermore, within Nikon View NX2 and Capture NX2 software, it is possible to apply the same settings to an NEF (RAW) file recorded by a Nikon DSLR camera that has the PCS.

It is important to mention that full integration of the PCS with Nikon Capture NX2 means that the settings made within the PCS on the D3100 are only really relevant if you shoot in the JPEG format. The values for the various parameters are embedded in those file types and cannot be altered at a later stage; at least not without a lot of trial-and-error testing, and even then, there is no guarantee the process will be successful. Since the full range of the PCS settings is also available in Nikon View NX2 and Nikon Capture NX2, it is possible to adjust all PCS settings at will subsequently if pictures are recorded in the NEF (RAW) format.

The Picture Control System offers six preset Picture Controls: Standard, Neutral, Vivid, Monochrome, Portrait, and Landscape. Depending on which item is selected, a range of attributes can be adjusted, including sharpening, contrast, brightness, saturation, and hue. The Monochrome item offers controls to simulate traditional contrast control filters used for black-and-white photography, and toning effects. The Standard, Vivid, Portrait, and Landscape items also have a Quick Adjust feature that allows sharpening, contrast, and saturation to be adjusted simultaneously. Plus, there is also an automated option to adjust sharpening, contrast, and saturation. Finally, a graphical display available on the camera's LCD screen maps contrast against saturation, to assist you in your understanding of how one group of settings relates to another. The PCS of the D3100 provides further flexibility as the user has the ability to modify each of the six preset Picture Control items to customize them.

In the P, S, A, and M exposure modes, it is possible to select one of the preset Nikon Picture Controls to suit the type of subject or scene being photographed. In GUIDE, AUTO, ⚡, and the six Scene modes, the D3100 selects one of the preset Nikon Picture Controls automatically, and there is no option to alter this selection. To select the Picture Control, open the Shooting menu and navigate to the [Set Picture Control] item, then press ▶ to display the six preset Nikon Picture Control options. Highlight the required option and press ⊛.

> There are six Nikon Picture Controls available on the D3100.

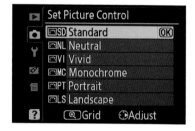

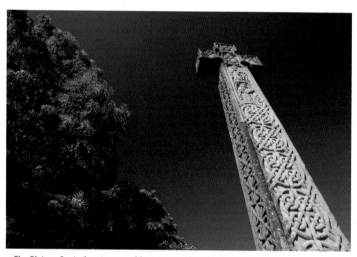

∧ The Picture Control system provides a tremendous level of control over many aspects of an image. Generally, it is best to use low amounts of saturation, contrast, and sharpening, because it is far easier to increase these during post-processing than to reduce them.

ITEM	SHARPENING	EFFECT
🖻SD STANDARD	3	Probably the most useful option for most shooting situations; modest levels applied to image attributes such as color saturation and contrast.
🖻NL NEUTRAL	2	Provides a good starting point for any image that will be subjected to extensive post-processing, as processing applied in camera is very restrained.
🖻VI VIVID	4	Useful for images that will be printed directly from the camera. Saturation and contrast are relatively high.
🖻MC MONOCHROME	3	Use for producing black-and-white images directly from the camera.
🖻PT PORTRAIT	2	Color rendition is optimized for skin tones, while sharpening is reduced.
🖻LS LANDSCAPE	4	Saturation of blues and greens tends to be boosted, plus sharpening level is raised.

HINT: There is no indication in the viewfinder as to which Picture Control is selected, but if you press the 🖷 button, the information will be shown in the information display.

MODIFYING PICTURE CONTROL ATTRIBUTES

The PCS enables you to modify any one of the six basic Nikon Picture Controls so that settings match a particular shooting situation more appropriately, or so you can use the settings for a specific creative purpose (note this option is only available in the P, S, A, and M exposure modes). However, it is not possible to create an entirely new custom Picture Control; you can only modify an existing set of parameters.

Start by navigating to the [Set Picture Control] item in the Shooting menu, then press ▶ to display the six preset Picture Control items. Highlight the required Picture Control and press ▶ to display the settings for the various attributes. Use ▲ and ▼ to select the required attribute, and use ◀ and ▶ to adjust its value.

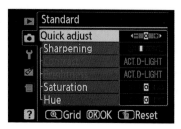 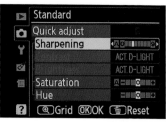

^ By default the Quick adjust option, where available, will be highlighted when entering the Picture Control adjustments.

^ Highlight the attribute to be adjusted and use ◄ and ► to change the value.

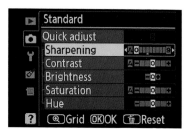

> Here, Sharpening has been set to zero for the Standard Picture Control.

Alternatively, with Picture Control settings that offer a [Quick adjust] option, you can use that to simply intensify or tone down all of the attribute settings that characterize that specific Picture Control (i.e., if you select +1 in [Quick adjust] for Portrait, it will reduce contrast even more and render skin tones even warmer than it normally does). When you adjust the level of a Picture Control setting, a yellow line is displayed beneath the previous level for your reference. To save the settings you have selected, press the ⊛ button. If a Picture Control is modified from its default settings, it will be marked with an asterisk. If at any time you want to restore a Picture Control to its original settings, press the 🗑 button, highlight [Yes], and press ⊛.

> The Standard Picture Control has been modified from its default settings.

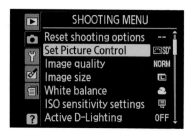

NOTE: To access the graphical display of contrast and saturation, in order to compare the current settings of those attributes with those of the other Picture Controls, press the 🔍 button (if the Monochrome option is selected, only the value for contrast is shown). You can use ▲ and ▼ to scroll through the list of available Picture Controls, which is shown to the right of the graph. Press the 🔍 button to return to the Picture Control menu.

NOTE: I would not recommend using the LCD screen of the D3100 to make any critical assessment of the sharpness, color, or contrast in an image. It simply does not have a sufficiently high resolution or the ability to display the full gamut of colors defined by the Adobe RGB color space, with greens being particularly restricted. Its capabilities are closer to the narrower gamut of sRGB.

The settings available for each of the Picture Control options are outlined in the following table:

OPTION	SETTINGS
Quick adjust	Choose values between ±2 to reduce (negative value) or enhance (positive value) the effect of the selected Picture Control. This option resets any manually adjusted settings; it is not available with the Neutral and Monochrome Picture Controls.
Sharpening	A (auto), or a manually set value between 0 (no sharpening) and 9 (maximum sharpening); available with all Picture Controls
Contrast	A (auto), or a manually set value between ±3; negative values reduce contrast, while positive values increase contrast; available with all Picture Controls
Saturation	A (auto), or a manually set value between ±3; negative values reduce saturation, while positive values increase saturation; available with all Picture Controls except Monochrome
Hue	Manually set value between ±3; available with all Picture Controls except Monochrome
Filter effects	Use to emulate the effect of contrast control filters used with traditional black-and-white photography; only available with Monochrome Picture Controls
Toning	Use to emulate the effect of chemical toners used in traditional black-and-white photography; only available with Monochrome Picture Controls

[Sharpening]: Sharpening is a process applied to digital data that can increase the apparent sharpness (acuity) of a picture. It is applied to correct the side effects of converting light into digital data, which often causes distinct edges between colors, tones, and objects in a digital picture to look ill defined (fuzzy). The process identifies an edge by analyzing the differences between neighboring pixel values. It then lightens the pixels immediately adjacent to the brighter side of the edge and darkens the pixels adjacent to the dark side of the edge. This causes a local increase of contrast around the edge, making it appear sharper; the higher the level of sharpening applied, the greater the contrast at the edge. Sharpening is not a method for rescuing an out-of-focus picture—remember once out of focus always out of focus!

If you select the automatic setting for this option, you surrender all control to the camera and have no way of ensuring consistency in the degree of sharpening it applies; the camera will vary the amount of sharpening according to the nature of the scene being photographed. Scenes with a high degree of fine detail will receive a greater degree of sharpening compared with scenes that contain large areas of continuous tone.

There is no single level of sharpening that is appropriate for all shooting conditions. Remember that, with JPEG files, sharpening is fixed by in-camera processing. Any sharpening applied in post-processing will be cumulative. With an NEF (RAW) file, the original in-camera sharpening can be removed, but only by selecting a different Picture Control option within Nikon Capture NX 2 and then adjusting the settings. The level of sharpening should be based on your ultimate intentions for the image (i.e., display on a webpage, publication in a book or magazine, or producing a print for framing). Therefore, it is often preferable to only apply sharpening during the final stages of post-processing, particularly if you want to work on images for a range of different output purposes. I would make the following suggestions with regard to in-camera sharpening when shooting with the D3100:

O For general photography, using JPEG format files that you intend to work on in post-processing, set sharpening to zero or a low value.

O For general photography, using JPEG format files that you intend to print directly from the camera without any further post-processing, set sharpening to a mid-range value.

o On occasions when you need to expedite the output of pictures for publishing on a webpage or in newsprint, use the JPEG format and set the sharpening level in the mid to high range. In this specific case, a slightly stronger degree of sharpening is probably more appropriate, as images will be viewed on computer monitors or at low reproduction resolutions. It is probably also more prudent because it will save valuable time in post-processing.

o If you shoot in the NEF (RAW) file format, I recommend setting sharpening to zero. Otherwise, there is a risk that any in-camera sharpening, when applied by a RAW file converter, will create a cumulative effect with any further sharpening that is subsequently applied by either the RAW file converter or during post-processing.

[Contrast]: The contrast control allows you to adjust the distribution of tones in an image and works by applying a curve control similar to those used in software for digital image post-processing. I feel the D3100 tends to err toward too much contrast when left at the default level in the Nikon Picture Controls, except in the Neutral option; therefore, I recommend that this control be used judiciously. It is important to remember that it is far easier to increase contrast at a later stage than it is to reduce it. This is especially important if you intend to subject the image to further contrast adjustments in post-processing.

NOTE: If Active D-Lighting is in operation, the contrast option in all Picture Controls will be disabled and the adjustment scale display will be replaced by "ACT. D-LIGHT," indicating that Active D-Lighting has been selected. To adjust contrast manually for the Picture Control, switch Active D-Lighting to [Off].

[Saturation]: Adjusting the saturation of an image changes the overall vividness (chroma) of color without affecting the brightness (luminance) of an image. A positive value increases saturation and a negative value decreases it. As with contrast, I have found the D3100 sets saturation a little too strongly for my liking in both the automatic option and at the default settings in the Standard, Vivid, and Landscape Picture Controls. I suggest you exercise restraint with the saturation control—overdoing it will make returning an image to a more natural-looking color a difficult task.

HINT: There will always be a degree of subjective opinion when assessing color, but I find the D3100 tends to produce a slightly oversaturated color. A combination of the Neutral Picture Control and Adobe RGB color space renders the most natural and neutral colors, so it probably represents a good reference point when adjusting other Picture Controls.

NOTE: If achieving consistent results is important to you, I recommend very strongly that you avoid using the A (auto) option for **[Contrast]** and **[Saturation]**. The levels applied by the D3100 with this setting will vary depending on the exposure level and is also influenced by the position of the subject in the frame area.

[Hue]: The RGB color model (sRGB or Adobe RGB), used by the D3100 to produce images, is based on combinations of red, green, and blue light. By mixing two of these colors, a variety of different colors can be produced. If the third color is introduced, the hue of the final color is altered. For example, applying a positive adjustment will cause reds to look more orange, greens more blue, and blues more purple. If you apply a negative adjustment, the hue shifts so that red is more purple, blue is more green, and green is more yellow.

HINT: Personally, I believe that unless you need to produce images direct from the camera, it is better to leave adjustment of contrast, saturation, and hue until post-processing. Appropriate software offers a far greater degree of control over these adjustments.

[Filter Effects]: In the Monochrome Picture Control, there are options to select filter effects that emulate the results of using contrast control filters with traditional black-and-white film. The purpose of these filter effects is to modify the tonal response of the sensor to certain wavelengths (colors) of light. The options available in the D3100 are **[Off]** (default), **[Yellow]**, **[Orange]**, **[Red]**, and **[Green]**. Just like their optical filter counterparts, these filter effects reduce the amount of their complimentary color in the image. For example, the yellow, orange, and red options reduce the level of blue, making a blue sky appear darker;

the yellow filter has the least effect and the red, the greatest. The result is an increase in the level of contrast between the blue sky and any white clouds, making the clouds more prominent. The green option reduces the amount of red, making red and orange colors appear darker. This option can be useful for enhancing the range of skin tones in a portrait picture and making them appear more natural, or for separating the tones of the various shades of green in landscape photography. My advice is to experiment with these options to determine if, how, and when they will best suit your needs.

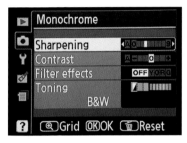

‹ The screen for the Monochrome Picture Control is slightly different, as it has options to apply filter effects and toning.

[Toning]: In addition to the filter effects described above, the Monochrome Picture Control also offers a range of options that emulate the effects of traditional chemical toning of black-and-white prints. The options include [B&W] (default), [Sepia] (yellowish-brown), [Cyanotype] (blue tint), [Red], [Yellow], [Green], [Blue-green], [Blue], [Purple-blue], and [Red-purple] (similar to selenium toning). Once you have selected the [Toning] option and selected the desired tone, press ▼ to highlight the saturation control displayed below the tone options, and use ◄ and ► to adjust the saturation of the toning effect (this is not available with the [B&W] option).

NOTE: Regardless of the toning option selected, the D3100 always saves a black-and-white picture recorded in the NEF (RAW) format as an RGB file. Therefore, it can always be converted back to a full-color image using the Picture Control utility in Nikon View NX2 or Nikon Capture NX2.

COLOR SPACE

A color space (sometimes called color gamut) defines the range of colors that are available for reproduction and what particular RGB values should represent those colors in the digital image file. Unless you know your pictures will only ever be displayed on a computer monitor (i.e., as part of a webpage) or you will be using a direct printing method with no intention of carrying out any post-processing, I would recommend using the Adobe RGB color space option on the D3100. It provides the widest range of colors, permitting more subtle rendition and well-graduated tonal transitions. This increases the flexibility of an image file that will be subjected to post-processing, and the quality of any print made from that image file produced by an appropriate printing process. Although, to reap these benefits, it is essential that any software used for post-processing also handles the image file in the same Adobe RGB color space (i.e., you use a color-managed workflow, working with a properly color-profiled computer monitor). The sRGB color space is more suited to an image that will be used directly from the camera with no post-processing.

To choose a color space, highlight the [Color space] item in the Shooting menu and press ▶ to display the two choices: [sRGB] (default) and [Adobe RGB]. Highlight the required option and press ⑩ to confirm the selection, returning to the Shooting menu.

NOTE: While it comes very close, the Adobe RGB color space option on the D3100 does not appear to be capable of reproducing the complete gamut of the full Adobe RGB color space, as the camera does not replicate some of the green values. The LCD screen on the D3100 falls short of being able to display even the sRGB color space, so it certainly doesn't show the full gamut of the Adobe RGB space. Therefore do not attempt to make a critical assessment of color from the camera's display.

HINT: It is essential that any software used for post-processing be set to the same color space as the image file recorded by the camera. Otherwise, it is more than likely that the application will assign its own default color space and you will lose control over the rendition of colors.

Active D-Lighting (not to be confused with the **[D-Lighting]** option available in the Retouch menu) applies a localized adjustment of contrast to improve detail in areas of deep shadow and bright highlights. It can be thought of as an automated dodge-and-burn effect, as opposed to a global adjustment to contrast. It is designed for use with Matrix metering, which assesses scene contrast, and is intended for situations where the scene has a naturally high level of contrast. If necessary, it will modify the exposure level by reducing it accordingly. The amount of adjustment is quite modest, typically 0.3 EV or 0.7 EV, to preserve highlight detail. Then, after the exposure has been made and while the

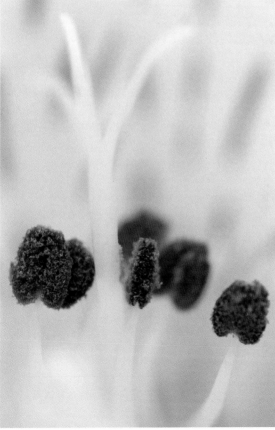

> Active D-Lighting will help to retain detail in bright highlights by reducing the exposure level; it must be used with Matrix metering.

image data is being processed, the shadow and middle tones are adjusted to optimize the dynamic range recorded by the camera by adjusting the tone curve applied to the image data. This feature is intended for any shooting situation where the level of contrast between the deepest shadows and brightest highlights is high. However, its use should be considered with some care; unlike the normal D-Lighting feature in the Retouch menu, where a copy file is created, Active D-Lighting affects the original exposure level.

I recommend practicing restraint if you use the Active D-Lighting, because this function affects exposure. If the effect of the Active D-Lighting is too strong, it may compromise the tonal range of the entire image—especially if the contrast in the scene is very high and images are recorded in the JPEG format. Any adjustment applied by Active D-Lighting to an NEF (RAW) file can always be removed later, using Nikon Capture NX2 software. To maintain optimal image quality, I suggest you avoid using Active D-Lighting at ISO settings of 800 or above.

To select the Active D-Lighting from the Information Display, press the █ button and then press the ⊕ button. Move the cursor to the Active D-Lighting ⊞ item and press ⊛. Highlight either [Off] or [On] using the Multi Selector, and then press ⊛. Active D-Lighting can also be selected via the menu system. Highlight the [Active D-Lighting] item in the Shooting menu and press ▶ to display the options of [Off] or [On]. Highlight the required option and press ⊛ to confirm the selection and return to the Shooting menu. Alternatively, selection of Active D-Lighting can be assigned to the Fn button via the [Buttons] item in the Setup Menu. Once assigned, simply press the Fn button to open the Information Display and highlight the ADL item; keep the button pressed and rotate the Command dial to toggle between [Off] and [On].

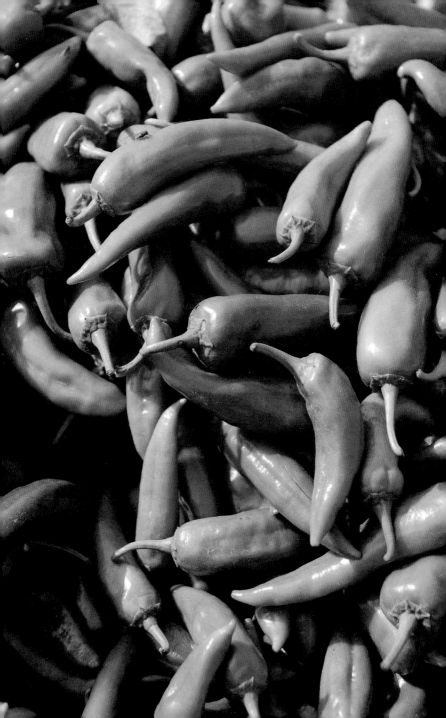

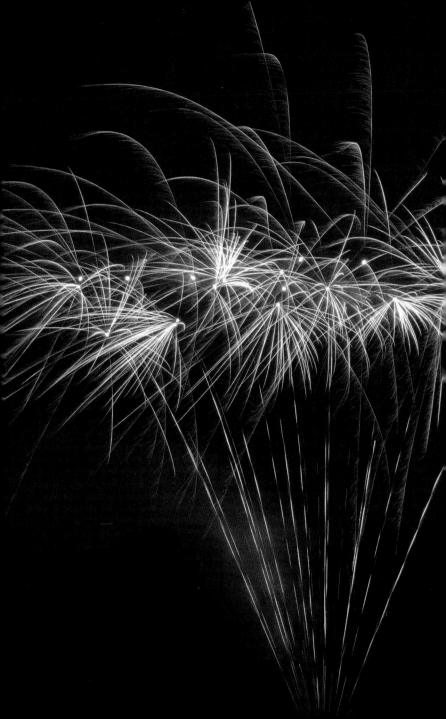

The Menu System

The control of many of the features and functions on the D3100 relies on an extensive and comprehensive menu system that is displayed on the LCD monitor. It is divided into five main sections:

o Playback menu: Used to review, edit, and manage the pictures stored on the inserted memory card.

o Shooting menu: Used to select and set a number of camera controls, such as release mode, autofocus, metering, and the built-In flash. It also allows the user to influence the quality and appearance of the pictures being recorded by the camera. This menu contains several special features, such as the Picture Control, Active D-Lighting, and White Balance.

o Setup menu: Used to establish the basic configuration of the camera. Once the settings for the items in this menu are set, they generally are not changed very frequently. It also contains the option for formatting a memory card and the self-cleaning function of the optical low-pass filter.

o Retouch menu: This menu is only available when a memory card containing picture files is inserted in the camera. It offers a range of items that enable the user to crop, enhance, and add effects to a picture and save it as a separate copy without affecting the integrity of the original picture file. Plus, the D3100 has the ability to process and convert NEF (RAW) files in camera and save the new file in the JPEG format, as well as perform very basic editing of video recordings made in the D-Movie mode.

o Recent Settings menu: This menu shows up to 20 menu settings used most recently. Menu items are shown in chronological order, with the most recently used item at the top of the list.

The menu system of the D3100 comprises a total of 52 main menu items, many of which have numerous submenus. To help overcome the challenges such an extensive and complex menu system can bring, the Recent Settings menu provides quick access to the 20 most recently used menu items. Since each page in the menu system can only display seven items, a lot of time can be spent scrolling through pages and options, using the Multi Selector to reach a desired setting. It is not possible to rearrange the order of the items in any of the menus, which compounds the amount of navigation required; in many cases, items that a user is most likely to want to access are located beyond the first page of the menu display. Finally, as far as navigating the menu system is concerned, it is important to remember that the Information Display can be used to access a limited number of menu items directly. Where such an alternative route is available, I would recommend using it, as this will improve the efficiency of camera handling with the benefit of lower battery power consumption by reduced use of the monitor screen.

ACCESSING MENUS

To access any of the menus, push the MENU button and press ◀ to highlight one of the five tabs used to identify each menu (top to bottom): ▣ Playback menu, ◘ Shooting menu, Ⴤ Setup menu, ☑ Retouch menu, and ▤ Recent Settings menu.

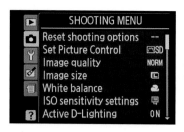

∧ The required menu is selected by highlighting the appropriate icon in the left column.

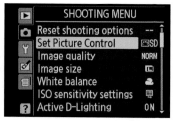

∧ To enter the desired menu, press ▶, and a menu item will be highlighted.

When you have highlighted the required menu tab, the chosen menu will be displayed to the right of the five tabs. Press ▶ to enter the selected menu and highlight an option. To navigate to a specific menu item, press ▲ or ▼. To display the sub-options available for a selected menu item, press ▶. Again, use ▲ or ▼ to highlighted the desired sub-option and press the ◉ button to confirm the selection. To exit the menu system, either press the shutter release button lightly to the halfway position or press the MENU button twice.

NOTE: Most menus have multiple pages, so keep scrolling up or down using ▲ or ▼ to access options not shown on the first page displayed.

NOTE: Pressing ▶ generally has the same effect as pressing ◉. However, there are some menu options that can only be selected by pressing ◉.

NOTE: If a menu option is displayed in gray it cannot be accessed. This can be for one of a number of reasons, including the current camera settings, state of the memory card, or condition of the battery.

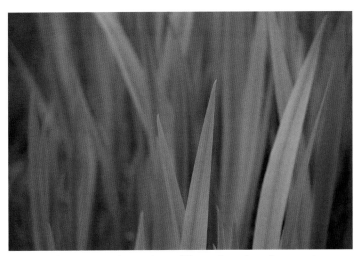

∧ The D3100's menu system is extensive, enabling you to configure the camera to your specific requirements for the specific subject.

The ▶ Playback Menu will only be displayed if a memory card is currently installed in the camera.

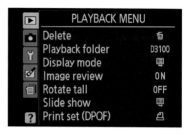

DELETE IMAGES

By using the **[Delete]** option in the Playback menu, you can choose to erase individual images, a group of images, or all of the images on the card.

HINT: To delete images one by one from the D3100, it is quicker and easier to use the H button on the rear of the camera. However, using the Delete function in the Playback menu to erase a group of images will probably save a lot of time.

To delete a group of images:

1. Highlight the **[Delete]** item in the Playback menu and press ▶.
2. Highlight ▦ **[Selected]** and press ▶.
3. Thumbnails of all of the images stored on the inserted memory card will be displayed on the monitor screen, regardless of whether they are stored in different folders. Scroll through the images using the Multi Selector; a yellow frame will be displayed around the selected image. To see an enlarged view of the selected image, press and hold the ⊕ button.
4. To select the highlighted image for deletion, press the ⊕▦ button. The 🗑 icon will appear in the upper right corner of the thumbnail image.
5. Once all the files to be deleted have been selected, press the ⊛ button.
6. The total number of images to be deleted will be displayed, along with two options: **[No]** or **[Yes]**. Highlight the required option and press the ⊛ button to complete the process.

To delete a group of images taken on a selected date:

1. Highlight the **[Delete]** item in the Playback menu and press ▶.
2. Highlight DATE **[Select date]** and press ▶.
3. A list of all the dates on which images and video files have been recorded for the files stored on the installed memory card will be displayed. Highlight the required date using ▲ or ▼, and then press ▶ to place a check mark against the date. Repeat this process for each date where images are to be deleted.
4. Once the date(s) have been selected, press the ⊛ button.
5. A warning message will be displayed, "Delete all images taken on selected date?" along with two options: **[No]** or **[Yes]**. Highlight the required option and press the ⊛ button to complete the process.

To delete all images:

1. Highlight the **[Delete]** item in the Playback menu and press ▶.
2. Highlight **[All]** and press ▶.
3. Highlight either **[No]** or **[Yes]** as required.
4. Press the ⊛ button to complete the process.

NOTE: Deleting all of the images on the card in this manner does not have the same effect as formatting the memory card; to prevent any problems with the memory card, it should be formatted following the correct procedure (see pages 120-122 for full details).

NOTE: It is not possible to delete pictures that have been protected.

HINT: If you select a high volume of pictures for deletion, the duration of the process can become lengthy. To avoid draining the camera battery and placing additional wear and tear on the camera, it is preferable to manage the images stored on the memory card by connecting it to a computer via a card reader.

PLAYBACK FOLDER

The **[Playback folder]** item in the Playback menu allows you to determine which images on the installed memory card will be displayed during Playback. There are two options available:

○ **[Current]:** (default) Only the images in the folder currently selected for **[Active Folder]** in the Setup menu will be displayed during Playback.

○ **[All]:** All of the images stored on the installed memory card can be displayed, regardless of the folder they are in or the camera used to record them, provided it conforms to the Design Rule for Camera File System (DCF). All Nikon digital cameras and most other current digital cameras are DCF compatible.

To select the **[Playback folder]** option:

1. Highlight the **[Playback folder]** item in the Playback menu and press ▶.
2. Highlight the desired option using ▲ or ▼.
3. Press ⊛ to confirm the selection.

DISPLAY MODE

The **[Display mode]** option on the D3100 determines which pages of image information, in addition to the File Information and Overview Data pages, are available during single-image Playback, as well as the transition effects apparent when scrolling through the images. The **[Detailed photo info]** option allows you to choose whether or not to display **[Highlights]**, **[RGB histogram]** and **[Data]** (a range of pages, depending on camera settings and use of a GPS device, which show information about the image).

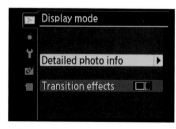

∧ Here are the **[Display mode]** options with the **[Detailed photo info]** option selected.

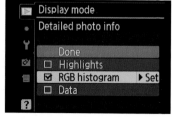

∧ The **[Detailed photo info]** submenu is shown here with the **[RGB histogram]** option turned on.

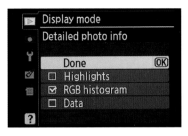

‹ To save the selected options, [Done] must be highlighted and ⊛ pressed.

To select an option(s) for [Detailed photo info]:

1. Highlight the [Display mode] item in the Playback menu and press ▶.
2. Highlight the [Detailed photo info] item and press ▶.
3. Highlight the desired option using ▲ or ▼, and then press ▶; a check mark will appear in the box to the left of the option title.
4. Repeat step 2 for any other desired option(s).
5. Finally, highlight [Done] and press ⊛ to confirm the selection and return to the Playback menu.

The [Transition effects] option on the D3100 determines the transition effect between images as you scroll through them in full-frame single-image Playback (note this will not be used with information pages selected under the [Display mode] item). There are three options: [Slide in], [Zoom/fade], and [None]. Since the first two options increase the delay between the display of each image, which lengthens the time the monitor screen is active and drains more battery power, I recommend setting this item to [None]. To select an option under [Transition effects]:

1. Highlight the [Transition effects] item in the Playback menu and press ▶.
2. Highlight the required option.
3. Press ⊛ to confirm the selection.

IMAGE REVIEW

The **[Image review]** option in the Playback menu determines if an image will be displayed on the monitor screen immediately after it is recorded. There are situations when reviewing every image recorded by the camera immediately is undesirable, such as when shooting in low-light conditions where the light from the screen is a distraction. When weighing the necessity of immediate image review, you should consider that the monitor screen consumes a relatively large amount of power, considerably increasing the drain on the battery. My recommendation is to switch this option off and use the ▶ button whenever you wish to review an image. To select **[Image review]**:

1. Highlight the **[Image review]** item in the Playback menu and press ▶.
2. Highlight **[On]** or **[Off]** (default).
3. Press ⊗ to confirm the selection.

ROTATE TALL

The **[Rotate Tall]** option determines whether pictures shot in the vertical (portrait) format are displayed automatically in that orientation or in the horizontal (landscape) format during Playback. Displaying an image in the vertical orientation on the monitor screen will decrease the overall size of the image to about 2/3 the size of an image displayed horizontally, as a horizontal image uses the full viewing area of the screen.
To select **[Rotate Tall]**:

1. Highlight the **[Rotate Tall]** item in the Playback menu and press ▶.
2. Highlight **[On]** or **[Off]**.
3. Press ⊗ to confirm the selection.

NOTE: The **[Auto Image Rotation]** option in the Setup menu must be turned on for the Rotate Tall function to operate.

SLIDE SHOW

The Slide Show option in the Playback menu allows you to view all of the images stored on the current memory card in sequential order. This can be a useful and enjoyable feature, especially if the camera is connected to view the images on a television or external monitor screen.

To use **[Slide Show]**:

1. Highlight the **[Slide Show]** item in the Playback menu and press ▶.
2. **[Start]** will be highlighted. To commence the slide show immediately, press the ⊗ button.
3. To select the display duration for each image, highlight **[Frame interval]** and press ▶ to display the four options: 2, 3, 5, or 10 seconds. Highlight the desired interval and press ⊗ to confirm the selection, returning to the **[Slide Show]** page of the Playback menu.
4. To set the transition effect between images displayed in the slide show, highlight **[Transition effects]** and press ▶ to display the three options: **[Zoom/fade]**, **[Cube]**, and **[None]**. Highlight the desired option and press ⊗ to confirm the selection, returning to the **[Slide Show]** page of the Playback menu.

After applying settings in steps 3 and 4 above, repeat step 2 above to start the slide show. There are a variety of controls available when the Slide Show function is active:

- O To return to the previous image, press ◀.
- O To skip to the next image, press ▶.
- O To display and scroll the photo information pages, press ▲ or ▼.
- O To pause the display, press the ⊗ button. A submenu with three options will be displayed: **[Restart]**, **[Frame Interval]**, or **[Exit]**. Highlight as required and press ⊗ to select the option.
- O To stop the slide show and return to the Playback menu, press the MENU button.
- O To stop the slide show and return to the Playback mode (full-frame or thumbnail view), press ▶.
- O To stop the slide show and return to the Shooting mode, press the shutter release button down halfway.

At the end of the slide show display, a menu will be displayed with the following options: **[Restart]**, **[Frame Interval]**, **[Transition effects]**, or **[Exit]**. This is the same menu that is displayed when the slide show is paused by pressing the ⊗ button. Highlight the required option and press ⊗.

HINT: Due to the protracted use of the monitor screen, the slide show function can consume a significant amount of battery power, especially if a large number of images are stored on the memory card. Ensure you use a fully charged battery or the EH-5a AC adapter with EP-5A power connector.

PRINT SET (DPOF)

The **[Print Set (DPOF)]** item in the Playback menu enables the user to create and save instructions that will enable a set of images to be automatically printed by a DPOF-compatible printing device (see pages 284-288 for more details).

◻ *SHOOTING MENU*

The following are the various items available in the Shooting menu of the D3100.

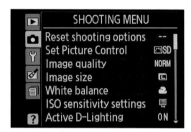

RESET SHOOTING OPTIONS

To select **[Reset shooting options]**:

1. Highlight the **[Reset shooting options]** item in the Shooting menu and press ▶.
2. Highlight **[No]** or **[Yes]**.
3. Press ⊛ to confirm the selection.

By selecting **[Yes]**, this item allows the user to reset the items listed in the table on the following page to their default settings with a single action.

OPTION	DEFAULT SETTING
FOCUS POINT	Center
FLEXIBLE PROGRAM	Off
AE-L/AF-L BUTTON HOLD	Off
VIEWFINDER FOCUS MODE	Auto-Servo AF
LIVE VIEW / MOVIE FOCUS MODE	Single-Servo AF
FLASH MODE: 🏕, ⚘, 🌼, ❀	Auto Front-Curtain Sync
FLASH MODE: 🌃	Auto Slow Sync
FLASH MODE: P, A, S, M	Front-Curtain Sync
EXPOSURE COMPENSATION	Off
FLASH COMPENSATION	Off

SET PICTURE CONTROL

The Picture Control System allows the user to set specific controls that determine how the D3100 will perform image processing. The D3100 has six standard Nikon Picture Controls: Standard, Neutral, Vivid, Monochrome, Portrait, and Landscape (see pages 156-165 for more details).

IMAGE QUALITY

The [Image quality] option in the Shooting menu allows the user to select the file format for images recorded by the camera. The D3100 can record images in JPEG or NEF (RAW) formats. (See pages 122-131 for more details.)

IMAGE SIZE

Image size determines the file size, or resolution, of an image. Image Size is expressed as the number of pixels used in the file. Image size adjustments will only apply to images saved using the JPEG format. NEF (RAW) files are always saved at the camera's highest resolution. (See pages 129-131 for more details.)

WHITE BALANCE

The [White balance] option in the Shooting menu allows you to select the color temperature at which the images you are shooting will be balanced and processed. (See pages 145-156 for more details.)

ISO SENSITIVITY

ISO Sensitivity in the D3100 emulates the sensitivity to light of film bearing the same ISO number. The higher the ISO number the greater the sensitivity to light. (See pages 45-49 for more details.)

ACTIVE D-LIGHTING

The Active D-Lighting feature (not to be confused with the [D-Lighting] item in the Retouch menu) can be used to optimize the exposure settings when using Matrix metering. Since the effects of Active D-Lighting are applied during the processing of an image file, it is not possible to reverse them when recording JPEG files. The effects of Active D-Lighting on an image recorded in the NEF (RAW) format can be altered subsequently using appropriate Nikon software. (See pages 167-168 for more details.)

AUTO DISTORTION CONTROL

Auto Distortion Control is a proactive feature that operates while the camera is processing image data after a picture has been recorded (it is not the same as the reactive [Distortion Control] item in the Retouch menu that can be used to correct an image that has already been saved to the memory card installed in the camera). It is intended to reduce the effects of linear distortion that often occurs, particularly at the periphery of the frame, where straight lines are not rendered as straight. Typically a wide-angle lens causes barrel distortion that makes lines bow outward away from the center of the picture, while long telephoto lenses cause pincushion distortion, where lines bend inward. This option is only available with D- and G-type Nikkor lenses (PC, fisheye, and certain other lenses are excluded). Select [On] to have the camera correct linear distortion automatically, but be aware that this may result in the edge of the image being cropped out of the final picture; image-processing time is also extended.

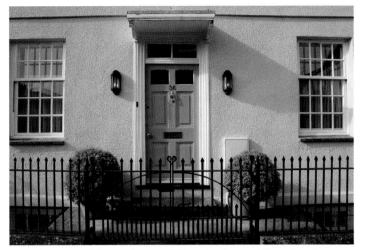

^ Many lenses, especially zoom lenses, exhibit varying degrees of linear distortion, such as the barrel distortion evident in this shot (notice how straight lines bow away from the center of the picture). The Auto Distortion Control feature will help to correct for this effect.

COLOR SPACE

The range of colors capable of being displayed in an image recorded by the D3100 is determined by the Color Space setting. The D3100 provides two options for color space: **[Adobe RGB]** and **[sRGB]**. The color space determines the range (gamut) of colors that will be available in an image file for color reproduction and should be chosen according to how the image will be processed after it has been exported from the camera. (See page 166 for more details.)

NOISE REDUCTION

Unlike other Nikon DSLR cameras that have a separate Noise Reduction feature for long exposures and high ISO settings, the D3100 combines these into a single function. Images taken at shutter speeds of 8 seconds or longer and / or an ISO setting of 800 or above with the D3100 will often exhibit higher levels of electronic noise. Noise is the result of amplification processes that are applied to the data captured by the sensor, especially at high ISO settings, which is then compounded by the higher internal temperature of the camera due to the extended shutter speed. It manifests as irregularly placed bright, colored pixels that disrupt the appearance of an image, particularly in areas of even tonality. The [Noise reduction] item in the Shooting menu will help reduce the appearance of noise. To select [Noise reduction]:

O Highlight the [Noise reduction] item in the Shooting menu and press ▶.
O Highlight [On] or [Off] (default) as required.
O Press the ⊛ button to confirm the selection and return to the Shooting menu.

If [On] is selected for [Noise reduction], the processing time for each recorded image will be equal to the duration of the shutter speed used for the exposure. While the image data is being processed "Job nr" will appear, blinking, in place of the shutter speed and aperture value displays in the control panel. No other picture can be recorded while "Job nr" is displayed and image processing is in progress. If [Off] is selected for [Noise reduction], Noise Reduction is only applied at sensitivity settings above ISO 800, although the level of adjustment is less than when this function is set to [On], and no Noise Reduction is performed for long exposures.

NOTE: The process used by the D3100 to perform Noise Reduction involves the camera making a second exposure, known as a "dark frame exposure," during which the shutter remains closed, but the camera maps the sensor and records the values of each pixel. Sometimes a pixel can lock up and retain a value that is erroneous; this can often occur if the sensor gets hot due to prolonged usage, such as in a long exposure, or due to a high ambient temperature. After mapping the sensor for "hot" (overly bright) pixels, the camera subtracts the "dark frame" photodiode values from the photodiode values of the main exposure in an effort to reduce the effect of noise in the final image.

HINT: Nikon states that when the Long-Exposure Noise Reduction feature of the D3100 is on, it will operate whenever the shutter speed exceeds 8 seconds. In testing, I have found the D3100 to be remarkably noise free, even at exposure durations of several minutes, so it is not necessarily essential to use this feature whenever the shutter speed duration becomes protracted.

Hint: Noise Reduction will affect the resolution of fine detail and, at high levels, the brightness of colors. The ISO noise performance of the D3100 is extremely good, with very clean images being produced at ISO settings up to (and including) ISO 800. The random, almost film-like grain quality caused by noise in D3100 images from around ISO 1600 on up is not, for the most part, troublesome until the sensitivity is pushed beyond ISO 3200.

NOTE: The in-camera Noise Reduction for higher ISO sensitivities does not offer the same level of control as found in dedicated noise reduction software. Unless you must use the in-camera options, I recommend applying noise reduction during post-processing.

AF-AREA MODE

The options available in this item determine how the autofocus point is selected (see pages 83-88 for more details when shooting pictures using the viewfinder, and pages 133-135 for more details when using Live View or recording in D-Movie mode).

AF-ASSIST

The D3100 has a built-in lamp that activates to assist autofocus operation in low-light shooting situations. **[AF-assist]** determines whether the lamp operates or not. If **[ON]** is selected, the lamp will illuminate in Single-Servo autofocus (AF-S) when **[Auto-area]** is selected for the AF-Area mode, or when **[Single point]**, **[Dynamic-area]**, or **[3D-tracking (11 points)]** AF is selected and the center AF point is used. The options are as follows:

- O **[On]** (default): The built-in lamp activates to assist autofocus operation in low-light shooting situations.
- O **[Off]**: The lamp does not light regardless of the level of ambient illumination.

HINT: As discussed in the section of this book that deals with the autofocus system of the D3100 (see pages 89-90 for more information), I consider this lamp to be of little practical value and recommend you select the **[Off]** option for this item.

METERING

The options available in the [Metering] item determine the pattern used by the TTL metering system of the D3100 (see pages 49-53 for more details).

MOVIE SETTINGS

The options available in the [Movie settings] item determine the quality (resolution) of movies and whether sound is recorded while using the D-Movie mode of the D3100 (see page 142 for more details).

BUILT-IN FLASH

Use the [Built-in flash] item to select the Flash mode for the built-in Speedlight of the D3100 when shooting in P, S, A, and M modes. (See pages 238-240 for more details).

ᵠ *SETUP MENU*

The Setup menu is used to establish the basic configuration of the camera. Once the settings for most of the items in this menu are made, it is unlikely they will be changed very frequently.

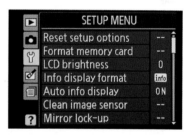

RESET SETUP OPTIONS

To select [Reset setup options]:

1. Highlight the [Reset setup options] item in the Setup menu and press ▶.
2. Highlight [No] or [Yes].
3. Press ⊛ to confirm the selection.

By selecting **[Yes]**, you are able to reset all the items listed below to their default settings in a single action.

OPTION	DEFAULT SETTING
LCD Brightness	0
Info Display Format	Graphic; Background color: Green
Auto Info Display	On
Clean Image Sensor – Clean at	Startup & shutdown
HDMI – Output Resolution	Auto
HDMI – Device Control	On
Time Zone and Date—Daylight Saving Time	Off
Auto Image Rotation	On
Auto Timers Off	Normal
Self-Timer Delay	10 seconds
Beep	On
Rangefinder	Off
File Number Sequence	Off
Buttons—**Fn** button	ISO Sensitivity
Buttons—**AE-L/AF-L**	AE/AF Lock
Buttons—AE Lock	Off
Slot Empty Release Lock	Release locked
Date Imprint	Off
GPS—Auto Meter-Off	Enable
Eye-fi Upload	Enable

FORMAT MEMORY CARD

A new memory card should always be formatted when it is first placed into the D3100. It is also a good idea to format any memory card you insert into the camera, even if the card has been formatted using a computer. This is particularly important if you use your memory cards between different camera bodies. Before you format any memory card, ensure that any image files stored on the card have been saved to another storage device.

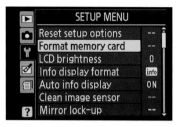
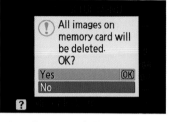

⌃ Here, the [Format memory card] item is
selected in the Setup menu.

⌃ A warning message is displayed during
the formatting process before the action is
actually completed.

LCD BRIGHTNESS

The brightness of the LCD monitor on the back of the camera is set to
a default value, but can be adjusted to help improve the appearance of
any displayed image or page of information. To adjust LCD brightness:

1. Highlight the [LCD Brightness] option from the Setup menu and press ▶.
2. Adjust the brightness value up or down by pressing ▲ or ▼.
3. Press the ⊛ button to confirm the screen brightness value.

A negative value reduces screen brightness, while a positive value
increases screen brightness. The screen displays a grayscale to help you
judge the effect of the brightness level on the full tonal range present in
your images.

HINT: I consider the default value for the screen brightness level to be too
high. For a more accurate assessment of images, I suggest setting screen
brightness to -1.

INFO DISPLAY FORMAT

The D3100 offers two different styles for the Information Display: [Classic]
and [Graphic]. To select a style for the Information Display:

1. Select the [Info display format] item in the Setup menu and press ▶.
2. Highlight the desired option from [Classic] or [Graphic] and press ▶.
3. The [Classic] and [Graphic] options offer a choice of background color.
   Choose [Blue], [Black], or [Orange] for [Classic], and choose [Green],
   [Black], or [Brown] for [Graphic]. Press ⊛ to confirm your selection.

I recommend using the [Classic] display because it offers the greatest clarity although the [Graphic] display may be more helpful to less experienced photographers because it provides a visual representation of the lens aperture and shutter speed. When the camera is turned to shoot a picture in the vertical format, the Information Display is rotated accordingly.

AUTO INFORMATION DISPLAY

If [On] is selected, the Information Display will be shown on the monitor screen once the shutter release button is pressed down halfway. When [Off] is selected for the [Image review] item in the Playback menu, the Information Display will also be shown immediately after an exposure is made. If [Off] is selected for [Auto information display], it will be necessary to press the 🔳 button to view the Information Display.

CLEAN IMAGE SENSOR

This option is used to automatically clean the optical low-pass filter by vibrating it (see pages 293-295 for more details).

MIRROR LOCK-UP

This option is used for manual cleaning or inspection of the optical low-pass filter (see pages 296-299 for more details).

VIDEO MODE

The [Video mode] item allows you to select the type of signal used by any video equipment, such as a DVD player or television, to which your camera may be connected. This option should be set before connecting your camera to the device with an appropriate A/V cord (see page 189 for more details).

HDMI

The [HDMI] option allows you to select the output resolution to an HDMI viewing device and can be used to enable remote control of the D3100 from HDMI devices that support the HDMI-CEC (High-Definition Multimedia Interface—Consumer Electronic Control) standard. These options should be set before connecting your camera to the HDMI device with an appropriate HDMI cord.

Use the [Output resolution] item to select the format for images to be output to the HDMI device. If [Auto] is selected, the D3100 will set the appropriate format automatically.

If [On] is selected for the [Device control] item, when the D3100 is connected to a device that supports the HDMI_CEC standard and both devices are turned on, options for Play and Slide Show will be displayed on the HDMI device screen, and its remote control can be used in place of the camera's Multi Selector and ® buttons during Playback of full-frame images or a slide show. If [Off] is selected for the [Device control] item, the remote control for the HDMI device cannot be used to control the D3100 for image display purposes.

FLICKER REDUCTION

The [Flicker reduction] item is intended to help reduce the effects of banding that can occur when using Live View or the D-Movie mode under fluorescent or mercury-vapor lighting. Choose the frequency that matches that of the local AC power supply. In very bright conditions this item may not be particularly effective; in such conditions set the camera to either M or A exposure modes and use a small aperture (large f/number).

> The available
options for the
[Flicker reduction]
item in the Setup
menu.

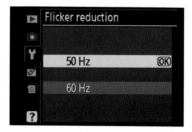

TIME ZONE / DATE

The [Time zone and date] item enables you to set and change the date and time recorded by the camera's internal clock and how it is displayed. To set the internal clock:

1. Highlight the [Time zone and date] item in the Setup menu and press ▶ to display the menu options.

2. Use ▲ and ▼ to highlight [Time zone] and press ▶ to display a map of world time zones.

3. Press either ◀ or ▶ to select the appropriate time zone, and press ⊛ to confirm the selection and return to the [Time zone and date] menu.

4. Now, use ▲ and ▼ to highlight the [Date and time] option, and press ▶ to display the date / time clock. Use ▶ to select each item in turn and adjust as needed by using ▲ and ▼ until the full date and time have been entered.

5. Press ⊛ to confirm the settings and return to the [Time zone and date] menu.

6. Next, highlight the [Date format] option and press ▶ to display the list of choices. Use ▲ and ▼ to highlight the desired date format and press ⊛ to confirm the selection.

7. Finally, use ▲ and ▼ to highlight the [Daylight saving time] option and press ▶ to display the two choices; the default setting for [Daylight saving time] is [Off]. If daylight saving time is in effect in the current time zone, highlight [On] and press ⊛ to confirm the selection.

To exit the menu system and return the camera to its Shooting mode, press the shutter release button halfway down.

HINT: If you travel to a different time zone, it is only necessary to adjust the [Time zone] option; the date and time will be automatically adjusted for the selected time zone. The only other option that may need to be adjusted is the [Daylight saving time] option.

HINT: The internal clock is not as accurate as many wristwatches or domestic clocks, so it is important to check it regularly.

LANGUAGE

The **[Language]** option in the Setup menu of the D3100 allows you to select one of 20 languages for the camera to use when displaying menus and messages. To select the language, press the MENU button and highlight the required option under the **[Language]** item using ▲ or ▼. Press the ⊛ button to confirm and lock your selection. If you wish to change the language at any time after the initial setup, repeat the procedure just described.

IMAGE COMMENT

The **[Image comment]** feature of the Setup menu allows you to attach a short note or reference to an image file. Comments can be up to 36 characters long and may contain letters and / or numbers. Since the process requires each character to be input individually, this is not a feature you will use for every picture you take. However, as a way of assigning a general comment (i.e., the name of a location / venue / event) or attaching notice of authorship / copyright, it is very useful. To attach an image comment:

1. Highlight the **[Image Comment]** option from the Setup menu and press ▶.
2. Highlight **[Input Comment]** from the options list and press ▶.
3. To enter your comment, highlight the character you wish to input by using the Multi Selector and press ⊛ to select it. If you accidentally enter the wrong character, rotate the Command dial to move the cursor over the unwanted character and press the 🗑 button to erase it.
4. Press the ⊛ button to save the comment and return to the **[Image comment]** options list.
5. To actually attach the comment to your photographs, highlight the **[Attach Comment]** option, and then press ▶. A small check mark will appear in the box to the left of the option.
6. Finally, highlight **[Done]** and press the ⊛ button to confirm the selection.

If you wish to exit this process at any time without attaching the comment, prior to step 5, simply press the MENU button. When the check mark is present in the **[Attach comment]** option of the **[Image comment]** item, the saved comment will be attached to all subsequent images shot on the D3100. To prevent the comment from being attached to an image, simply return to the [Image comment] menu and uncheck the [Attach comment] box by highlighting the option and pressing ▶. The Image Comment will remain stored in the camera's memory and can be attached to future images simply by rechecking the [Attach comment] box. The comment will be displayed on the third page of the photo Information Display, available in single-image Playback. It can also be viewed in Nikon View NX2 or Capture NX2 software.

AUTO IMAGE ROTATION

The D3100 automatically recognizes the orientation of the camera as it records an image: horizontal, vertical—rotated 90° clockwise, or vertical—rotated 90° counter-clockwise. At its default setting, the camera stores this information, so the image will be automatically rotated during Playback. It will also be displayed in the correct orientation on a computer with compatible software. If you do not want the camera to record the shooting orientation, the [Auto image rotation] feature can be switched off. To set [Auto image rotation]:

1. Highlight the [Auto image rotation] item from the Setup menu and press ▶.
2. Highlight [On] or [Off] as required.
3. Press ⓞⓚ to confirm the selection.

NOTE: If you shoot with the camera tilted up or down it may not record the orientation correctly. In this case it is probably easier to select [Off] and rotate the pictures in appropriate software, such as Nikon View NX2 or Nikon Capture NX2.

NOTE: The [Rotate tall] item in the Playback menu must also be turned on for images to be displayed in the orientation in which they were originally taken during Playback on the camera. However, if the [Image review] item in the Playback menu is set to [On], images taken in a vertical format will not be rotated for image review because the camera will already be in the correct orientation.

The [Dust Off ref photo] item of the D3100 is designed specifically for use with the Image Dust Off function in Nikon Capture NX2. The image file created by this function creates a mask that is electronically "overlaid" on an NEF (RAW) file, enabling the software to reduce or remove the effects of shadows that are cast by dust particles on the surface of the optical low pass filter. To obtain a reference image for the Dust Off Ref Photo function you must use a CPU-type lens (Nikon recommends use of a lens with a focal length of 50mm or more). This function can only be used with NEF (RAW) files; it is not available for JPEG or TIFF files.

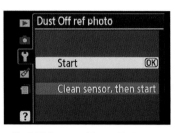

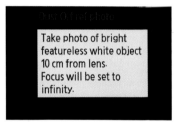

^ The initial screen of [Dust Off ref photo] item options in the Setup menu

^ The D3100 displays an instruction message for how to capture the [Dust Off ref photo].

To use [Dust Off ref photo]:

1. Highlight the [Dust off ref photo] option from the Setup menu and press ▶.

2. [Start] and [Clean sensor, then start] will be displayed on the monitor screen. Highlight [Start] and press ⊛ to begin the process: "rEF" will appear in the viewfinder and the following message will be displayed on the LCD screen: "Take photo of bright featureless white object 10 cm from lens. Focus will be set to infinity." If [Clean sensor, then start] is selected and ⊛ is pressed, the camera will vibrate the low-pass filter before displaying the messages just described.

3. Point your camera at a featureless white subject positioned approximately 4 inches (10 cm) from the front of the lens.

4. Press the shutter release button all the way down (focus will be set automatically to infinity).

Once you have recorded the Image Dust Off reference data file, it can be displayed in the camera during Playback. It appears as a grid pattern with "Image Dust Off ref photo" displayed within the image area (see above screen shot). A Dust Off reference data file can be identified by its file extension, which is NDF; these files cannot be viewed using a computer.

NOTE: If the reference target is too bright or too dark, the camera will probably not be able to acquire Dust Off reference data. In this case a warning will be displayed on the monitor screen: "Exposure settings are not appropriate. Change exposure settings and try again." Either use an alternative target or change the level of illumination.

HINT: This feature is reasonably effective, but the dust particles can be dislodged and shift between shots, providing no guarantee that this technique will be completely successful if you save only one reference file. The best approach is to shoot several reference files during the course of a shoot and use the one that was made closest to the time of the exposure you need to correct.

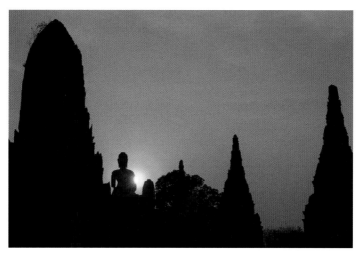

^ It is important to keep the D3100's low-pass filter clean, otherwise dust and other unwanted material will cause dark spots in an image, which will be particularly noticeable in areas of continuous tones, such as a clear sky.

AUTO OFF TIMERS

This item determines how long the monitor screen stays on if no camera functions are performed during menu display and image Playback (through the [Playback/menus] item), how long an image is displayed after shooting (through the [Image review] option), and how long exposure meters, the viewfinder, and Information Displays stay on when no camera function is performed (through the [Auto meter-off] selection). The options are: [Short], [Normal] (default), [Long], and [Custom]. The standard times are show in the chart. The [Custom] option requires a time to be selected for each selection, and then [Done] must be highlighted before pressing the ⊛ button.

	PLAYBACK / MENUS	IMAGE REVIEW	LIVE VIEW	AUTO METER OFF
Short	8 seconds	4 seconds	30 seconds	4 seconds
Normal	12 seconds	4 seconds	30 seconds	8 seconds
Long	20 seconds	20 seconds	3 minutes	1 minute

HINT: Selections under this item should be considered in respect to the power drain the LCD screen causes; the best advice is to set the shortest duration that is still convenient.

> Here, the [Auto off timers] options are shown, with the [Custom] option highlighted.

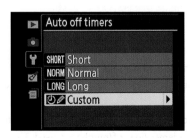

SELF-TIMER DELAY

This item controls the duration of the shutter release delay in the Self-Timer mode. **[Self-timer delay]** options are as follows:

- **[2 s]**: 2 seconds
- **[10 s]**: 10 seconds (default)

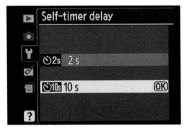

< The **[Self-timer delay]** item options, with the default setting of 10 seconds highlighted.

> **HINT:** Set the duration of the delay to match the shooting situation; using a duration that is unnecessarily long will just increase the drain on battery power.

BEEP

Select **[On]** to have an audible warning sound when the Self-Timer is counting down, the camera attains focus in AF-S (Single-Servo), or focus locks in Live View. Select **[Off]** to cancel any audible warning. In Ⓠ Quiet Shutter release mode, this item is not available, but there will still be no warning sound.

> **HINT:** This is a matter of personal preference, but the audible warning can be a distraction in many shooting situations. For that reason, I recommend selecting **[Off]** for this item; Q will be displayed in the control panel to confirm the warning is switched off.

RANGEFINDER

Available in all exposure modes except M (Manual), the exposure indicator scale can be used to assist manual focusing by showing whether focus has been acquired, and if not, where the focus point is located. This feature requires that a lens with a maximum aperture of f/5.6, or larger (lower f/number) is used. The function does not operate in Live View or the D-Movie mode. The options are as follows:

○ **[On]**: The exposure indicator scale shows the state of manual focus.
○ **[Off]** (default): The analog exposure scale functions normally.

INDICATOR	DESCRIPTION	INDICATOR	DESCRIPTION
	Focus has been acquired		Focus point slightly behind subject
	Focus point slightly in front of subject		Focus point is significantly behind subject
	Focus point is significantly in front of subject		Camera cannot determine correct focus

FILE NUMBER SEQUENCE

This option controls whether file numbering continues in a consecutive sequence from the last number used when a memory card is formatted, a new folder is created, or a new memory card is inserted in the camera, or if it is reset to 0001. The options are as follows:

○ **[On]** (default): Whenever a memory card is formatted or a new memory card is inserted in the camera, file numbering continues consecutively from the last number used or the largest number in the current folder, whichever is higher. If the current folder contains a photograph numbered 9999, a new folder will be automatically created, and numbering will be reset to 0001.
○ **[Off]**: File numbering is reset to 0001 whenever a memory card is formatted, a new folder is created, or a new memory card is inserted in the camera.
○ **[Reset]**: The same as the **[On]** option, except that the file number for the next picture that is taken is assigned by adding one to the largest file number in the current folder. If that folder is empty, file numbering is reset to 0001.

HINT: If you expect to shoot pictures using more than one memory card, I strongly suggest that you use the **[On]** option. Otherwise, you will potentially end up with duplicate file numbers and names, which can become very confusing once images are saved to your computer.

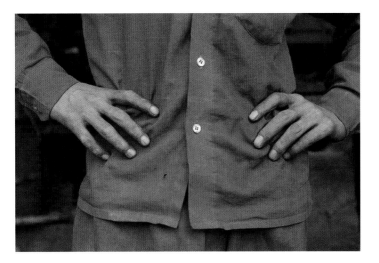

^ The Function button can be assigned a variety of roles to help improve the general handling qualities of the D3100, so that when you see a shot you don't want to miss, you can quickly make the necessary settings without having to navigate menu screens.

BUTTONS

Fn Function Button: The Fn button, located on the front of the camera below the ⚡ button, can be assigned a variety of different functions using the **[Fn Button]** item within the **[Buttons]** option. The options are as follows:

- O **[Image quality/size]**: Press the Fn button and rotate the Command dial to select the image quality and size.

- O **[ISO sensitivity]**: Press the Fn button and rotate the Command dial to select the ISO sensitivity value.

- O **[White balance]**: Press the Fn button and rotate the Command dial to select the White Balance value (only available in P, S, A, and M modes).

- O **[Active D-Lighting]**: Press the Fn button and rotate the Command dial to select the ADL level (only available in P, S, A, and M modes).

AE-L/AF-L Button: The AE-L/AF-L button, located on the rear of the camera to the right of the viewfinder eyepiece, can be assigned a variety of different functions using the [AE-L/AF-L button] item within the [Buttons] option. The options are as follows:

- ☐ [AE/AF lock] (default): Focus and exposure are locked when the AE-L/AF-L button is pressed.
- ☐ [AE lock only]: Only exposure is locked when the AE-L/AF-L button is pressed.
- ☐ [AF lock only]: Only focus is locked when the AE-L/AF-L button is pressed.
- ☐ [AE lock (hold)]: Exposure is locked when the AE-L/AF-L button is pressed and remains locked until the button is pressed again or the exposure meter turns off automatically.
- ☐ [AF-ON]: Autofocus is initiated when the AE-L/AF-L button is pressed. Pressing the shutter release button will not activate autofocus.

NOTE: If [AF-ON] is selected the Vibration Reduction (VR) feature, available on some Nikkor lenses, will not operate when the AE-L/AF-L button is pressed; VR is only activated by pressing the shutter release button. If you do use the technique of locking focus via the AE-L/AF-L button, when you decide to take a picture press the shutter release button and pause briefly when it is depressed halfway to allow the VR system to activate and settle, before pressing it all the way down to operate the shutter.

AE Lock: This option determines how the exposure value can be locked using the [AE lock] item within the [Buttons] option. The options are as follows:

- ☐ [Off] (default): The exposure is only locked by pressing the AE-L/AF-L button.
- ☐ [On]: The exposure can be locked by either pressing the AE-L/AF-L button or pressing the shutter release button down halfway.

HINT: This is a matter of personal preference, but if you wish to recompose the picture after taking a meter reading, having the exposure locked by simply pressing the shutter release button can be convenient.

SLOT EMPTY RELEASE LOCK

This item allows the shutter to operate without a memory card being installed in the camera. The options are as follows:

O **[Release locked]** (default): The shutter release is disabled if no memory card is installed in the camera.

O **[Enable release]**: The shutter release operates if no memory card is installed in the camera. The camera stores no images; however, the last recorded image is displayed in Demo mode.

HINT: Disaster potentially looms with this item if it is set to the **[Enable release]** option—you do not want the camera to operate as though it is recording pictures when, in fact, there is no memory card installed!

DATE IMPRINT

This item enables date information to be imprinted within the image area as it is recorded.

OPTION	DESCRIPTION
Off	No information is recorded.
Date	The Date or Date and Time information is recorded within the image area.
Date and Time	
Date Counter	Number of days between date of shooting and a selected date is recorded. Up to three different dates can be stored in this option; after a date is selected for the first time, enter a date and press ⊗ to access the [Choose date] and the [Display options] pages.

NOTE: The date information format is the same as for the **[Time zone and date]** item in the Setup menu. This item is not available with NEF (RAW) recording and cannot be added to or removed from pictures already saved to the memory card.

The D3100 uses a folder system to organize images stored on the installed memory card. The [Storage folder] option in the Setup menu allows you to select which folder the images you are currently recording will be saved in and enables you to create new folders. If you do not use any of the folders options, the camera will automatically create a folder named 100D3100, in which the first 999 pictures recorded by the camera will be stored. If you exceed 999 pictures, the camera will create a new folder named 101D3100; a new folder will be created for each set of 999 pictures. The three-digit prefix is only displayed when the memory card is connected to a computer, either directly from the camera or via a card reader.

You can create your own folder(s) and name them for your reference. You can assign a five-character folder title; a three-digit number between 100 and 999 always prefixes the title. If you use multiple folders on a single memory card, you must select one "active" folder to which all images will be stored until an alternative folder is chosen.

NOTE: If the folder that has reached full capacity (i.e., 999 images) is folder number 999D3100, the camera will disable the shutter release button and prevent you from making an exposure. You will have to create a new folder with a lower number, or choose another folder on the memory card that still has space for new images. Likewise, the shutter release button will be disabled if the active folder contains a picture numbered 9999.

To create a new folder:

1. Highlight the [Storage folder] item in the Setup menu and press ▶.
2. Highlight the [New] option and press ▶.
3. Designate the name / number of the new folder by using the keypad of letters and numbers that are displayed on the monitor screen. Use the Multi Selector to select the required character and press ⊗ to input it. To move the cursor, rotate the Command dial.
4. To delete a character at the current cursor position, press the 🗑 button.
5. Press ⊕ to confirm the action and return to the Setup menu.
6. Press MENU to exit without creating a new folder name.

To select an existing folder:

1. Highlight the **[Storage folder]** item in the Setup menu and press ▶.
2. Highlight the **[Select folder]** option and press ▶.
3. A list of the folders currently stored on the memory card is displayed; highlight the folder you wish to use by pressing ▲ or ▼.
4. Press ⑳ to confirm the action and return to the Setup menu.

The **[Rename]** option allows an existing folder name to be changed. The **[Delete]** option allows all empty folders on the memory card to be deleted.

HINT: Folders may be useful if you expect to take pictures of a variety of subjects (i.e., various different locations on a vacation), but with the relatively low cost of memory cards it is probably easier, and more efficient, to use multiple cards.

HINT: Personally, I believe that using multiple folders is time consuming, potentially confusing, and fraught with danger! If you have more than one Nikon digital camera and move cards between them, the different cameras will not be able to display images stored in folders created by another camera. If the second camera then creates a new folder, it will have a higher prefix number than the folder created by the first camera. Even multiple folders created by the D3100 can present problems in other cameras, as new images will be saved to the currently selected folder with the highest prefix number. I would rather use a browser application such as Nikon View NX2 to organize my image files.

GPS

Using the dedicated Nikon GP-1 GPS unit connected to the accessory terminal of the D3100 makes it possible for the camera to record GPS information when a picture is taken.

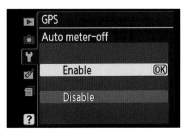

‹ The options available under the **[Auto meter off]** item in the **[GPS]** submenu

As soon as the camera confirms communication with the connected GPS device, GPS will be displayed in the Information Display. If the GPS icon is shown blinking, it means the GP-1 is still searching for a GPS signal and any picture taken will not include GPS data. If the GPS icon is not displayed, it means the camera has received no new GPS data from the GP-1 for at least 2 seconds, and again, no GPS data will be recorded if a picture is taken.

The information recorded when an exposure is made with the GPS icon displayed includes current latitude, longitude, altitude, time, and heading (see note below). The time provided by the GPS device uses Universal Time Coordinated (UTC) data and is independent of the camera's internal clock. To view GPS data, open an image in single-image Playback and use the Multi Selector to scroll through the photo information pages until the GPS Data page is displayed. The [GPS] item in the Setup menu has two options:

○ **[Auto meter off]:** Allows you to choose whether or not the exposure meters will turn off automatically when a GPS unit is attached. Highlight **[Auto meter off]** and press ▶ to display the two sub-options:

  ● **[Enable] (default):** If no camera operation is performed for the period selected at **[Auto off timers]** in the Setup menu, the exposure meter will turn off automatically. While this reduces drain on the camera's battery, it may prevent GPS data from being recorded because if the camera's meter is turned off, the GPS device may also switch off or go into a standby mode. If the shutter release is then pressed all the way down to record an exposure without pausing, there may be insufficient time for the GPS device to reactivate.

  ● **[Disable]:** The camera's exposure meter will not turn off automatically while the GP-1 GPS device is connected. GPS data will always be recorded, as the GP-1 device will also remain active.

○ **[Position]:** Is only available if a GPS device is connected and GPS communication is confirmed; if not, the **[Position]** item is grayed out in the menu. When communication is established with the GP-1, the camera displays current latitude, longitude, altitude, and date / time (UTC data).

EYE-FI UPLOAD

The wireless communication-enabled Eye-Fi memory cards can only be used in their country of purchase. This item is only displayed when a dedicated Eye-Fi memory card is installed in the D3100. To upload JPEG files directly from the camera to the predetermined destination, select **[Enabled]**. If the Wi-Fi signal is not sufficiently strong, image upload will not take place. In areas where Wi-Fi is unavailable or wireless devices are prohibited ensure the **[Disable]** option is selected.

FIRMWARE VERSION

When **[Firmware version]** is selected from the Setup menu, the current versions of the firmware installed on the camera are displayed on the monitor screen. To check the current firmware installed on your camera, highlight the **[Firmware version]** option from the Setup menu and press ▶. The details of the firmware are displayed on the next page. Press ⊛ to return to the Setup menu. Firmware updates can be downloaded from any of the Nikon technical support websites. To check for current updates visit: www.nikon.com.

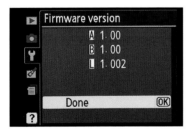

✍ *RETOUCH MENU*

The Retouch menu enables you to create retouched (modified), trimmed (cropped), or resized versions of the image files saved on a memory card installed in the camera. When the features in this menu are applied to an image, a new copy of the file is created and stored on the same memory card. The original image file remains on the card in its original, unmodified form.

While I feel options available in the Retouch menu are a useful aspect of camera control, I believe it is important to keep them in perspective. The items available in this menu cannot be considered anywhere near as sophisticated as their equivalent adjustments in any good image-editing software. They are intended to provide a quick, convenient, and largely automated method of producing a modified version of the original image without the use of a computer. As such, they offer an unprecedented level of control when using in-camera processing to produce a finished picture directly from the camera.

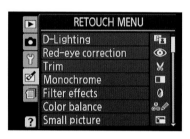

SELECTING IMAGES

To select an image directly from the Retouch menu, open the Retouch menu, highlight the desired function, and press ▶ to select it and display a set of thumbnail images on the monitor screen to choose from. For some items, a further menu of options may be displayed before the thumbnail images. In these cases, highlight the required option and press ▶ again to continue to image selection. Use the Multi Selector to scroll through the thumbnail images; a yellow border will frame the currently selected picture. To view an image full-frame, press and hold ⊕. Once you have selected the picture to be modified and copied, press ⊛ to display the retouch options (see details below for each Retouch menu item). To cancel the process at any time, press the MENU button. To apply the retouch option and save the new copy image, press ⊛.

Alternatively, it is possible to access the Retouch menu directly from full-frame Playback. Display the picture to be modified on the monitor screen and press the ⊛ button. The Retouch menu will be displayed; highlight the required item by using ▲ and ▼ and press ▶ to open the options for that item. To return to the full-frame Playback, press ▶. Press ⊗ to create the retouched copy. An ✍ icon in the upper left of the image identifies the retouched copy file.

IMAGE QUALITY AND SIZE

The image quality and size of the copy image created by the Retouch menu will depend on the quality and size of the original image file(s). The selected option within the Retouch menu may also affect image size and quality. Except in the case of the [Trim], [Small picture], [Image overlay], and [NEF (RAW) processing] options, the following explains how image size and quality will be affected:

- O Copies created from JPEG images are the same size and quality as the original file.
- O Copies of NEF (RAW) files are saved as JPEG files with [Large] and [Fine] selected for size and quality.

The copy the [Image overlay] option creates is always saved at the image quality and size currently set on the camera, regardless of the fact that this option is only available with NEF (RAW) images. If you wish to save the copy image as an NEF (RAW) file, ensure the image quality on the camera is set to NEF (RAW) before you apply the [Image overlay] option.

NOTE: In most cases, up to ten effects from the Retouch menu can be applied to a single image. However, each effect can only be applied to a given file once, with the exception of the [Image overlay] option. If an option is displayed grayed out, it is not available.

⊞ *D-LIGHTING*

The D-Lighting feature of the Retouch menu brightens shadow areas to reveal more detail. It is not an overall brightness control; its application is selective. By modifying the tone curve applied to the image, it only affects the shadow areas of the recorded image and preserves the mid- and highlight tones.

Select the image (as described on pages 206-207) and press the ⊛ button to display two thumbnail images: one unmodified (left) and the other modified (right). You can select three levels of D-Lighting: low, normal, or high by using ▲ and ▼. To view the preview image full-frame, press and hold ⊕. Once you have decided which level is most appropriate, press the ⊛ button to apply the change and create the copy image. You can press the MENU button to cancel the function without making any changes.

👁 *RED-EYE REDUCTION*

This option is only available with pictures taken using either the built-in Speedlight of the D3100 or an external Nikon Speedlight. Select the image (as described above) and press ⊛. If no flash was used for the chosen exposure, a small yellow box containing a cross is displayed over the thumbnail image, and the image cannot be selected. If flash was used but the camera cannot detect the presence of red-eye, a message stating "Unable to detect red eye in selected image" will be displayed.

If the D3100 detects what it considers to be a red-eye effect, the image will be displayed with a small navigation window; press and hold the ⊕ button to zoom into the image. You can navigate around the image to view other areas of the picture not visible by using the Multi Selector; the area currently displayed on the monitor screen is shown with a yellow border in a navigation window. To scroll rapidly to another area of the picture, press and hold the Multi Selector down.

If you can see the effects of red-eye in the selected picture, press ⊛ to cancel the zoom control and return to the full-frame Playback and then press ⊛ again. The D3100 will then create a copy image automatically, using processed image data, to reduce the red-eye effect.

NOTE: Since this is a completely automated process, it is possible for the camera to inadvertently select an image not affected by red-eye but containing an area that looks like red eye; this is why it is important to double check the preview image before confirming the operation of the process.

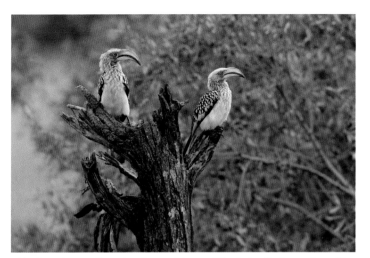

∧ The Retouch menu offers a broad range of image editing tools, allowing you to modify a picture in-camera, such as a Trim feature that allows you to crop in on a subject. Keep in mind, though, that you will almost always get better results using dedicated image editing software on a computer.

✄ TRIM

The **[Trim]** option enables you to crop (trim) the original image to exclude unwanted areas. Highlight the **[Trim]** option in the Retouch menu and press ▶ to display a set of thumbnail images. Select the image (as described above) and press ⊛. The selected image is displayed on the LCD monitor, along with a yellow frame to show the crop area; you can move the crop frame around the image using the Multi Selector. Press the ⊟ button to reduce the size of the crop area. Use the 🔍 button to increase the size of crop area; the crop size is displayed in the top left corner of the image in pixel dimensions (width x height). It is also possible to adjust the aspect ratio of the cropped area; rotating the Command dial allows you to switch between 3:2, 4:3, 5:4, 1:1, and 16:9. Once you have decided on the location, size, and aspect ratio of the crop area, press ⊛ to create the cropped copy. The new copy image will be displayed on the LCD monitor. Press the MENU button to return to the Retouch menu display.

NOTE: Copies created from NEF (RAW), NEF (RAW) + JPEG, or TIFF (RGB) files have an image quality of JPEG [Fine]. Copies created from JPEG files have the same image quality as the original.

The size of the copy file varies with the selected crop size and aspect ratio, as follows:

ASPECT RATIO	RANGE OF AVAILABLE IMAGE SIZES (IN PIXELS)
3:2	3840 x 2560, 3200 x 2128, 2560 x 1704, 1920 x 1280, 1280 x 856, 960 x 640, 640 x 424
4:3	3840 x 2880, 3200 x 2400, 2560 x 1920, 1920 x 1440, 1280 x 960, 960 x 720, 640 x 480
5:4	3600 x 2800, 2992 x 2400, 2400 x 1920, 1808 x 1440, 1200 x 960, 896 x 720, 608 x 480
1:1	2880 x 2880, 2400 x 2400, 1920 x 1920, 1440 x 1440, 960 x 960, 720 x 720, 480 x 480
16:9	3840 x 2160, 3200 x 1800, 2560 x 1440, 1920 x 1080, 1280 x 720, 960 x 536, 640 x 360

☐▬ *MONOCHROME*

This item allows you to save the copied image in one of three monochrome effects: **[Black-and-white]** (grayscale), **[Sepia]** (brown tones), or **[Cyanotype]** (blue-and-white tones). In all three cases the image data is converted to black and white using an algorithm dedicated to this feature; it is a different algorithm than the one used for the **[Monochrome]** option in the Picture Controls. The image data for the black-and-white copy is still saved as an RGB file (i.e. it retains its color information).

> Shown here is the Setup menu with the **[Monochrome]** item highlighted.

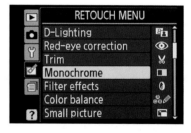

RETOUCH MENU
D–Lighting
Red-eye correction
Trim
Monochrome
Filter effects
Color balance
Small picture

Select the image as described on pages 206-207. With this item you must select the desired option before the thumbnail images are displayed. If you select either the **[Sepia]** or the **[Cyanotype]** options, the appropriate color shift is applied after the copy picture is converted to black and white. The degree of the color shift can be adjusted using ▲ to increase and ▼ to decrease the effect. Once you are satisfied with the preview image, press ⊛ to save the copy picture.

❶ *FILTER EFFECTS*

The [Filter effects] option in the Retouch menu offers choices that simulate the results of effect filters that were more commonly used with film photography. Select the image as described above. With this item the desired option must be selected before the thumbnail images are displayed.

- ○ [Skylight]: Nikon describes this option as emulating the effect of a Skylight filter. The effect is very subtle, reducing the amount of blue in the image by a very modest amount.
- ○ [Warm tone]: This effect increases the amount of red in the image and produces a result similar to the use of a Wratten 81-series color correction filter. Again, the effect is subtle; proper White Balance control should eliminate the need to use it.
- ○ [Red intensifier]: Intensifies red; use the Multi Selector to select one of three levels: ▲ to increase and ▼ to decrease the effect.
- ○ [Green intensifier]: Intensifies green; use the Multi Selector to select one of three levels: ▲ to increase and ▼ to decrease the effect.
- ○ [Blue intensifier]: Intensifies blue; use the Multi Selector to select one of three levels: ▲ to increase and ▼ to decrease the effect.
- ○ [Cross screen]: Adds a starburst effect to point light sources in the image. This option has a number of sub-items, providing greater control over the effect.
- ○ [Number of points]: Select from 4, 6, or 8.
- ○ [Filter amount]: Choose the brightness of the light sources affected.
- ○ [Filter angle]: Select the angle of the star points.
- ○ [Length of points]: Select the length of the star points.
- ○ [Confirm]: Use to preview the effects of the filter (to preview in full-frame press the ⊕ button).
- ○ [Save]: Create the retouch copy.
- ○ [Soft]: Adds a soft filter effect; use the Multi Selector button to select one of three levels: 1 (high), 2 (medium), or 3 (low).

In all [Filter effects] options, a preview image is displayed showing the effect of the selected item on the original image; press ⊛ to apply it and create the copy image.

⬚⬚✎ *COLOR BALANCE*

The [Color balance] item is used to produce a copy image with a modified color balance from the original file. Select the image (as described above) and press ⊛ to display the control options.

A thumbnail image of the selected picture is displayed alongside histograms for the composite RGB, red, green, and blue channels. Below the thumbnail is a two-dimensional CIE color space map with a vertical and horizontal axis aligned on its center. The central point of the color space map represents the color balance of the original file. Press the Multi Selector up to increase the level of green and down to increase the level of magenta. Pressing the Multi Selector to the left increases the level of blue, and to the right increases the level of amber. The black square cursor will shift position accordingly. The histograms will reflect the altered color distribution and the thumbnail image can be used to preview the effect.

⬚ *SMALL PICTURE*

The [Small picture] item offers options to reduce the resolution of the original image to create a copy that has a far smaller file size:

- ○ 640 x 480 pixels: Suitable for playback on a television set.
- ○ 320 x 240 pixels: Suitable for display on web pages.
- ○ 160 x 120 pixels: Suitable for sending as an attachment to e-mail.

NOTE: If the [Small picture] item is selected from the [Retouch menu] (rather than from single-image Playback), it is necessary to select the image size as the first step and then select the picture(s) to which the process will be applied.

NOTE: Copies created by [Small picture] cannot be further modified.

NOTE: Small copy files created with the [Small picture] option have file names that begin with "SSC_" and end with the file extension ".JPG" (e.g. SSC_0001.JPG).

To use this option via the Retouch menu, proceed as follows:

1. Open the Retouch menu, highlight **[Small picture]**, and press ▶ to display two options: **[Select image]** and **[Choose size]**.

2. Highlight **[Choose size]**, and then press ▶ to display the three size options (listed above), and highlight the required size.

3. Press ⊛ to confirm your choice and return to the previous page.

4. Highlight **[Select picture]** and press ▶ to display the thumbnail images. The currently selected image is shown framed by a yellow border.

5. Use the Multi Selector to highlight a desired image (the yellow border will shift accordingly) and press ⊞ to select it (a small ⊡ appears in the top right corner of the thumbnail to indicate it has been selected). Press ⊕ to view an enlarged picture.

6. Repeat as required. Once you have selected all the images you want to reduce in size, press ⊛. A confirmation page will be displayed indicating how many images will be processed.

7. Select **[Yes]** to proceed with the process, or **[No]** to return to the previous page. If you select **[Yes]**, press ⊛ to apply the effect and save the copy picture(s).

NOTE: Images saved using the **[Small picture]** item are displayed with a gray border during full-frame Playback, thumbnail Playback, and when a picture selection dialog page is displayed. It is not possible to use the ⊕ zoom function with these images.

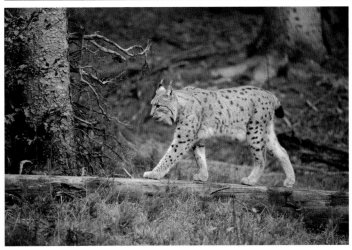

⌃ The Retouch menu items can be useful if you want to modify a picture and do not have ready access to a computer, such as when travelling.

[Image overlay] enables the merging of a pair of NEF (RAW) files, combining them to form a single, new image (the original image files are not affected by this process). The images to be used do not have to be taken in consecutive order, but must have been recorded by a D3100 and be stored on the same memory card. To use [Image overlay]:

1. Highlight the [Image overlay] option in the Retouch menu and press the ▶ button. The [Image overlay] page will open with [Image 1] highlighted.

2. To select the first picture, press ⊛; a thumbnail view of all NEF (RAW) files stored on the memory card will be displayed. Scroll through the images using the Multi Selector to highlight the image you wish to select.

3. Press ⊛ and the selected image will appear in the [Image 1] box and the [Preview] box.

4. Adjust the gain value of [Image 1] by pressing ▲ and ▼. The effect of the gain control can be observed in the preview box. (The default value is x1.0; x0.5 cuts the gain in half, while selecting x2.0 doubles the gain.)

5. Highlight the [Image 2] box and repeat steps 2 – 4 above.

6. Once you have adjusted the gain of both images to achieve the desired effect, highlight the [Preview] box by pressing ◀ or ▶. Highlight [Overlay] using ▲ or ▼ and press ⊛ to display a preview of the combined images. If the result is satisfactory press the ⊛ button to save the new image; otherwise press ⊠ to return to the previous step.

7. To save the image without displaying a preview, highlight [Save] at step 6 above, instead of [Overlay], and press the ⊛ button. The new image will be displayed full-frame.

The image will be saved on the memory card using the Image Quality and Image Size settings currently selected on the camera. Image attributes such as White Balance, sharpening, color mode, saturation, and hue will be copied from the image selected as [Image 1]. The shooting data is also copied from [Image 1]. Image Overlays saved as NEF (RAW) files use the same compression and bit depth as the original files; overlays saved as JPEG files utilize size-priority compression.

This item can be used to create JPEG format copies of pictures saved and stored on the installed memory card at an image quality of NEF (RAW) or NEF (RAW) + JPEG. To use **[NEF (RAW) processing]**:

1. Highlight **[NEF (RAW) processing]** in the Retouch menu and press ▶.
2. Select the required NEF (RAW) picture from the displayed thumbnail pictures by pressing the Multi Selector; note, only NEF (RAW) pictures will be displayed. Press ⊛ to select the highlighted picture.
3. A preview image is now displayed next to a menu of options:
    a. **[Image quality]**: Choose image quality from JPEG Fine, JPEG Normal, or JPEG Basic.
    b. **[Image size]**: Choose image size from Large, Medium, or Small.
    c. **[White balance]**: Choose White Balance settings, specify fluorescent lighting type, and apply White Balance Fine-Tuning. (Photographs taken at a White Balance of Preset Manual can only be subjected to Fine-Tuning from the Preset Manual White Balance option, and the **[Preset manual]** sub-option is only available for pictures taken at this White Balance setting.)
    d. **[Exposure compensation]**: Adjust the exposure level ±2 EV.
    e. **[Set Picture Control]**: Choose a Picture Control option.
4. Highlight the required option and press ▶. Select the required setting and press ⊛ to return to the preview image and menu display. Repeat the selection process for any other options to be used.
5. Once all settings have been adjusted, highlight EXE.
6. Press ⊛ to create and save a JPEG format copy and return to full-frame Playback.
7. Press the MENU button to return to full-frame Playback without creating a JPEG copy image.

NOTE: The Exposure Compensation option should be treated with caution, as the ±2 EV range is overly optimistic. The extended dynamic range of NEF (RAW) files recorded by the D3100 does permit some adjustment to the exposure level, but only across a far more limited range if image quality is to be preserved. I would suggest that ±1.7 EV is the practical limit of adjustment using this option, and preferably lower. To maximize image quality, the original exposure should be as accurate as possible.

NOTE: The Exposure Compensation option cannot be selected if the original picture was taken with Active D-Lighting.

NOTE: The [White balance] option cannot be selected for a copy image created using the [Image overlay] feature. Preset Manual White Balance is only available if the original image was recorded using the Preset Manual White Balance.

NOTE: [White balance] and [Set Picture Control] options are not available for images recorded using the 🔲 mode or any Scene mode.

📷 QUICK RETOUCH

This item can be used to make a rapid enhancement to color saturation and contrast; the D3100 will apply D-Lighting accordingly to increase the brightness of strongly backlit subjects. Select an image as described above and press ⓞ to display the image, alongside a preview of the adjusted image. Use ▲ or ▼ to select one of three values: [Low], [Normal], or [High]. Press and hold ⊕ to view the preview image full-frame, and press ⓞ to make the copy image. To return to the normal full-frame Playback, press the ▶ button.

HINT: This is about as "quick and dirty" as it gets as far as image adjustment goes; this item should only be considered when the need to expedite an image with adjusted color saturation and contrast is immediate and imperative!

📷 STRAIGHTEN

If you shoot a picture and then find that it is not aligned as it should be—for example, a horizon line slopes to one side—this item can be used to straighten the image. The image can be rotated by up to 5°, in steps of approximately 0.25°, by pressing ▶ to turn the image clockwise, or ◀ to turn the image counterclockwise. A pattern of gridlines is displayed on the monitor screen to assist in aligning the image. The edge of the image will be trimmed to produce a square copy. Press ⓞ to create the copy image. To return to full-frame Playback without copying the image, press the ▶ button.

⊕ DISTORTION CONTROL

Optical distortion from a lens can cause straight lines close to the edge of the frame to appear bowed. Typically, wide-angle lenses produce barrel distortion that causes lines to bend outward away from the center of the image, while telephoto lenses cause pincushion distortion that causes lines to bend inward toward the center of the image. This item corrects for such optical distortion. The **[Auto]** option applies correction automatically, and then the user can refine the correction using the Multi Selector. Alternatively, you can select the **[Manual]** option and press ▶ to reduce barrel distortion or ◀ to reduce pincushion distortion. The greater the degree of correction the more the peripheral area of the original frame will be cropped. Press ⊛ to copy the picture and save the adjustments. To return to normal full-frame Playback without copying the image, press the ▶ button.

NOTE: The **[Auto]** option is not available if the **[Auto distortion control]** item in the Shooting menu is set to **[On]**.

⊞ FISHEYE

This item modifies an image to emulate the appearance of a picture taken using a fisheye lens. This type of lens is not corrected to render straight lines as straight but, instead, with an increasing amount of distortion the further the line is from the center of the frame. Select **[Fisheye]** and press ▶ to display the thumbnail images. Select the required image and press ⊛. Press ▶ to increase the (barrel) distortion or ◀ to reduce the effect. Be aware that greater distortion will result in more of the image being cropped at the edges. Press ⊛ to copy the retouched picture. To return to normal full-frame Playback without copying the image, press the ▶ button.

⊗ COLOR OUTLINE

This item converts a conventional color picture into an outline image that can be used as a starting point for a drawing or painting. Select **[Color outline]** and press ▶ to display the thumbnail images. Select the required image and press ⊛. The image is displayed as a monochrome line drawing. Press ⊛ to save the effect and copy the image. To cancel the process, press the ▶ button.

▲ *PERSPECTIVE CONTROL*

This item is used to correct the perspective of an image: for example, the converging vertical lines that occur when shooting a picture of a tall building with the camera tilted upward. Select **[Perspective control]** and press ▶ to display the thumbnail images. Select the required image and press ⓘ. Use the Multi Selector to adjust the image as required, using the scales displayed along the bottom and left side of the LCD monitor screen as a guide. Press ⓘ to save the adjusted copy image. To cancel the process, press the ▣ button.

▒ *MINIATURE EFFECT*

This option is intended to emulate the effect of using a Nikkor PC-E Tilt / Shift lens when shooting pictures with a tilt movement applied. By altering the focus characteristics by reducing the depth of field to a very narrow region, it creates an effect as though the viewer is looking at a model of the scene. For the best results, shoot pictures to be converted with this item from a high vantage point.

1. Select **[Miniature effect]** and press ▶ to display the thumbnail images.
2. Select the required image and press ⓘ. The image is displayed full-frame with a narrow oblong box marked with a yellow outline.
3. If the picture is in a horizontal (wide) format, press ▲ and ▼ to determine the area of focus (the area confined within the yellow box).
4. Press ◀ and ▶ to position the area of focus if the picture is in a vertical (tall) format.
5. Press and hold ⊕ to view the preview image full-frame.
6. Press ⓘ to save the copy image.
7. To cancel the process, press the ▣ button.

EDIT MOVIE

This item allows you to trim video clips recorded in the D-Movie mode or to save a selected frame from a video clip as a JPEG file picture.

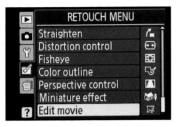

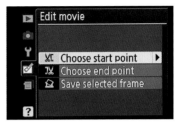

ʌ The **[Edit movie]** item, shown highlighted in the Setup menu, can only be used with files created through the D-movie mode.

ʌ When you select **[Edit movie]** from the Retouch menu, you will see the options shown above.

To trim a movie clip from the Retouch menu, choosing where it will begin:

1. Select **[Edit movie]** and press ▶ to display the options.
2. Select **[Choose start point]** and press ▶ to display a thumbnail of the movie clips stored on the memory card.
3. Select the required movie clip and press ⊗. The clip will begin to play back.
4. Press ▲ to pause the clip and display **[Proceed]**.
5. Select **[Yes]** to delete all frames prior to the displayed frame and save a new trimmed copy of the video clip, starting at the point selected.

To trim a movie clip from the Retouch menu, choosing where it will end:

1. Select **[Edit movie]** and press ▶ to display the options.
2. Select **[Choose end point]** and press ▶ to display a thumbnail of the movie clips stored on the memory card.
3. Select the required movie clip and press ⊗. The clip will begin to play back.
4. Press ▲ to pause the clip and display **[Proceed]**.
5. Select **[Yes]** to delete all frames after the displayed frame and save a new trimmed copy of the video clip, ending at the selected point.

To select an individual frame and save it as a JPEG picture through the Retouch menu:

1. Select **[Edit movie]** and then press ▶ to display the options.
2. Select **[Save selected frame]** and press ▶ to display a thumbnail of the movie clips stored on the memory card.
3. Select the required movie clip and press ⊛.
4. Press ⊛ again and the clip will begin to play back. Press ▼ to pause the playback.
5. To save the currently displayed frame, press ▲.
6. Highlight and press ⊛ to create a JPEG picture.

Alternatively, it is possible to edit a movie clip directly from full-frame Playback:

1. Display the movie clip full-frame on the monitor screen by pressing the ▶ button, and by pressing ◀ or ▶.
2. Play the movie clip back by pressing ⊛. Use the ⊛ button to start and resume playback and press ▼ to pause the playback. To trim the opening section of the movie clip, pause on the first frame you wish to retain, alternatively to trim the end of the movie clip, pause on the last frame you wish to retain.
3. Press the **AE-L/AF-L** button to display the **[Edit movie]** item from the Retouch menu.
4. To create a copy that includes the current frame and all subsequent frames, highlight **[Choose start point]** and press ⊛. To create a copy that includes the current frame and all preceding frames, select **[Choose end point]** and press ⊛.
5. Press ▲ to delete all frames before or after the current frame (for **[Choose start point]** or **[Choose end point]**, respectively).
6. Highlight **[Yes]** and press ⊛ to save the edited copy.

The saved copy can be trimmed further by repeating the movie-editing process through either method.

NOTE: A movie clip must be at least 2 seconds long to be edited.

Use this item to compare a retouched copy with the original (source) file, as follows:

1. Select either a picture that has been retouched or a retouched copy (indicated by the ☑ icon) during full-frame Playback for **[Before and after]**.

2. Press ⊛ to display the original source image to the left and the retouched copy on the right. The options used to create the copy are displayed above the two images.

3. Use ◄ and ► to switch between the two images; the selected version is shown with a yellow border.

4. Press and hold 🔍 to view an enlarged view of the selected image.

5. If the image was created using the **[Image overlay]** option, use ▲ and ▼ to view the second source image.

6. Press the ▶ button to return to the Playback mode.

7. To return to Playback mode with the selected image displayed, press ⊛.

NOTE: There must be at least one retouched image or retouched copy file stored on the selected memory card for the **[Before and after]** item to be available in the Retouch menu.

NOTE: The **[Before and after]** item can only be accessed when the Retouch menu is accessed by pressing ⊛ during full-frame Playback.

🗐 *RECENT SETTINGS*

The Recent Settings menu combines the most recently used items from the other four menus into one easily accessible list; up to a maximum of 20 menu items will be displayed. As different menu items are used, they will be added automatically to the top of the Recent Settings menu list in the chronological order in which they were selected and used.

To display the Recent Settings menu, press MENU and select 🗐 from the tabs displayed along the left of the monitor screen. To scroll through these items, use ▲ and ▼, and use ⊛ to select the highlighted item. To remove an item from the Recent Settings menu, highlight it and press 🗑. A confirmation dialog box will be displayed; press 🗑 again to delete the item.

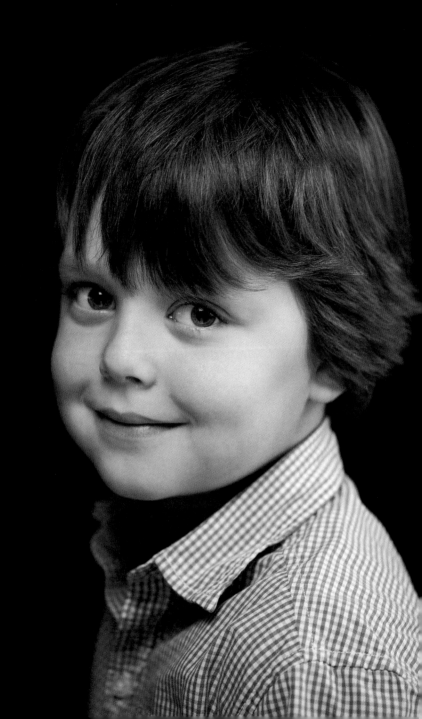

Nikon Flash Photography

Before we take a look at the flash capabilities of the D3100, it is helpful to understand some basics about the physics of light and flash exposure. One of the most important principles that influences flash exposure is the Inverse Square Law. It states that light from a point light source, such as a flash unit, falls off as it travels over a distance by the inverse of the square of that distance. Put simply, if you double the distance from a light source, its intensity drops by a factor of four because as light travels from the source it spreads out illuminating a wider area. So, at double the distance from the source, light covers four times the area. At four times the distance, the light covers sixteen times the area, so its intensity is reduced to one sixteenth of its intensity at the original distance.

Besides being aware of the Inverse Square Law, it is also essential to appreciate how exposure of light from a flash unit is influenced by the ISO sensitivity, lens aperture, and shutter speed controls of a camera. Just as when exposing for ambient light, the amount of light required for exposure from a flash occurs in direct proportion to the ISO setting on a camera. So, if the ISO value is doubled, the amount of light required from the flash to maintain the same flash exposure level (assuming no other factors change) is halved; conversely, if the ISO value is halved, the flash output must be doubled to maintain the same flash exposure level. Equally, altering the lens aperture, which controls how much light passes through the camera lens, has the same effect on flash exposure as altering the ISO level. So, if the aperture is changed from f/8 to f/5.6, to allow twice as much light to pass through the lens, the flash only needs to output half as much light to maintain the same flash exposure level (again, assuming no other factors are altered). If the lens aperture is changed from f/8 to f/11, to allow only half as much light to pass through the lens, the flash output must be doubled to maintain the same flash exposure level.

The intensity of the light produced by an electronic flash unit is always the same; therefore, the flash exposure is controlled by the duration of the flash output. At its maximum output of light, the duration of the flash pulse from a modern Nikon Speedlight flash unit is typically about 1/1000 of a second; as the amount of light output from the flash is reduced from its maximum level, the duration of the flash pulse becomes even briefer. Yet, the fastest flash synchronization (sync) speed of the D3100 is 1/200 second—the briefest shutter speed at which the opening and closing of the shutter allows the light from the flash to be recorded fully by the camera. Therefore, provided the shutter speed is set to either the flash sync speed or a slower (longer) shutter speed, it has no effect on the flash exposure. The only time the shutter speed is of any consequence when shooting with flash is if ambient light is also being recorded as part of the overall exposure. In this case, the ambient light exposure will be influenced by the shutter speed, but it still has no effect on the flash exposure.

Because a flash unit emits a precise, fixed amount of light (based principally on the flash-to-subject distance, ISO setting, and lens aperture) the light from the flash will only illuminate the subject properly at a specific distance. Therefore, any element in the scene closer to the flash than the subject will be overexposed and anything farther away will be underexposed. The degree of over- or underexposure will depend on how much closer or farther away the element is in relation to the flash unit, since the intensity of the light will be determined by the effect of the Inverse Square Law described previously.

Finally, the output of an electronic flash unit, often referred to as its power, is quantified by a value known as its guide number (GN); the higher the guide number, the more powerful the flash unit. Guide numbers are quoted as a distance (feet or meters) for a given ISO level and angle of view (usually expressed as a lens focal length). For example, the built-in Speedlight of the D3100 has a GN of 39 feet (12 m) at ISO 100, 18mm. When comparing guide numbers, make sure that the same units are used for linear measurement, ISO value, and focal length (see the section, "Manual Flash Exposure Control" on pages 246-247 for details on how to use the GN value to calculate flash output manually).

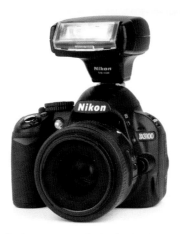

^ The D3100 with Nikon's most compact flash unit, the Nikon SB-400 Speedlight. Its flash head can be tilted for bounce flash (but not rotated) making it more versatile than the built-in flash.

THE CREATIVE LIGHTING SYSTEM

The most sophisticated method of Flash Exposure Control developed by Nikon to date is the Nikon Creative Lighting System (CLS). This system is far more refined than the fundamental principles on which Flash Exposure Control was originally based; it encompasses a range of features and functions that are as much a part of the cameras themselves, as the Speedlights. Features include: intelligent through-the-lens (i-TTL) Flash Exposure Control, the Advanced Wireless Lighting (AWL) system that provides wireless control of multiple Speedlights using i-TTL, Flash Value (FV) Lock, Flash Color Information Communication, Auto FP High-Speed Sync, and Wide-area AF-Assist to improve autofocus accuracy with cameras such as the D300s, which have multiple AF points covering a large part of the frame area. Currently, CLS compatibility encompasses the D3100, together with the D3-series, D2-series, D700, D300-series, D200, D90, D5000, D3000, D80, D70-series, D60, D50, D40-series, and

F6 cameras, including the internal Speedlight units of those models that possess them. The CLS includes the following external Nikon Speedlights: SB-900, SB-800, SB-700, SB-600, SB-400, and SB-R200. However, some of the listed camera models do not support all the features of the CLS.

The Auto FP High-Speed Sync and FV Lock features are not available with the D3100 when used with either its built-in Speedlight or an external CLS compatible Speedlight. Furthermore, its built-in Speedlight does not have a Commander mode for remote control of compatible Speedlights using the AWL system, and there is no Repeating Flash mode (although this feature is supported with compatible external Speedlights).

TTL FLASH MODES

When used in combination with a CPU-type lens, the D3100 supports two methods of TTL-controlled flash exposure with its built-in flash unit or a compatible external Speedlight. To select TTL flash control for the built-in Speedlight. When shooting in the P, S, A, or M exposure modes (TTL flash control is always used in any other exposure mode), open the Shooting menu and navigate to the [Built-in flash] item and press ▶. Highlight [TTL] and press ⊛. When using an external Speedlight, the flash mode is selected via the controls of the Speedlight.

i-TTL BALANCED FILL-FLASH

This is Nikon's third generation of TTL Flash Exposure Control—the most sophisticated to date. When the D3100 is set to Matrix metering, a D- or G-type Nikkor lens is mounted on the cameras, and the built-in Speedlight (or an external Speedlight such as the SB-600, SB-800, or SB-900) is activated, i-TTL Balanced Fill-Flash will attempt to balance the ambient light to the flash output.

It is important to note that whenever you see the term "i-TTL Balanced Fill-Flash," existing ambient light and flash are being mixed in a fully automated process to produce the final exposure. How the two light sources are mixed and in what proportion will depend on a wide variety of factors, including ISO sensitivity, lens aperture, exposure mode, Exposure Compensation value, brightness of both the ambient and flash illumination, and the nature of the scene being photographed.

Fill Flash is a recognized lighting technique in which the flash is used to supplement the main ambient light source. The level of illumination provided by the flash is generally weaker than the ambient light; its purpose is to provide a small amount of additional light in the shadows and other under-lit areas of a scene to help reduce the overall level of contrast. Many photographers also use this technique when shooting portraits to put a small catch light in their subject's eyes.

When the camera is in Manual exposure mode (M), only the flash exposure is determined by the i-TTL system. However, when i-TTL is used with any of the D3100's automated exposure modes, the camera has full control of the exposure for both the ambient light and flash output. It assesses the flash output level and the ambient light in an attempt to

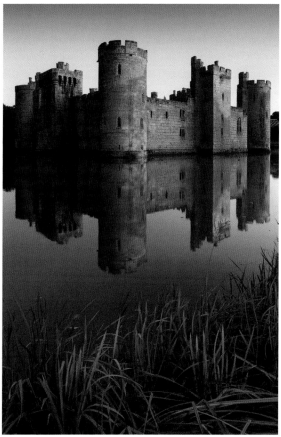

> It may not seem an obvious situation to use flash, but the grass in the foreground was in deep shade, so some fill-flash was used to add light to this area of the picture.

create a balanced exposure using both light sources. To achieve this, the D3100 will often adjust the exposure for either the ambient light or the flash output, and sometimes both.

Consequently, any compensation applied by the user to adjust either the ambient light exposure or flash output lLevel is frequently overridden (or even ignored). This often results in a picture with too much flash exposure, spoiling the Fill-Flash effect. The lack of user control also makes it difficult to achieve consistent, repeatable results.

STANDARD i-TTL FLASH

This flash mode differs from the i-TTL Balanced Fill-Flash mode in that the measurement of ambient light in the scene remains wholly independent of the flash output control, and is not integrated in any way with the flash exposure calculations.

So, if you want to achieve consistent, repeatable results when using a true Fill-Flash technique—where the flash is the supplementary light—I recommend that you use standard i-TTL flash. This is because any Flash Output Compensation or Exposure Compensation you have set will be applied without influence from the camera. Likewise, in any situation where you wish to use flash as the main source of illumination and have control over the flash output level, as well as the exposure of ambient light, I also suggest you select standard i-TTL flash.

The i-TTL Balanced Fill-Flash is the default Flash Exposure Control method for the built-in flash unit of the D3100. The only way to override this is to set the camera to Spot metering, which causes the camera to use Standard i-TTL Flash control. When using the Nikon SB-400, SB-600, SB-700, SB-800 and SB-900 Speedlights the Flash Exposure Control method is selected directly on the flash unit; but if you set the D3100 to Spot metering, the camera will override this selection and always use standard i-TTL flash control.

i-TTL FLASH EXPOSURE CONTROL

i-TTL offers an enhanced and refined method of Flash Exposure Control. Currently, the SB-900, SB-800, SB-700, SB-600, SB-400, and SB-R200 are the only external Speedlights that support i-TTL and the CLS, while the SU-800 Wireless Speedlight Commander can be used to control any of these units with the exception of the SB-400. If any other external

Nikon Speedlight is attached to the D3100, TTL Flash Exposure Control is not supported; this applies to all earlier Speedlights, even DX-types, designed for earlier Nikon DSLR cameras. The i-TTL system works in the following way with the D3100:

○ i-TTL uses fewer monitor pre-flashes than other systems, but they have a higher intensity. This greater intensity improves the efficiency of obtaining a measurement from the TTL flash sensor. By using fewer pulses, the amount of time taken to perform the assessment is reduced, which enables the camera to perform this process before lifting the reflex mirror.

○ The D3100 uses its 420-pixel RGB metering sensor located in the prism head for TTL control of flash exposure, regardless of whether the camera is used with its built-in Speedlight, a single external Speedlight, or multiple Speedlights controlled via an SU-800 wireless Speedlight commander in the AWL system. In all cases, monitor pre-flashes are always emitted before the reflex mirror is raised.

○ The i-TTL system of the D3100 is designed to work with ISO sensitivities between 100 and 3200; at the Hi 1 (ISO 6400) and Hi 2 (ISO 12,800) settings, Flash Exposure Control may be less accurate.

The following is a summary of the sequence of events used to calculate flash exposure by the D3100 when it is used with the built-in Speedlight, or external CLS Speedlights, and a D- or G-type Nikkor lens:

1. Once the shutter release is pressed, the camera reads the focus distance from the D- or G-type lens.
2. The camera sends a signal to the Speedlight to initiate the pre-flash system, which then emits the monitor pre-flashes (pulses of light) from the Speedlight(s).
3. The light from these pre-flashes is bounced back from the scene, through the lens and onto the 420-pixel RGB metering sensor (via the reflex mirror).
4. The information from the pre-flashes gathered by the 420-pixel RGB metering sensor is analyzed, along with measurements of the ambient light in the scene and information supplied by the focusing system. The camera then determines the amount of light required from the Speedlight(s) and sets the duration of the flash discharge accordingly.
5. The reflex mirror lifts up, out of the light path to the shutter, and the shutter opens.

6. The camera sends a signal to the Speedlight(s) to initiate the main flash discharge, which is quenched the instant the amount of light pre-determined in Step 4 has been emitted.

7. The shutter closes at the end of the predetermined shutter speed duration, and the reflex mirror is lowered to its normal position.

NOTE: In the D3100, the emission of the monitor pre-flashes occurs before the reflex mirror is raised. Thus, there is a slight chance that during the short delay between the mirror being raised and the shutter opening, the light from the pre-flash may cause the subject to blink.

FLASH OUTPUT ASSESSMENT

The most crucial phase in the sequence described above is step 4, which is the point when the required output from the flash is calculated. As stated previously, this is accomplished using the 420-pixel RGB metering sensor that is positioned in the viewfinder head of the D3100. The ability of this sensor is enhanced by the Scene Recognition System (SRS), which made its debut in the original D300 in mid-2007. A diffraction grating located immediately in front of the metering sensor separates the light falling on it, from both the reflected monitor pre-flash illumination and the ambient light, into its component colors. This enables the sensor to recognize shapes and objects by the distribution of color and contrast, enabling it to work more effectively and efficiently. The Scene Recognition System only operates with Matrix metering and is particularly sensitive to skin tones; however, if Center-Weighted or Spot metering is selected, the D3100 uses a simple grayscale metering system—in other words, it is not sensitive to color.

When Matrix metering is used, this evaluation of the shape and color of elements in the scene is performed together with conventional assessments of the overall levels of brightness and the level of contrast. This information is then combined with information from the autofocus (AF) system. The camera assesses the brightness of each of the 420-pixels on the RGB metering sensor, and then compares them relative to each other to establish scene contrast while it looks for patterns. For example, a distribution of bright pixels in the upper part of a frame and darker pixels in the lower part may be indicating a light sky above the subject area. The metering system assumes the subject is covered by the active AF point(s); by checking which AF point(s) report focus, it can determine the location of the subject within the frame. Provided a D- or G-type Nikkor lens, or a third-party lens that supports communication of focus distance, is mounted on the camera, the metering system will also integrate the approximate subject distance into the calculations for flash output.

Once the camera has collected all the information pertaining to the shapes, colors, brightness, and range of contrast in the scene, it compares these values against brightness pattern information from actual photographs held in a stored database of over 30,000 sample exposures, covering an enormous range of lighting conditions. If the first comparison generates an evaluation that conflicts with the stored exposure data, the pattern of pixels may be re-assessed and then a further analysis performed. For example, if any group of pixels reports an abnormally high level of brightness in comparison to the others on the sensor, the metering system will usually ignore this information in its flash exposure calculations. This can occur if there is a highly reflective surface, such as glass or water in a part of the scene; this could result in a bright reflection of the light from the flash that would otherwise cause the metering system to underexpose the picture.

FOCUS INFORMATION

As described above, when using Matrix metering and a D- or G-type Nikkor lens, focus information is provided to the metering system in two forms: camera-to-subject distance and the level of focus/defocus at each AF point. The basic strategy of the Matrix metering system is to optimize flash output while avoiding overexposure; therefore, in most cases, the focus distance information will influence which pixels of the RGB metering sensor affect ambient exposure and flash output calculations. For example, if the subject is positioned in the center of the frame and the lens is focused at a middle to long distance, the camera will assess all the pixels on the sensor but place slightly more emphasis on those at the center of the frame. In this situation, if flash is the main source of illumination and the background is much further away from the flash than the subject, it is likely to result in a typical "party picture" where the subject is well lit by the flash but set against a completely black background (due to flash fall-off). Conversely, assuming the subject is positioned in the center of the frame, the lens is focused at a short distance, and the level of illumination is fairly even across the frame area, the camera will generally place slightly more emphasis on those pixels that cover the outer part of the frame area and slightly less on the central ones as it attempts to prevent loss of highlight detail in the subject. However, an exception to this occurs if the camera detects a very high level of contrast between the central and outer areas of the frame; in this situation, the metering system commonly reverses the emphasis and weights the exposure calculations according to the information received from pixels at the center of the frame area to ensure exposure accuracy in this region.

Essentially, what the camera is trying to do in both cases just described is prevent overexposure of the subject. As each AF point is checked for its degree of focus, individual focus point information is integrated with focus distance information. This provides the camera with information about the probable location of the subject within the area of the scene. Using the examples given in the previous paragraph, the metering system knows that the central AF point has acquired focus while the other AF points each report varying levels of defocus. Therefore, exposure is calculated on the assumption that the subject is in the center of the frame, and the camera biases its computations according to the focus distance information it receives from the lens.

However, it is important to understand that other twists occur in this story of interaction between exposure calculation and focus information. For example, when you acquire and lock focus on a subject using the center AF point and then recompose the shot so that the subject is located elsewhere in the frame, the camera will generally use the exposure value it calculated when it first acquired focus. However, if it assesses that the level of brightness detected by the pixels at the center of the frame has changed significantly from the level when focus was first acquired, the camera can and often does adjust its flash exposure calculations—sometimes not necessarily for the better. Unfortunately the D3100 lacks the Flash Value (FV) Lock feature of more sophisticated Nikon camera models, so it may be necessary to apply a Flash Output Compensation to help improve flash exposure accuracy in such situations.

NOTE: A D- or G-type Nikkor lens, or a third party lens with equivalent specification, must be mounted on the camera for the focus distance information to be accurately assessed.

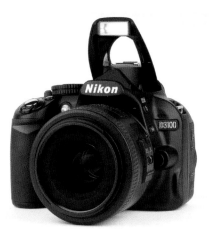

^ The D3100's small, built-in Speedlight can be useful as a fill-flash, but its proximity to the lens axis and fixed position limit it as a main light source.

THE BUILT-IN SPEEDLIGHT

The D3100's built-in Speedlight has an automatic flash Guide Number of 39 feet (12 m) at ISO 100, 68°F (20°C), and 43 feet (13 m) for manual flash. The camera's maximum flash synchronization speed in all exposure modes is 1/200 second, regardless of the type of Speedlight that is used; unlike some more sophisticated models, the D3100 does not support the Auto FP high-speed flash sync feature of the CLS. To prevent errors, the D3100 will not allow a shutter speed above 1/200 second to be set when either the built-in Speedlight or an external Speedlight is being used.

The subject must be further from the camera than the minimum flash range of 2 feet (0.6 m); the camera may not calculate a correct flash exposure at shorter distances. If the camera is set to one of the automatic Scene modes that support use of flash and the meter determines that flash is needed, the built-in Speedlight will pop up automatically. In P, S, A, and M exposure modes, it must be activated manually by pressing the 🗲 Flash mode button that is located immediately below the 🔳 Flash Exposure Compensation icon on the lower left side of the viewfinder head.

The built-in Speedlight draws its power from the camera's main battery—extended use of the flash will have a direct effect on battery life.

As soon as the flash unit pops up, it begins to charge. The flash-ready symbol ⚡ appears in the viewfinder to indicate charging is complete and the flash is ready to fire. If the flash fires at its maximum output, the same flash-ready symbol will blink for approximately three seconds after the exposure has been made. This indicates the flash is not yet ready for another exposure, warning of the potential for underexposure. The flash-ready symbol operates in exactly the same way when using an external Speedlight.

> The ⚡ Flash mode button for the built-in flash can be seen toward the top of this picture. It is located just below the flash housing, to the right-hand side of the lens mount (if you're holding the camera upright and looking at the front of it).

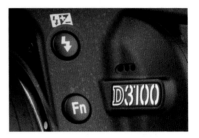

RANGE, APERTURE, AND ISO SENSITIVITY

The built-in flash unit's shooting range will vary depending on the values set for the lens aperture and ISO sensitivity:

LENS APERTURE AT ISO						RANGE	
100	200	400	800	1600	3200	METERS	FEET
1.4	2	2.8	4	5.6	8	1.0 – 8.5	3.25 – 27.92
2	2.8	4	5.6	8	11	0.7 – 6.0	2.33 – 19 .66
2.8	4	5.6	8	11	16	0.6 – 4.2	2 – 13.75
4	5.6	8	11	16	22	0.6 – 3.0	2 – 9.83
5.6	8	11	16	22	22	0.6 – 2.1	2 – 6.92
8	11	16	22	32	-	0.6 – 1.5	2 – 4.92
11	16	22	32	-	-	0.6 – 1.1	2 – 3.58
16	22	32	-	-	-	0.6 – 0.7	2 – 2.33

LIMITATIONS

While the built-in Speedlight of the D3100 is not as powerful as an external Speedlight, it can still provide a useful level of illumination at short ranges, especially for the purpose of fill flash, since it supports

Flash Output Compensation. However, if you want to use the built-in Speedlight as the main light source, you should be aware of the following:

- O The Guide Number (GN) is limited, thus flash shooting ranges are relatively short (see table on the previous page).
- O The proximity of the flash head is much closer to the central lens axis when compared to an external flash; hence, the likelihood of red-eye occurring is significantly increased.
- O This close proximity of the built-in Speedlight to the central lens axis often means that the lens obscures the output of the flash, especially if a lens hood is in place. For example, the obstruction of the light from the flash may cause a shadow to appear on the bottom edge of the picture if the camera is held in a horizontal orientation.
- O The angle of coverage achieved by the built-in Speedlight is limited and only extends to cover the field-of-view of a lens with a focal length of 18mm or more. If used with a shorter focal length lens, the flash will not be able to illuminate the periphery of the frame and these areas will appear underexposed. Even at the widest limit of coverage, it is not uncommon to see a noticeable fall-off of illumination (vignetting) in the corners of the frame.
- O The built-in Speedlight draws its power from the camera's battery, so extended use will exhaust it quite quickly.

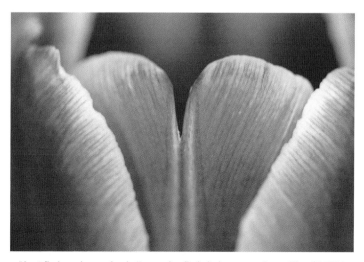

^ Direct flash can be very harsh. Here, a ring flash device was used on a Nikon SB-700 to produce a softer, shadowless light.

The built-in flash can be used with CPU lenses (i.e., all AF and Ai-P types) with focal lengths between 18mm and 300mm. Regardless of the lens, the built-in flash has a minimum range of 2 feet (0.6 m) making it impossible to use with the close focus distances of macro lenses. Furthermore, it is not possible to use the built-in Speedlight with the AF-S 14–24mm f/2.8G ED—light is obscured regardless of the focal length with this lens. The built-in flash may be unable to illuminate the entire frame area evenly when using the following lenses at focus distances less than those given in the following table:

LENS	ZOOM POSITION	MINIMUM DISTANCE WITHOUT VIGNETTING
AF-S DX Nikkor 10–24mm f/3.5–4.5G ED	24 mm	2.5 m / 8.2 ft.
AF-S DX Zoom-Nikkor 12–24mm f/4G IF-ED	20 mm	3 m / 9.8 ft.
	24 mm	1 m / 3.25 ft.
AF-S 16–35mm f/4G VR	28 mm	1.5 m / 4.9 ft.
	35 mm	1 m / 3.25 ft.
AF-S DX Nikkor 16–85mm f/3.5–5.6G ED VR	24–85 mm	No vignetting
AF-S Zoom-Nikkor 17–35mm f/2.8D IF-ED	24 mm	2 m / 6.6 ft.
	28 mm	1 m / 3.25 ft.
	35 mm	No vignetting
AF-S DX Zoom-Nikkor 17–55mm f/2.8G IF-ED	28 mm	1.5 m / 4.9 ft.
	35 mm	1 m / 3.25 ft.
	45–55 mm	No vignetting
AF Zoom-Nikkor 18–35mm f/3.5–4.5D IF-ED	24 mm	1 m / 3.25 ft.
	28–35 mm	No vignetting
AF-S DX Zoom-Nikkor 18–70mm f/3.5–4.5G IF-ED	18 mm	1 m / 3.25 ft.
	24–70 mm	No vignetting
AF-S DX NIKKOR 18–105mm f/3.5–5.6G ED VR	18 mm	2.5 m / 8.2 ft.
	24 mm	1 m / 3.25 ft.
AF-S DX Zoom-Nikkor 18–135mm f/3.5–5.6G IF-ED	18 mm	1 m / 3.25 ft.
	24–135 mm	No vignetting
AF-S DX VR Zoom-Nikkor 18–200mm f/3.5–5.6G IF-ED	24 mm	1 m / 3.25 ft.
AF-S DX NIKKOR 18–200mm f/3.5–5.6G ED VR II	35–200 mm	No vignetting

LENS	ZOOM POSITION	MINIMUM DISTANCE WITHOUT VIGNETTING
AF Zoom-Nikkor 20–35mm f/2.8D IF	24 mm	2.5 m / 8.2 ft.
	28 mm	1 m / 3.25 ft.
	35 mm	No vignetting
AF-S NIKKOR 24mm f/1.4G ED	24 mm	1 m / 3.25 ft.
AF-S NIKKOR 24–70mm f/2.8G ED	35 mm	1.5 m / 4.9 ft.
	50 mm	1 m / 3.25 ft.
	70 mm	No vignetting
AF-S VR Zoom-Nikkor 24–120mm f/3.5–5.6G IF-ED	24 mm	1 m / 3.25 ft.
	28–120 mm	No vignetting
AF-S NIKKOR 24–120mm f/4G ED VR	24 mm	2.5 m / 8.2 ft.
AF-S NIKKOR 28–300mm f/3.5–5.6G ED VR	28 mm	1.5 m / 4.9 ft.
	35 mm	1 m / 3.25 ft.
AF-S Zoom-Nikkor 28–70mm f/2.8D IF-ED	35 mm	1.5 m / 4.9 ft.
	50–70 mm	No vignetting
AF-S VR Zoom-Nikkor 200–400mm f/4G IF-ED	250 mm	2.5 m / 8.2 ft.
	350 mm	2 m / 6.6 ft.
AF-S NIKKOR 200–400mm f/4G ED VR II	200 mm	5 m / 16.4 ft.
	250 mm	3 m / 9.8 ft.
	300 mm	2.5 m / 8.2 ft.
	350–400 mm	No vignetting
PC-E NIKKOR 24mm f/3.5 ED *	24 mm	3 m / 9.8 ft.

* When not shifted or tilted.

HINT: Always remember to remove the lens hood to prevent the flash's light from being obscured and causing a shadow.

FLASH SYNCHRONIZATION

Flash Synchronization (sync) modes determine when the flash is fired in relation to the opening and closing of the shutter, and should not be confused with the Flash Exposure Control modes described earlier (i.e., i-TTL Balanced Fill-Flash, Standard i-TTL Flash, or Manual Flash). The availability of a particular Flash Sync mode will depend on the exposure mode selected via the Mode dial. In turn, the choice of Flash Sync mode will influence the range of available shutter speeds (see the Shutter Speed Restrictions chart on page 241).

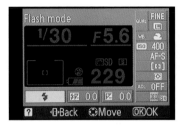

^ The flash mode can be accessed via the Information Display, as shown here.

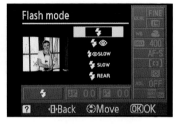

^ The available flash modes for the selected exposure mode are listed beside example pictures.

To set a Flash Sync mode on the D3100, press the 🔳 button to activate the Shooting Information display on the monitor, and then press the 🔧 button to place the cursor in the shooting information. Use the Multi Selector to highlight the flash mode in the Shooting Information display, and then press the ⊛ button. Use ▲ and ▼ to highlight the required flash mode and press ⊛ to select it. The options available are as follows when using the 🔅, 🔆, 🔆, and ♣ Modes:

- o ⚡ Auto Flash: The built-in flash will pop up automatically if the camera determines that the ambient light level is low or the subject is strongly backlit.

- o ⚡👁 Auto Flash with Red-Eye Reduction: This operates in the same way as Auto flash, except the Red-Eye Reduction lamp will illuminate briefly before the flash fires. When using the built-in flash, the Red-Eye Reduction lamp lights for approximately one second before the main flash output; with an external Speedlight, a short series of low-intensity light pulses are emitted before the main output. The purpose is to try to induce the pupils in the subject's eye to constrict, thus reducing the risk of red-eye.

- o ⊕ Flash Off: Operation of the flash unit is cancelled regardless of the prevailing light conditions.

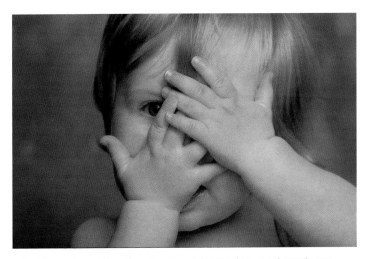

^ Flash is a useful tool that allows the photographer complete control over the way a subject is lit. Here, light from a Nikon SB-700 was bounced off a white reflector to produce a soft, broad light.

HINT: This mode not only alerts your subject that you are about to take a picture, but it also causes a delay in the shutter's operation, by which time you may have missed the shot! Personally, I never bother with this feature. Red-eye can easily be removed in post-processing.

Using ▣ Mode:

- ○ ⚡👁AUTO/SLOW Auto Flash with Slow Sync and Red-Eye Reduction: This operates in the same way as Auto flash with Slow Sync, except the Red-Eye Reduction lamp will illuminate briefly before the flash fires.

- ○ ⚡AUTO/SLOW Auto Flash with Slow Sync: The built-in flash pops up automatically when the camera detects low light. This option differs from ⚡ flash, because it offers an extended range of shutter speeds between 1/200 and 1 second to enable the camera to record the ambient light.

- ○ ⚘ Flash Off: Operation of the flash unit is cancelled regardless of the prevailing light conditions.

Using P and A Modes:

○ 🔆 Fill Flash: The built-in flash will pop up only if the 🔆 button is pressed. The flash fires as soon as the shutter has opened.

○ 🔆👁 Fill Flash with Red-Eye Reduction: This operates in the same way as Fill Flash, except the Red-Eye Reduction lamp will illuminate briefly before the flash fires.

○ 🔆👁SLOW Slow Sync with Red-Eye Reduction: This operates in the same way as Slow Sync flash, except the Red-Eye Reduction lamp will illuminate briefly before the flash fires.

○ 🔆SLOW Slow Sync: This operates in the same way as Fill Flash, except all shutter speeds between 30 seconds and 1/200 second are available. It is useful for recording low-level ambient light as well as those areas of the scene or subject illuminated by the flash (see below for a full description).

○ 🔆REAR Rear-Curtain Sync: The flash fires immediately before the shutter closes. As with Slow Sync flash, all shutter speeds between 30 seconds and 1/200 second are available; it is not only useful for recording low-level ambient light as well as those areas of the scene or subject illuminated by the flash, but also for creating motion blur trails that appear to follow a moving subject (see below for a full description). SLOW is displayed in the shooting information once the setting for this mode is completed.

Using M and S Modes:

○ 🔆 Fill Flash: The built-in flash will pop up only if the 🔆 button is pressed. The flash fires as soon as the shutter has opened.

○ 🔆👁 Fill Flash with Red-Eye Reduction: This operates in the same way as Fill Flash, except the Red-Eye Reduction lamp will illuminate briefly before the flash fires.

○ 🔆REAR Rear-Curtain with Slow Sync: The flash fires immediately before the shutter closes. All shutter speeds between 30 seconds and 1/200 second are available; it is not only useful for recording low-level ambient light and those areas of the scene or subject illuminated by the flash, but also for creating motion blur trails that appear to follow a moving subject (see the page 248-249 for a full description).

NOTE: If an external Speedlight is attached to the D3100, the flash will fire in every exposure mode, with the exception of ⊘—even in modes that do not support the use of the built-in Speedlight, such as ⛰.

When using the built-in Speedlight of the D3100, the range of available shutter speeds varies according to the selected exposure mode as follows:

MODE	SHUTTER SPEED RANGE
AUTO ✳ ☺ P, A	1/200 – 1/60 second
⬛	1/200 – 1 second
✳ S	1/200 – 30 seconds
M	1/200 – 30 seconds, ʙᴜ ʟ ʙ

The following table summarizes how the shutter speed and lens aperture values are influenced by the selected exposure mode when an external Speedlight is used:

EXPOSURE MODE	SHUTTER SPEED	LENS APERTURE
Programmed-Auto (P)	Set automatically by camera between 1/200 – 1/60 second [1]	Set automatically by the camera
Shutter-Priority (S)	Value between 1/200 – 30 seconds available for selection by the user	
Aperture-Priority (A)	Set automatically by camera between 1/200 – 1/60 second [1]	Value selected by the user
Manual (M)	Value between 1/200 – 30 seconds, plus ʙᴜ ʟ ʙ available for selection by the user	

[1] Shutter speed may be set as slow as 30 seconds in Slow Sync, Slow Rear-Curtain Sync, and Slow Sync with Red-Eye Reduction flash modes.

> The SB-600 (shown here) and
the SB-700 are small, compact
external flash units that increase
the flexibility and creativity
of using flash with the D3100
considerably.

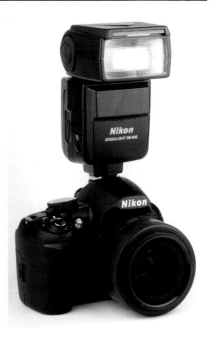

The D3100 offers full i-TTL Flash Exposure Control with five external
Nikon Speedlights that are compatible with the CLS:

- O SB-R200 with a GN of 33 feet (10m) at ISO 100

- O SB-400 with a GN of 69 feet (21 m) at ISO 100

- O SB-600 with a GN of 98 feet (30 m) at ISO 100 with the flash head set
  to 35mm

- O SB-700 with a GN of 92 feet (28 m) at ISO 100 with the flash head set
  to 35mm

- O SB-800 with a GN of 125 feet (38 m) at ISO 100 with the flash head set
  to 35mm

- O SB-900 with a GN of 111 feet (34 m) at ISO 100 with the flash head set
  to 35mm (and with Normal light distribution selected)

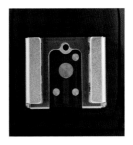

> The external Speedlights can be mounted on the accessory shoe on the top of the D3100.

243

	FLASH UNIT					ADVANCED WIRELESS LIGHTING					
						COMMANDER			REMOTE		
FLASH MODE/FEATURE		SB-900 SB-800	SB-700	SB-600	SB-400	SB-900 SB-800	SB-700	SU-800[1]	SB-900 SB-800	SB-700 SB-600	SB-R200
i-TTL	i-TTL balanced fill-flash for digital SLR[2]	✓[3]	✓[3]	✓[3]	✓[4]	✓	✓	✓	✓	✓	✓
AA	Auto aperture[2]	✓[5]	—	—	—	✓[6]	—	✓[6]	✓[6]	—	—
A	Non-TTL auto	✓[5]	—	—	—	✓[6]	—	✓[6]	✓[6]	—	—
GN	Distance-priority manual	✓	✓	—	—	—	—	—	—	—	—
M	Manual	✓	✓	✓	✓[7]	✓	✓	✓	✓	✓	✓
RPT	Repeating flash	✓	—	—	—	✓	—	✓	✓	✓	—
AF-assist for multi-area AF[2]		✓	✓	✓	—	✓	✓	✓	—	—	—
Flash Color Information Communication		✓	✓	✓	✓	✓	✓	—	—	—	—
REAR	Rear-curtain sync	✓	✓	✓	✓	✓	✓	✓	✓	✓	✓
👁	Red-eye reduction	✓	✓	✓	✓	✓	✓	—	—	—	—
Power zoom		✓	✓	✓	—	✓	✓	—	—	—	—
Auto ISO sensitivity control		✓	✓	✓	✓	—	—	—	—	—	—

1 Only available when SU-800 is used to control other flash units.
2 CPU lens required.
3 Standard i-TTL flash for digital SLR is used with Spot metering or when selected with flash unit.
4 Standard i-TTL flash for digital SLR is used with Spot metering.
5 Selected with flash unit.
6 Auto aperture (AA) is used regardless of mode selected with flash unit.
7 Can be selected with camera.

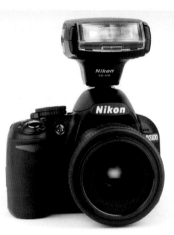

^ The SB-400 Speedlight is one of five accessory flash units compatible with the D3100.

All models except the SB-R200 can either be attached to the camera directly or via the dedicated Nikon TTL remote flash cords: SC-28, SC-29, or the now discontinued SC-17. The SB-R200 can only be controlled as part of the Nikon Advanced Wireless Control (AWL) flash system via either the SU-800 commander unit or the SB-700, SB-800, and SB-900 Speedlights when used as master flash units.

The five Speedlights that can be attached to the accessory shoe of the D3100 offer additional versatility because their flash heads can be tilted and—in the case of the SB-600, SB-700, SB-800, and SB-900—swiveled for bounce flash. Unlike earlier Nikon Speedlights, which cancelled monitor pre-flashes if the flash head was tilted or swiveled for bounce flash, the SB-400, SB-600, SB-700, SB-800, and SB-900 emit pre-flashes regardless of the flash head orientation. The four latter units also have an adjustable auto zoom-head (SB-600: 24-85mm, SB-700: 14-120mm, SB-800: 24-105mm, SB-900: 12-200mm) that controls the angle of coverage and a wide-angle diffuser to allow them to illuminate an even wider field of view. With the diffuser, the SB-600 and SB-800 can cover down to 14mm, while the SB-900 can cover down to 12mm.

NOTE: If the SB-400 is attached to the D3100 and turned on, the **[Built-in flash]** item in the Shooting menu changes to **[Optional flash]**, which allows **[TTL]** or **[Manual]** to be selected for the Flash Control mode.

When used with the D3100, the SB-900 and SB-700 automatically adjust their zoom head to match the coverage of the lens focal lengths with the camera's DX-format sensor. However, this is not the case with other Speedlights. Thus, the zoom head coverage of the SB-600 and SB-800 is set to correspond to the field of view of lens focal lengths based on the assumption that the Speedlight is attached to a camera with an FX-format (35mm or full-frame) sensor. Because the smaller DX-format sensor of the D3100 causes an effective reduction in the angle of view of any given lens focal length, the flash will illuminate a greater area with the D3100 than is necessary. Consequently, this will restrict the potential shooting range and squander flash power. In this situation, use the following table to adjust the zoom head position and thus maximize the performance of the flash unit:

FOCAL LENGTH (MM)	ZOOM HEAD POSITION (MM)
14	20
18	24
20	28
24	35
28	50
35	50
50	70
70	85
85	105[1]

[1]Available on SB-800 only

AUTOMATIC FLASH WITH THE SB-800 AND SB-900

When using the SB-800 and SB-900 Speedlights with the D3100, there are two additional non-TTL flash modes available; these are selected on the Speedlight:

Auto Aperture (AA): In this mode, the SB-900 and SB-800 read the ISO sensitivity setting, lens aperture, and the command to fire the flash from the camera automatically. The AA flash mode can be used in Aperture-Priority or Manual exposure mode. The flash output level is determined using a sensor on the front panel of the Speedlight to monitor the flash exposure, and as soon as this sensor detects that the flash output has been sufficient, the flash pulse is quenched. If between exposures you decide to alter the focal length or change the lens aperture, the Speedlight will adjust its output accordingly to maintain a correct flash exposure. The problem with this option is that the sensor does not necessarily "see" the same scene as the lens does, which can lead to inaccuracies in flash exposure.

Automatic (A): This is the only automatic, non-TTL flash mode available with the SB-800 and SB-900 Speedlights. It can be used in Aperture-Priority or Manual exposure mode. Like in the AA mode, a sensor on the front of the SB-800, SB-900, or DX-type Speedlight monitors flash levels and shuts off the flash when the Speedlight calculates that sufficient light has been emitted. However, the lens aperture and ISO sensitivity values must be set manually on the Speedlight to ensure that the subject is within the flash shooting range. As with the AA mode, the sensor does not necessarily "see" the same scene as the lens does, which can lead to inaccuracies in flash exposure.

MANUAL FLASH EXPOSURE CONTROL

In Manual flash mode (available in P, S, A, and M exposure modes only), you set the output of the Speedlight (built-in or external) to a fixed level. In this situation, it is necessary to calculate the correct lens aperture as determined by the flash-to-subject distance and the Guide Number (GN) of the Speedlight. To select Manual Flash control for the built-in Speedlight, open the Shooting menu and navigate to [Built-in Flash] and press ▶. Highlight [Manual] and press ⓞⓚ. When using an external Speedlight, the flash mode is selected via the controls of the Speedlight.

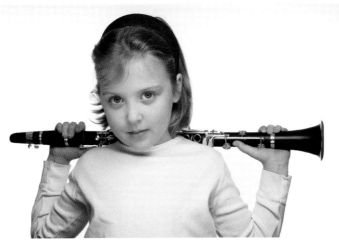

∧ In a studio situation, where you shoot under controlled conditions, using manual flash will ensure consistent, repeatable results.

For example, at its base sensitivity of ISO 100, the built-in Speedlight of the D3100 has a guide number (GN) of 43 ft (13 m). The [Built-in Flash] item determines the output level of the built-in Speedlight in Manual flash; a value between 1/1 (full output) to 1/32 can be selected. Since there is only one specific exposure value for any given level of sensitivity (ISO) at a particular flash-to-subject distance, it is necessary to calculate the lens aperture required to record a proper exposure. Use the following equation:

Aperture = GN / Distance

For example, with the built-in Speedlight of the D3100 set to 1/1 (full output) at a flash-to-subject distance of 11 feet (3.4 m), the lens aperture required to obtain a correct exposure of the subject will be f/4 (4 = 43/11). Similar calculations will have to be performed when using an external Speedlight in Manual flash mode. Check the Guide Number (GN) for the particular Speedlight model and ensure that you conduct the calculations using the same unit of distance throughout.

SLOW SYNCHRONIZATION FLASH

The camera will normally set a shutter speed that is within the restricted range of 1/60 to 1/200 second when using the built-in flash or a compatible external Speedlight, and the camera is in Program (P) or Aperture-Priority (A) exposure mode. The actual speed that is used within this narrow range depends on the level of ambient light (the brighter the conditions, the shorter the shutter speed).

This restriction can have a significant effect on the overall exposure. For example, if you photograph a subject outside at night or in a dark interior, any area of the scene illuminated by ambient light alone will be lit dimly compared with those areas that will be illuminated by the flash. It is more than likely that the level of ambient light will not be sufficient for a proper exposure within this restricted range of shutter speeds; consequently, these areas of the scene will be underexposed. A typical photograph taken under these conditions has a well-exposed subject set against a dark, featureless background.

To prevent this, select the appropriate Slow Sync mode. This enables the camera to use a wider range of slower shutter speeds, extending from 1/200 second to the longest available shutter speed of 30 seconds. Therefore, the camera will be able to select a more appropriate shutter speed for the low level of ambient light, ensuring the correct exposure can be achieved for the background (remember, the flash output will have little if any effect in this region because the intensity of light from the flash will diminish according to the Inverse Square Law). However, the flash output will be controlled for a proper exposure of the subject and its surroundings.

> **HINT:** Since the shutter speed may be quite slow when using Slow Sync flash mode, consider using a tripod or other camera support to avoid the effects of camera shake.

REAR-CURTAIN SYNCHRONIZATION

If a subject you want to photograph is moving, it is possible to achieve some interesting effects by using Slow Sync flash mode in combination with a slow shutter speed—the flash will illuminate the subject briefly to record it as sharp while the slow shutter speed will record the ambient light, resulting in the subject's ambient motion trail being recorded as a blur. Rear-Curtain Sync fires the flash at the end of the exposure, just before the shutter closes, causing the motion trail to be recorded in a natural-looking manner—following the moving subject.

This technique can be particularly effective when Rear-Curtain Sync flash mode is used in either Shutter-Priority (S) or Manual (M) exposure mode. Alternatively, in Programmed-Auto (P) or Aperture-Priority (A) exposure modes, use Slow Rear-Curtain Sync flash mode. In each case, it will cause the blur from the subject's movement to appear as though it is following the sharp image of the subject formed by the flash illumination, producing a more natural appearance of the subject's movement.

FLASH OUTPUT COMPENSATION

Flash Compensation is used to modify the level of flash output. To set Flash Compensation on the D3100, press the ⓘnfo button to display the shooting information on the monitor, and then press the ⚡️ button to place the cursor in the Shooting Information Display. Use the Multi Selector to highlight the Flash Compensation option ⚡⎌ and then press the ⓚ button. Use ▲ and ▼ to highlight the required level of compensation and press ⓚ to confirm the setting. This method can be used with either the built-in Speedlight or a compatible external Speedlight.

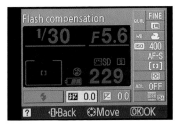

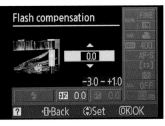

∧ The Flash Compensation option, shown highlighted in the Information Display

∧ Flash Output Compensation can be adjusted in steps of 0.3 EV.

Alternatively, Flash Compensation can be applied by pressing and holding the ⚡ and ⚡⎌ buttons, while turning the Command dial. Whichever way you decide to apply the compensation, ⚡⎌ will be displayed in the viewfinder once a compensation value is set. Compensation can be set over a range of +1 EV to –3 EV in steps of 0.3 EV. To restore normal flash output, set the Flash Compensation back to ± 0.0.

Flash Output Compensation can also be applied directly on compatible external Speedlights (the SB-900, SB-800, SB-700, and SB-600). If Flash Output Compensation is applied on both the D3100 and an external Speedlight at the same time, the effect is cumulative. For example, applying a value of +1 EV to both the camera and external Speedlight results in a Flash Output Compensation of +2 EV.

As discussed earlier in this chapter, the default i-TTL Balanced Fill-Flash mode will automatically apply Flash Compensation based on scene brightness, contrast, focus distance, and a variety of other factors. The level of automatic adjustment applied to flash output by the D3100 will often cancel out any compensation value entered manually. Since there is no way of telling what the camera is doing, you will never have control of the flash exposure. To regain control, set the flash mode to Standard i-TTL by either selecting Spot Metering on the camera (this is the only option for the built-in Speedlight) or by setting the Flash Control mode on an external Speedlight accordingly; in the latter case, ensure that only TTL is displayed in the control panel of the Speedlight for the flash mode, not TTL-BL.

FLASH COLOR INFORMATION

When Automatic White Balance is selected on the D3100 and you are using with the SB-900, SB-800, SB-700, SB-600, or SB-400 Speedlights (directly mounted on the camera), the external flash unit automatically transmits information to the camera about the color temperature of the light it emits. The camera will then use this information to adjust its final White Balance setting in an attempt to match the color temperature of the light from the flash and the color temperature of the prevailing ambient light.

NOTE: The Flash Color Information feature will only operate with the Automatic White Balance option, it is unavailable with any other White Balance option.

WIDE-AREA AF-ASSIST ILLUMINATOR

The purpose of the AF-Assist Illuminator built into the SB-900, SB-800, SB-700, and SB-600 external Speedlights and the SU-800 wireless commander unit, is to facilitate autofocus in low-light situations. In order to match the broader spread of the multiple AF points in many CLS-compatible cameras, the frame area covered by the AF-Assist Illuminator in these Speedlights is much wider than with previous non-CLS types. These external lamps are also much more powerful than the built-in AF-Assist Illuminator of the D3100, which has the further disadvantage of being obstructed by many Nikkor lenses due to its proximity to the lens mount.

When a compatible external Speedlight with an AF-Assist Illuminator is used off the camera (see section below), the light emitted by the lamp may not be reflected with sufficient strength to be effective if it strikes the subject at an oblique angle. In this situation, consider using the Nikon SC-29 TTL flash cord, which has a built-in AF-Assist Illuminator in its terminal block that attaches to the camera accessory shoe. This places the AF-Assist Illuminator immediately above the central axis of the lens to help improve the accuracy of autofocus.

OFF-CAMERA FLASH

When you work with a single external Speedlight, it is often desirable to take the flash off the camera. As mentioned already, there are multiple different dedicated Nikon cords for this purpose: the SC-17 (discontinued), SC-28, and SC-29. All three cords are 4.9 feet (1.5 m) long; up to three SC-17 or SC-28 cords can be connected together to extend the operating range away from the camera. Whenever you take a Speedlight off the camera and use any TTL flash mode that will incorporate focus distance information in the flash output computations, take care as to where you position the flash. If the Speedlight is moved closer or further away than the camera-to-subject distance, the accuracy of the flash output may be compromised—the TTL flash control system works on the assumption that the flash is located at the same distance from the subject as the camera. Likewise, when using Manual Flash Exposure Control, remember to calculate the lens aperture based on the flash-to-subject distance, not the camera-to-subject distance. The benefits of taking a Speedlight off the camera include:

- Increasing the angular separation between the central axis of the lens and the flash head will significantly reduce the risk of the red-eye effect with humans or eye-shine with pets and other animals.
- In situations where it is not practical to use bounce flash, moving the flash off-camera will usually improve the quality of the lighting. This is especially evident in the degree of modeling it provides when compared to the typical flat, frontal lighting produced by a flash mounted directly on the camera.
- By taking the flash off-camera and directing the light from the Speedlight accordingly, it is often possible to control the position of shadows so that they become less noticeable.
- When using Fill Flash, it is often desirable to direct light to a specific part of the scene to help reduce the level of contrast locally.
- An SB-900, SB-700, or SB-800 Speedlight connected to the camera via one of Nikon's dedicated TTL cords can be used as the master/commander flash to control multiple Speedlights off-camera using the Advanced Wireless Lighting system (see below).

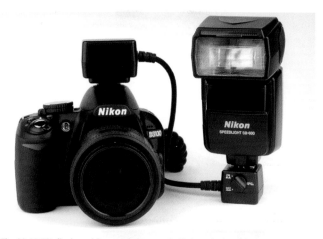

˄ The SC-29 TTL flash cord is one of three cords that can be used to connect external Speedlights to the D3100. It is shown here with the SB-600 Speedlight. Note the built-in AF-Assist lamp on the terminal positioned in the camera's accessory shoe.

WIRELESS FLASH CONTROL

Wireless flash control is compatible with the SB-900, SB-800, SB-700, SB-600, and SB-R200 Speedlights, together with the SU-800 Wireless Speedlight Commander unit. It allows for one or more remote Speedlight(s) to be operated and controlled wirelessly in P, A, S, and M exposure modes. The remote Speedlights can be used in a variety of flash modes: TTL, Auto Aperture (for use with remote SB-900/SB-800 Speedlights only), or Manual.

Up to three independent groups of remote Speedlights can be used via one of four dedicated communication channels. The built-in Speedlight of the D3100 does not support this feature, so it is necessary to use either an SB-900, SB-700, or SB-800 Speedlight as the master/commander flash. Alternatively, the SU-800 Wireless Speedlight Commander unit can be used instead of a Speedlight. In master flash or flash commander mode, these units communicate with the remote Speedlights via pulsed infrared light (IR).

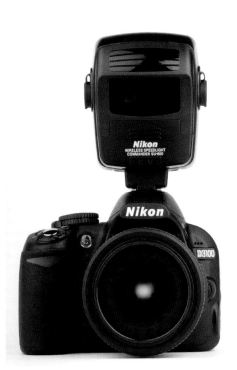

‹ The SU-800
Commander Unit
enables independent
control via wireless
communication of
up to three separate
groups of compatible
Nikon Speedlights;
each group can
consist of one or more
Speedlight(s).

When the following units are used as the master flash or commander unit for wireless control of compatible remote Speedlights (SB-900, SB-800, SB-700 and SB-R200), the effective range of operation is:

○ SB-900 / SB-800 / SB-700: When either the SB-900, SB-700, or SB-800 Speedlight is used as a master flash, the maximum effective operating range between it and the remote Speedlights is 33 feet (10 m) within 30˚ of the central axis of the lens, and 16 feet (5 m) within 30 to 60˚ of the central axis of the lens.

○ SU-800: The SU-800 is a dedicated IR transmitter (i.e., unlike flash units that emit control signals as part of a full spectrum emission, the SU-800 only emits IR light). It is more powerful than Speedlights that can perform the master flash role and is capable of controlling remote SB-900, SB-800, and SB-600 Speedlights from up to 66 feet (20 m).

○ SU-800 & SB-R200: Nikon states that when the SU-800 is used as the commander unit, the maximum effective operating range between it and remote SB-R200 Speedlights is 13 feet (4 m) along the central axis of the lens, and 9.8 feet (3 m) within 30° of the central axis of the lens.

I have found the quoted maximum operating ranges for the components of the Advanced Wireless Lighting system to be very conservative. For example, I have used both SB-900 and SB-800 Speedlights as master and remote units at ranges outwards of 100 feet (30 m) or more, particularly in situations where there have been reflective surfaces like walls and foliage close by to aid transmission of the IR control signals—this is three times greater than the suggested maximum range. However, in bright sunlight, which contains a high level of naturally occurring IR light, you may find the practical limit of the operating range is reduced.

HINT: I have managed to use remote flash units successfully even without direct line-of-sight between the master flash/commander unit and the sensor on the remote Speedlight(s). However, every shooting situation is different, so my advice is to set up the lighting system to your requirements and always take test shots to ensure that it works as intended.

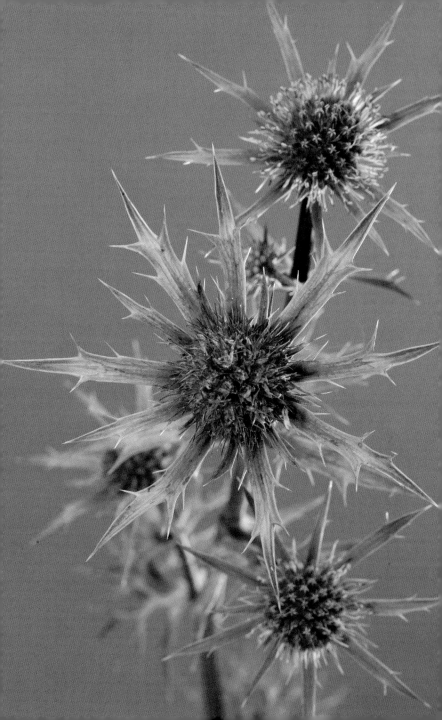

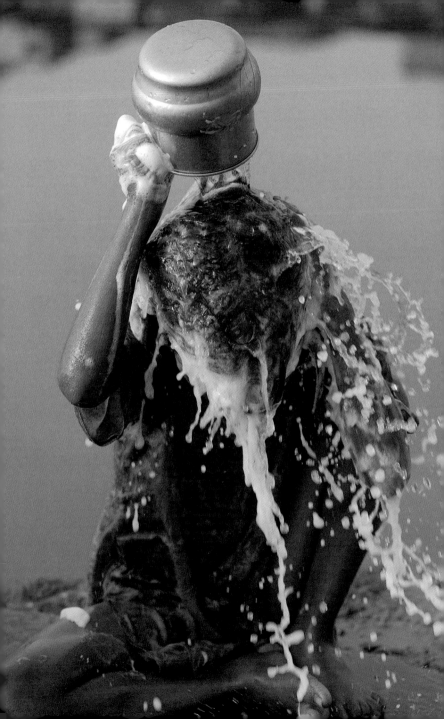

Nikon Lenses and Accessories

Nikon currently makes a range of approximately 60 lenses for their DSLR and film camera models. These lenses are known by their proprietary name, Nikkor. The "F" mount used on these Nikkor lenses is legendary; it has been used on all Nikon 35mm film and digital SLR cameras since the introduction of the original Nikon F SLR in 1959. As such, a great many of the lenses Nikon has produced in the past five decades can be mounted on the D3100, including most manual focus lenses that conform to the Ai lens mount standard.

The fullest level of compatibility is offered by current AF-S (D-type and G-type) and the earlier AF-I autofocus Nikkor lenses, both of which have an integral motor for driving the focus. The integral motor is necessary because, like its predecessor the D3000, the D3100 does not have its own built-in focusing motor. Excluding this motor reduces the weight of the camera by about 30 g (approximately one ounce) and enables the lens mount to be located closer to the base of the camera, helping to reduce the overall size of the camera body. This means any other type of Nikkor lens used on the D3100 must be focused manually; furthermore, the level of compatibility between the camera and lens is severely restricted if a non-CPU type lens (see pages 263-264) is attached to the camera.

Nikon also produces a range of software applications and camera accessories for the D3100. A vast amount of information and assistance with these products is available online. In addition, there is a wide range of other useful off-brand accessories available from other sources, some of which are referenced in the Resources section at the end of this chapter (see pages 274-275).

Whenever you attach or detach a lens from the D3100, make sure the camera is turned off. To attach a lens, identify the mounting index mark (white dot) on the lens and align it with the mounting index mark (white dot) next to the bayonet ring of the camera's lens mount. Enter the lens bayonet into the camera and rotate the lens counter-clockwise until it locks into place with an audible click. To remove a lens from the camera, press and hold the lens release button (located on the front of the camera to the left of the lens mount), and then rotate the lens until the two index marks are aligned before lifting the lens clear of the camera body. If you do not intend to mount another lens immediately, make sure you place the BF-1B body cap back on the camera to help prevent unwanted material from getting inside.

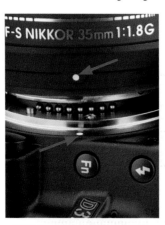
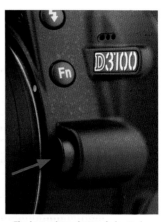

∧ When the mounting index marks on the D3100 body and a lens are aligned, the lens can be mounted to or released from the camera.

∧ The lens release button is located on the front of the camera, adjacent to the lens mount.

When using a CPU lens with an aperture ring, ensure it is set and locked to its minimum aperture value (highest f/number). If *FE E* appears, blinking, in the information display and viewfinder, the lens has not been set to its minimum aperture value and the shutter release will be disabled.

NOTE: The latest G-type Nikkor lenses lack a conventional aperture ring.

The designations of Nikkor lenses, particularly modern autofocus types, are peppered with initials. Here is an explanation of what some of these stand for:

O AF-type: These lenses are the predecessors to the later D- and G-type designs. They have a conventional aperture ring but do not communicate focus distance information to the camera.

O AF D-type: These lenses have a conventional aperture ring and an integral electronic chip that communicates information about lens aperture and focus distance between the lens and the camera body. Nikon refers to this chip as a central processing unit (CPU) but to be strictly accurate, it is an integrated circuit. A "D" appears on the lens barrel following the maximum aperture value.

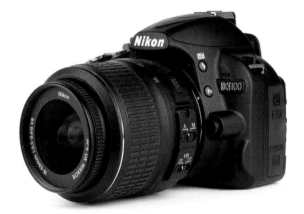

∧ The AF-S DX 18-55mm f/3.5-5.6 G is one of a number of Nikkor lenses designed specifically for the DX-format of the D3100.

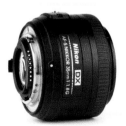

‹ A Nikkor CPU-type lens is readily identified by the electrical contact pins set around the lens mount flange; note the AF-S and G designations on the lens barrel.

o AF G-type: These lenses have no aperture ring and are only compatible with Nikon cameras that allow the aperture value to be set from the camera body. They contain an electronic chip that communicates information about lens aperture and focus distance between the lens and the camera body, similar to the D-type lenses. A "G" appears on the lens barrel following the maximum aperture value.

o AF-I: The predecessor to the AF-S lens type; these lenses have an integral focusing motor.

o AF-S: These lenses use a silent-wave motor (SWM) for focusing; alternating magnetic fields drive the motor, which moves the lens' elements to shift focus. This system offers the fastest autofocus of all AF Nikkor lenses. Most AF-S lenses have an additional feature that allows you to switch between autofocus and manual focus by simply taking hold of the focus ring, without needing to adjust any camera controls. "AF-S" appears on the lens barrel.

o DX: These lenses have been specially designed for use on Nikon small-format DSLR cameras. They project a smaller image circle than lenses designed for 35mm format cameras, and the light exiting their rear element is more collimated (actually parallel) to improve the efficiency of the photo diodes (pixels) on the camera's sensor. "DX" appears on the lens barrel.

o ED: To reduce the effect of chromatic aberration, Nikon developed a special type of glass known as Extra-Low Dispersion to bring various wavelengths of light to a common point of focus.

o IF: To speed up focusing, particularly with long focal length lenses, Nikon developed their internal focusing (IF) system. This system moves a group of elements within the lens so that it does not alter the length of the lens during focusing and prevents the front filter mount from rotating, facilitating the use of filters such as a polarizer.

o Nano Crystal Coat: This is a specialized lens coating that is applied to the surface of some lens elements to help reduce the level of light reflection, improving overall image quality. An "N" appears on the lens barrel.

o Non-CPU: Nikon uses the term "non-CPU" to describe any Nikkor lens lacking the components and electrical connections that enable communication of information between the lens and the camera body. With the exception of the PC-E 24mm f/3.5D, PC-E Micro 45mm f/2.8D, PC-E Micro 85mm f/2.8D, PC-Micro 85mm f/2.8D lens, and Ai-P type Nikkor lenses, all manual focus Nikkor lenses are non-CPU types.

o Micro-Nikkor: "Micro" is the name given to specialized lenses designed specifically for close-up and macro photography; the optical formula of these lenses is optimized for close focusing.

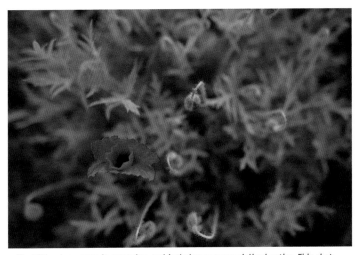

^ The Nikkor lens range is extensive, and includes many specialized optics. This shot was taken using the AF-S DX 35mm f/1.8G set to an aperture of f/2 to limit the depth of field.

- O PC-E: This is a special type of lens that offers the ability to shift and tilt the lens relative to the plane of the sensor in the camera to control perspective and depth-of-field. "PC-E" appears on the lens barrel.
- O VR: Vibration Reduction (VR) is Nikon's name for a sophisticated technology that enables a lens to counter the effects of camera shake and other vibrations. A set of built-in motion sensors that cause micro-motors to shift a dedicated set of lens elements are used to improve the sharpness of pictures. "VR" appears on the lens barrel.

LENS COMPATIBILITY

As mentioned previously in this chapter, the D3100 does not have an electric motor built into the camera to drive the focus action of those Nikkor AF lenses that lack their own integral AF motor; therefore, autofocus is ONLY supported with either the AF-S or the AF-I type Nikkor lenses. Other AF Nikkor lenses can be used with the D3100, but focusing must be performed manually.

Nikon classifies all AF-S, AF-I, and AF Nikkor lenses, plus manual focus Ai-P Nikkor lenses, as CPU-type lenses; these lenses can be readily identified by the electrical contact pins set around the edge of the lens mount bayonet flange. The following table provides details of the compatibility of CPU-type Nikkor lenses with the D3100:

CAMERA SETTING / LENS/ACCESSORY	Focus			Mode		Metering		
	AF	MF (with electronic rangefinder)	MF	Auto and scene modes; P, S, A	M	⊡ 3D	⊡ Color	⊙
AF-S, AF-I Nikkor [1]	✓	✓	✓	✓	✓	✓	—	✓[2]
Other type G or D AF Nikkor [1]	—	✓	✓	✓	✓	✓	—	✓[2]
PC-E Nikkor series	—	✓[3]	✓	✓[3]	✓[3]	✓[3]	—	✓[2, 3]
PC Micro 85mm f/2.8D [4]	—	✓[3]	✓	—	✓	✓	—	✓[2, 3]
AF-S/AF-I teleconverter [5]	✓[6]	✓[6]	✓	✓	✓	✓	—	✓[2]
Other AF Nikkor (except lenses for F3AF)	—	✓[7]	✓	✓	—	—	✓	✓[2]
Ai-P Nikkor	—	✓[8]	✓	✓	—	—	✓	✓[2]

[1] Use AF-S or AF-I lenses to get the most from your camera. Vibration Reduction (VR) is supported with VR lenses.
[2] Spot metering meters the selected focus point.
[3] Can not be used with shifting or tilting.
[4] The camera's exposure metering and flash control systems may not function as expected when the lens is shifted and/or tilted or an aperture other than the maximum aperture is used. With maximum effective aperture of f/5.6 or faster.
[5] AF-S or AF-I lens required.
[6] With maximum effective aperture of f/5.6 or faster.
[7] When the AF 80 200mm f/2.8, AF 35 70mm f/2.8, AF 28 85mm f/3.5 4.5 (New) or AF 28 85mm f/3.5 4.5 lenses are zoomed all the way in at the minimum focus distance, the In-Focus indicator may be displayed when the image on the matte screen in the viewfinder is not in focus. Focus manually until image in viewfinder is in focus.
[8] With maximum aperture of f/5.6 or larger.

USING NIKON AF-S/AF-I TELECONVERTERS

The Nikon AF-S/AF-I teleconverters can be used with the following AF-S and AF-I lenses:

- O AF-S VR Micro 105mm f/2.8G ED [1]
- O AF-S VR 200mm f/2G ED
- O AF-S VR II 200mm f/2G ED
- O AF-S VR 300mm f/2.8G ED
- O AF-S VR II 300mm f/2.8G ED
- O AF-S 300mm f/2.8D ED II
- O AF-S 300mm f/2.8D ED
- O AF-I 300mm f/2.8D ED

- AF-S 300mm f/4D ED [2]
- AF-S 400mm f/2.8D ED II
- AF-S 400mm f/2.8D ED
- AF-I 400mm f/2.8D ED
- AF-S 500mm f/4D ED II [2]
- AF-S 500mm f/4D ED [2]
- AF-I 500mm f/4D ED [2]
- AF-S 600mm f/4D ED II [2]
- AF-S 600mm f/4D ED [2]
- AF-I 600mm f/4D ED [2]
- AF-S VR 70–200mm f/2.8G ED
- AF-S VR II 70–200mm f/2.8G ED
- AF-S 80–200mm f/2.8D ED
- AF-S VR 200–400mm f/4G ED [2]
- AF-S VRII 200–400mm f/4G ED [2]
- AF-S 400mm f/2.8G ED VR
- AF-S 500mm f/4G ED VR [2]
- AF-S 600mm f/4G ED VR [2]

[1] Autofocus is not recommended. At close focusing distances, the maximum effective aperture is likely to be less than f/5.6.

[2] Autofocus is not guaranteed when used with the TC-17E II or TC-20 E II teleconverter, as maximum effective aperture is less than f/5.6; although in bright conditions or with good levels of contrast in the subject, it will often work quite well, but a little slower.

USING NON-CPU LENSES

Although the Nikon F mount has basically remained unchanged for almost fifty years, the design of modern cameras has moved on considerably. The introduction of electronic communication between the lens and camera for the purposes of exposure metering and autofocus has meant a number of changes have been introduced; as such, older non-CPU type lenses offer a very restricted level of compatibility with the D3100. In this case, the camera can only be used in Manual exposure mode (if you select another exposure mode, the camera disables the shutter release automatically). The lens aperture must be set using the aperture ring on the lens, and the autofocus system, TTL metering system, electronic analog exposure display, and TTL flash control do not function. However, provided the maximum effective aperture of the connected lens is f/5.6 or larger (smaller f/number), the electronic rangefinder does operate with the following non-CPU type lenses unless (otherwise stated):

- Ai-modified, Ai, Ai-S, and E-series Nikkor lenses
- Medical Nikkor 120mm f/4 (can only be used at a shutter speed of 1/100 or slower)
- Reflex Nikkor lenses (electronic rangefinder does not operate)
- PC Nikkor lenses (electronic rangefinder does not operate if the lens is shifted)
- Ai-type teleconverters (electronic rangefinder requires an effective aperture of f/5.6 or larger to operate)
- PB-6 Bellows focusing attachment (D3100 must be attached in vertical orientation but can be used subsequently in horizontal orientation)
- Extension rings PK-11A, PK-12, PK-13, and PN-11

INCOMPATIBLE LENSES AND ACCESSORIES

The following accessories and lenses are incompatible with the D3100. If you attempt to use them, it may damage the equipment.

- TC-16A AF teleconverter
- Non-Ai lenses
- Lenses that require the AU-1 focusing unit (400mm f/4.5, 600mm f/5.6, 800mm f/8, 1200mm f/11)
- Fisheye (6mm f/5.6, 7.5mm f/5.6, 8mm f/8, OP 10mm f/5.6)
- 2.1 cm f/4 (old type)
- K2 rings
- ED 180–600mm f/8 (serial numbers 174041–174180)
- ED 360–1200mm f/11 (serial numbers 174031–174127)
- 200–600mm f/9.5 (serial numbers 280001–300490)
- Lenses for the F3AF (AF80mm f/2.8, AF ED200mm f/3.5, TC-16 teleconverter)
- PC 28mm f/4 (serial number 180900 or earlier)
- PC 35mm f/2.8 (serial numbers 851001–906200)
- PC 35mm f/3.5 (old type)
- 1000mm f/6.3 Reflex (old type)
- 1000mm f/11 Reflex (serial numbers 142361–143000)
- 2000mm f/11 Reflex (serial numbers 200111–200310)

DEPTH-OF-FIELD CONSIDERATIONS

When a lens brings light to focus on a camera's sensor, there is only one plane of focus that is critically sharp. However, in the two-dimensional picture produced by the camera, there is a zone in front of and behind the plane of focus that is perceived to be sharp. This area of apparent sharpness is referred to as the depth of field, and its extent is influenced by the camera-to-subject distance together with the focal length and aperture of the lens in use.

If the focal length and camera-to-subject distance are constant, depth of field will be shallower with large apertures (low f/numbers) and deeper with small apertures (high f/numbers). If the aperture and camera-to-subject distance are constant, depth of field will be shallower with a long focal length (telephoto range) and deeper with a shorter focal length (wide-angle range). If the focal length and aperture are constant, depth of field will be greater at longer camera-to-subject distances and shallower with closer camera-to-subject distances. Depth of field is an important consideration when deciding on a particular composition, as it has a direct and fundamental effect on the final appearance of the picture.

A very important consideration concerning depth of field is that it is slightly less for images shot using the DX-format when compared with those taken on the FX-format cameras such as the Nikon D700 and D3-series models. This is due to the smaller size of the imaging area of the DX-format (23.1 x 15.4 mm) used in the D3100 as compared with the FX-format (36 x 23.9 mm); the DX-format picture must be magnified by a greater amount compared with the FX-format shot to achieve any given identical print size. Therefore, at normal viewing distances, details that appear to be sharp in a print made from an FX-format shot may no longer look sharp in a print of the same dimensions made from a DX-format shot. If you use the depth-of-field values given in tables for 35mm film, you will find they do not correspond to images shot on the DX-format with the same camera-to-subject distance and focal length. To guarantee that the depth of field in pictures taken on the DX-format is sufficiently deep, use the values for the next larger lens aperture. For example, if your lens is set to f/11, use the depth-of-field values for f/8 in the DX-format.

DIFFRACTION

Diffraction is an optical effect that, under certain circumstances, will limit the resolution you can achieve in a photograph. Assuming conditions of a uniform atmosphere (i.e., still, clear air), light waves will travel in straight lines. However, if those same light waves have to pass through a small hole, such as the aperture in the iris diaphragm of a camera lens, they become dispersed, or diffracted. At wide apertures (low f/numbers), the number of diffracted light waves is proportionally very small to the total number that pass through the aperture, hence the diffraction effect is negligible; but the proportion of diffracted waves increases as the size of the aperture is reduced, and the effect can become significant. After passing through a small aperture, the previously parallel light waves diverge, spreading out in different directions and, consequently, travel different distances between the iris diaphragm and the digital sensor, causing some light waves to shift out of phase and interfere with others. This process of interference creates a diffraction pattern that results in a general softening of detail in the image.

At a particular lens aperture (different for each lens and camera combination), the loss of resolution (softening) that occurs due to the effects of diffraction cancels out any gain in perceived sharpness due to increased depth of field. At this point, the camera lens is said to have become "diffraction limited." It is essential to know the diffraction limit for your lens(es) and different cameras, since there is no point in selecting aperture values beyond the diffraction limit, as image resolution will become increasingly degraded and exposure times extended with the risk of further loss of resolution through camera or subject movement.

I recommend you test each of your lenses with your D3100 to determine the diffraction limit for your own equipment. As a general rule, common with other Nikon DX-format camera models, I find that the D3100 diffraction limit is around f/11 to f/13; bear this in mind when you are looking to maximize depth of field by choosing smaller lens apertures.

SHUTTER SPEED CONSIDERATIONS

If you handhold your camera, it is worth remembering a rule of thumb concerning the minimum shutter speed needed to prevent a loss of sharpness due to camera shake. For the DX format, multiply the focal length of the lens by 1.5—the approximate magnification factor of the D3100 sensor compared with the FX-format—then take the reciprocal of this value and use it as the slowest shutter speed for shooting with that lens while handholding the camera. For example, a focal length of 300mm would require a minimum shutter speed of 1/450; the closest value available on the D3100 is 1/500.

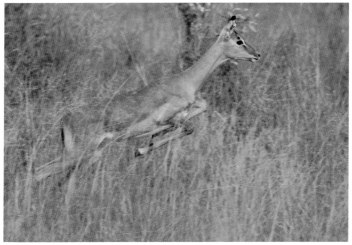

^ A shutter speed of 1/1000 second was required to capture the sharp detail of this leaping Impala.

The shutter speed can also be used for creative effect because it controls the way motion of the subject or camera is depicted in a photograph. Conventionally, a fast shutter speed is used to freeze motion in sports or action photography. However, slower shutter speeds can be used to create a degree of blur that will often evoke a greater sense of movement than a subject that is rendered pin-sharp. The panning technique is an example of a creative blur effect; using a slow shutter speed while moving the camera to track the subject results in the subject appearing relatively sharp against an increased level of blur in the background.

It is beyond the scope of this book to describe fully the features and functions of Nikon's dedicated software, but details can easily be obtained from the technical support sections of the websites maintained by the Nikon Corporation. The D3100 is supplied with a copy of Nikon View NX2, which incorporates the Nikon Transfer 2 application. The following section is intended to provide a brief overview of the three principal Nikon software applications in their current versions at the time of this writing:

- O Nikon Transfer 2 (version 2.0.2)
- O Nikon View NX2 (version 2.0.3)
- O Nikon Capture NX2 (version 2.2.6)

For Windows, the following operating systems are supported:

- O Microsoft Windows XP Professional (Service Pack 3 – 32-bit versions)
- O Microsoft Windows XP Home Edition (Service Pack 3 – 32-bit versions)
- O Microsoft Windows Vista (Service Pack 2 – 32 & 64-bit versions)
- O Microsoft Windows 7 (32 & 64-bit versions)

For Macintosh, the following operating systems are supported:

- O Mac OSX 10.4.11
- O Mac OSX 10.5.8
- O Mac OSX 10.6.4

NOTE: For information about Nikon software and to download updates to existing applications, I recommend you visit the various technical support websites maintained by Nikon. These can be accessed via www.nikon.com.

NIKON TRANSFER 2

Nikon Transfer 2 is Nikon's updated utility for downloading images from the camera or memory card to your computer. Nikon Transfer 2 provides a simple, intuitive workflow suitable for all users, from beginners to professionals. It is included as part of Nikon View NX2 (supplied with the D3100) and can also be downloaded for free from any of Nikon's technical support websites. Features include:

○ Automatic recognition / auto start after connecting a camera or inserting a CF / SD card
○ Transfers images from CD, external hard drive or other removable media
○ Transfers images to computer's hard drive
○ Easy selection and viewing of images on up to five external devices before transfer
○ Transfers image data to a primary destination and also to a backup location simultaneously
○ Adds metadata during transfer; both XMP / IPTC standards are supported
○ Selects the application the images are displayed in after transfer

NIKON VIEW NX2

View NX2 offers photographers a fast solution to the organization and classification of their digital images. This software uses your computer's file directory to display and browse images. Nikon View NX2 is included with the latest Nikon DSLR cameras, such as the D3100, and can also be downloaded for free from Nikon's website. Features include:

○ High-speed thumbnail and preview display
○ Three customizable workspaces that are selected according to the images being worked on: Browser, GeoTag, and Edit
○ D-Movie editing tools that allow selection of start and stop points of individual movie clips, frame grab, merging of movie and JPEG files with transition effects, and the ability to add audio tracks
○ A simple way to choose images, operating similarly to Explorer / Finder
○ Fast sorting using image rating and labeling classification systems, plus integration with GPS data recorded by the camera
○ Image enhancement tools, such as Sharpness, Contrast, and Brightness controls, along with tools such as Highlight and Shadow protection, D-Lighting, and Color Booster
○ Adjustment tools such as Crop, Straighten, and Auto Red-Eye Correction
○ Includes Picture Control Utility (including sharpening, contrast, saturation, hue, brightness, and black-and-white conversion)
○ Batch processing to convert file format, resize, rename, change settings, and save to multiple destinations

- Integration with Capture NX2
- Printing and email transmission
- IPTC/XMP data compatible (user settings retained when image is opened in other supported applications)
- Quick Adjustment features for NEF (RAW) images, including White Balance, exposure adjustment, correction for axial chromatic aberration, and creating custom curves
- Full integration with Nikon Picturetown—Nikon's online image storage and sharing service. Images can be uploaded directly from Nikon View NX2 via a simple drag and drop action, or stored images can be browsed directly from Nikon View NX2.

NIKON CAPTURE NX2

In mid-2008, Nikon released an updated version of Capture NX, Capture NX 2; while not an extensive re-working of the program, it does introduce some key improvements. As a general-purpose image editing application, Nikon Capture NX 2 is really quite good; all the adjustment features work with JPEG and TIFF files as well as with NEF (RAW) files. It incorporates the same unique U Point technology that permits complex selections of an area (or areas) within an image to be made with accuracy and speed that is far greater than can be achieved using other digital imaging software currently available. The program offers an extensive toolbox to enhance and modify any image file, regardless of whether it was saved in the NEF (RAW), TIFF, or JPEG format.

Capture NX 2 applies non-destructive image processing to NEF (RAW) files, which means that the original image data is never compromised. Each enhancement made is saved in an edit list with the original data and thumbnail. However, changes made to JPEG or TIFF files will alter the data of the original image. To avoid this from occurring, the image can be saved using a different file name or converted into Nikon's NEF (RAW) format. Parameters set on any Nikon camera-produced NEF (RAW) file—such as White Balance, sharpening, color mode, and saturation—are applied to the image when it is opened in Nikon Capture NX 2 for editing, so the camera settings are preserved. Key features in the latest iteration include:

- A new Workspaces option provides four pre-defined palette and toolbar configurations (Browser, Metadata, Multi-Purpose, and Edit) with support for two monitors, plus you can create your own custom

Workspace (desktop layout), which can be supported across one or two displays. The pre-defined and custom Workspaces can be assigned a keyboard shortcut to help improve efficiency. Option/Alt keys + keys 1 through 9 are assignable for this purpose.

O An improved image browser palette with an extended feature set that should lessen the need to switch between Capture NX and View NX for thumbnail viewing. There is also a new Favorite Folders option, which makes accessing frequently used folders very fast. The time to open an image from the image browser has been improved significantly.

O New Quick Fix and Adjust sections of the Edit List improve the general layout and access to key tools such as Exposure Compensation, levels and curves adjustments, contrast, saturation, and the new Highlight Protection and Shadow Protection controls.

O The U Point technology of Capture NX, which is the key to its image editing simplicity, has been extended to almost all photo adjustment tools, including Noise Reduction and Unsharp Mask, to enhance an already powerful feature for applying local changes to an image.

O Separate controls for the correction of both axial and lateral chromatic aberration

O There is a new Auto Retouch Brush that provides a one-click tool to remove the effects of dust spots and other blemishes in an image.

O Enhanced batch-processing speeds

O Advanced White Balance control with the ability to select a specific color temperature or sample from a gray point

O An advanced NEF (RAW) file control that permits attributes such as Exposure Compensation, sharpening, contrast, color mode, saturation, and hue to be modified after the exposure has been made, without affecting the original image data.

O The Image Dust Off feature, which compares an NEF (RAW) file with a reference image taken with the same camera to help reduce the effects of any dust particles on the low-pass filter.

O The D-Lighting tool, which emulates the dodge and burn techniques of traditional photographic printing to control highlight and shadow areas, producing a more balanced exposure.

O A Color Noise Reduction tool, which minimizes the effect of random electronic noise that can occur, especially at high ISO settings.

O An Edge Noise Reduction tool that accentuates the boundary between areas of an image to make them more distinct.

O The Color Moiré Reduction feature helps to remove the effects of moiré, which can occur when an image contains areas with a very fine repeating pattern.

- The LCH Editor, which allows for control of Luminosity (overall lightness), Chroma (color saturation), and Hue in separate channels.

- The Lens Vignette control to correct for uneven illumination across an image, particularly near the corners.

- The Fisheye Lens tool, which converts images taken with the AF Fisheye-Nikkor DX 10.5mm f/2.8G lens so they appear as though they were taken using a conventional rectilinear lens with a diagonal angle-of-view equivalent to approximately 120°.

> **NOTE:** Nikon Camera Control Pro 2, which enables remote control of the key shooting functions of some Nikon DSLR cameras from a computer, does not support the D3100.

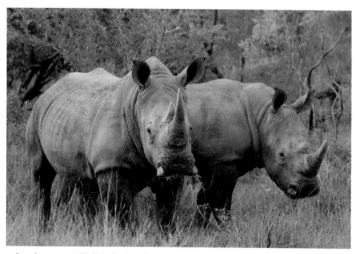

^ Carrying a spare EN-EL14 battery for your D3100 is always advisable when you expect to be in the field all day.

GENERAL NIKON ACCESSORIES

- AS-15: An accessory shoe adapter that has a standard PC sync socket for connecting the D3100 to a non-dedicated flash unit via a PC sync cable.

- BF-1B: Supplied with the D3100, a body cap that will help prevent dust from entering the camera; keep it in place at all times when a lens is not mounted on the camera.

CAUTION: The earlier BF-1 body cap cannot be used. It may damage the lens mount of the D3100.

○ DK-20: The standard viewfinder eyecup for the D3100; one is supplied with the camera.

○ DK-20C: Supplementary eyepiece correction lenses for use when the built-in diopter adjustment is insufficient.

○ DR-6: The right-angle viewfinder attachment.

○ EG-D2: The video cable to connect the D3100 to a TV set.

○ EH-5a: The multi-voltage AC adapter used to power the D3100.

○ EN-EL14: The dedicated Lithium-ion battery for the D3100; one is supplied with the camera.

○ EP-5A: The adapter required to connect the D3100 to the EH-5a multi-voltage AC adapter.

○ GP-1: The GPS unit for the D3100; it connects to the remote accessory terminal of the camera.

> The Nikon GP-1 GPS unit is shown here, attached to the D3100; the camera will record GPS data and embed it in the EXIF data of image files when this is attached. Nikon View NX2 software supports GPS data for GeoTagging of image files.

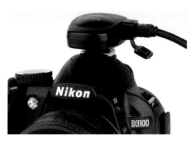

○ MC-DC2: The remote shutter release cord with lockable shutter release button.

○ MH-25: The multi-voltage AC charger for a single EN-EL14 battery; the MH-25 is supplied with the D3100.

○ SB-400: An external Speedlight (flash unit) for the D3100; it can be attached to the camera's accessory shoe or via the SC-28/SC-29 TTL flash cord.

○ SB-600: An external Speedlight (flash unit) for the D3100; it can be attached to the camera's accessory shoe or via the SC-28/SC-29 TTL flash cord.

○ SB-700: An external Speedlight (flash unit) for the D3100; it can be attached to the camera's accessory shoe or via the SC-28/SC-29 TTL flash cord.

- SB-800: An external Speedlight (flash unit) for the D3100; it can be attached to the camera's accessory shoe or via the SC-28/SC-29 TTL flash cord.
- SB-900: An external Speedlight (flash unit) for the D3100; it can be attached to the camera's accessory shoe or via the SC-28/SC-29 TTL flash cord.
- SB-R200: An external Speedlight (flash unit) for the D3100 intended for close-up and macro photography; it cannot be attached to the camera's accessory shoe but is fitted to an adapter ring that is attached to the front of the lens.

NOTE: Triggering the SB-R200 requires the use of the optional SU-800 Speedlight Commander unit or an SB-800/SB-900 Speedlight used in its Commander mode.

- SC-28: A TTL flash cord that maintains full functionality between a compatible external Speedlight and a D3100.
- SC-29: A TTL flash cord that maintains full functionality between a compatible external Speedlight and a D3100; the terminal unit that attaches to the camera has a built-in AF-assist lamp.
- SD-8a: An external battery pack for SB-900 or SB-800 Speedlights.
- SD-9: An external battery pack for SB-900 Speedlights.
- SK-6/SK-6a: A power bracket for SB-900 or SB-800 Speedlights; it attaches to the base of the D3100 allowing the flash to be mounted further from the central axis of the lens.
- UC-E4: A USB cable for connecting the D3100 to another USB-compliant device.

RESOURCES

A number of other manufacturers and suppliers provide equipment to compliment and enhance the performance of the cameras and flash accessories produced by Nikon. The following is a list of some that you may find useful:

- B&W: Manufacturers of filters and accessories; www.schneideroptics.com
- Gitzo: Manufacturers of tripods, monopods, and general camera support accessories; www.gitzo.com

- HDRsoft: Authors of the popular Photomatix high-dynamic range software; www.hdrsoft.com
- Kirk Enterprises: Manufacturers of camera and flash accessories, including flash brackets; www.kirkphoto.com
- Lastolite: Manufacturers of lighting accessories for portable flash units and a wide range of reflectors, diffusers, and other light modifying devices; www.lastolite.com
- Lee Filters: Manufacturers of both lens and lighting filters, including graduated filters; www.leefilters.com
- Lexar Media: Manufacturers of flash memory cards, including Secure Digital (SD) and high-capacity Secure Digital (SDHC) cards compatible with the D3100; www.lexar.com
- Lightshpere: A range of flash diffusion devices designed by photographer Gary Fong; www.garyfong.com
- Lumiquest: Manufacturers of flash modifiers and diffusers; www.lumiquest.com
- Manfrotto: Manufacturers of tripods, lighting stands, and flash support accessories; www.manfrotto.com
- Really Right Stuff: Manufacturers of an extensive range of camera, flash, close-up, and panoramic photography accessories; www.reallyrightstuff.com
- SanDisk: Manufacturers of flash memory cards, including Secure Digital (SD) and high-capacity Secure Digital (SDHC) cards compatible with the D3100; www.sandisk.com
- Singh-Ray: Manufacturers of camera lens filters, including graduated filter types; www.singh-ray.com

WEB SUPPORT

Nikon maintains product support and provides further information online at the following sites:

- www.nikon.com – Global gateway to Nikon Corporation
- www.nikonusa.com – Continental North America
- www.europe-nikon.com – Most European countries
- www.nikon-asia.com – Asia, Oceania, Middle East, and Africa

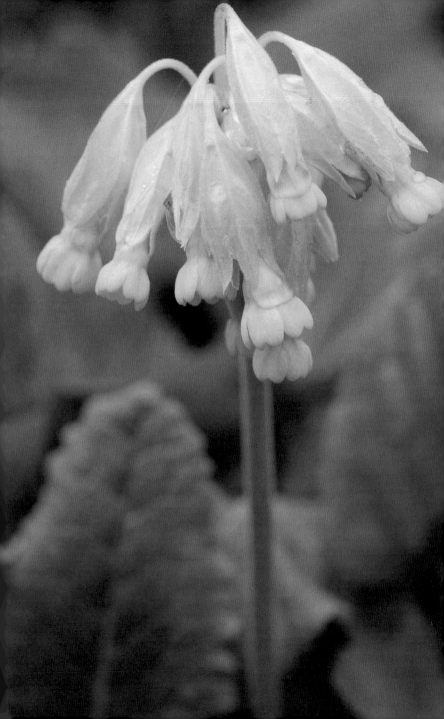

Digital Workflow

The world of digital photography requires that today's photographer be knowledgeable about what happens after the picture is taken, if they are to make the most of their images. This chapter covers everything from the different types of information stored with each image, camera-to-device connections, printing, digital workflow, to cleaning and troubleshooting the D3100.

IMAGE INFORMATION

You may be surprised to learn that, apart from image data, the picture files generated by the D3100 contain a wealth of other information, including the shooting parameters and instructions about printing pictures. This information is "tagged" to the image file using a number of common standards, depending on the sort of information saved with the image file. The supported standards are as follows:

DCF (v 2.0): Design Rule for Camera File System (DCF) is a standard used widely in the digital imaging industry for defining the camera's file management system. It includes the directory structure, file naming format, metadata format, and more.

DPOF: Digital Print Order Format (DPOF) is a standard used widely to enable pictures to be printed from a print order created and saved on a memory card.

PictBridge: A standard that permits an image file stored on a memory card to be outputted directly to a printer without needing to connect the camera to a computer or download image files from the memory card to a computer.

EXIF Data (v 2.21): The D3100 uses the EXIF (Exchangeable Image File Format) standard to tag additional information to each image file it records. Most popular digital imaging software is able to read and interpret the EXIF tags so the information can be displayed onscreen. The information recorded includes:

- Nikon (the name of the camera manufacturer)
- D3100 (the model number)
- Camera firmware version number
- Exposure information, including shutter speed, aperture, exposure mode, ISO, EV value, date / time, Exposure Compensation, flash mode, and focal length.
- Thumbnail of the main image

Examining EXIF data by either viewing the image information on the LCD screen or accessing the shooting data in appropriate software is a great teaching aid, as you can see exactly what the camera settings were for each shot. By comparing pictures and the shooting data, you can quickly learn about the technical aspects of exposure, focusing, metering, and flash exposure control.

Metadata: Metadata is any data that helps to describe the content or characteristics of a file. You may be familiar with viewing and perhaps adding some basic metadata through the File Info or Document Properties box found in many software applications and some operating systems. Most digital image management applications can search file properties and display them for you.

IPTC (DNPR) / XMP Metadata: Other metadata that can be tagged to an image file includes the use of a standard developed by the International Press Telecommunications Council (IPTC). Known as Digital Newsphoto Parameter Record (DNPR), it can append image information to include details of the origin, authorship, copyright, caption details, and keywords for searching purposes. Any application that is DNPR compliant will show this information and allow you to edit it. If you are considering submitting any pictures you shoot with the D3100 for publication, you should make use of DNPR (IPTC) metadata, as most publishing organizations require it to be present before accepting a submission.

Adobe's Extensible Metadata Platform (XMP) is an open standard digital labeling technology that allows metadata to be embedded into an image file. Any XMP-enabled software application allows descriptions and titles, searchable keywords, plus author and copyright information to be stored in a format that is easily understood by other software applications, hardware devices, and even file formats. Since XMP is extensible, it can accommodate existing metadata schemes.

The EXIF metadata recorded by the D3100 is not saved as standard IPTC / XMP metadata; however, standard IPTC / XMP metadata can be embedded automatically in images recorded by the D3100 during transfer by completing the appropriate IPTC / XMP data fields under the **[Embedded info]** tab in Nikon Transfer software. Nikon View NX2 (which includes Nikon Transfer 2) and Nikon Capture NX2 also support the EXIF, IPTC, and XMP standards.

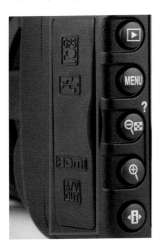

‹ The external connection terminals for the D3100 are located under the rubber cover on the left side of the camera. The D3100 can be connected to a TV via the A/V-OUT terminal, an HDMI device via the HDMI terminal, or a computer via the USB port.

AUDIO / VIDEO (A/V)

The optional Nikon EG-D2 A/V cord enables the D3100 to be connected to a television set or LCD screen for playback, or alternatively to a VCR or DVD player for recording of saved images. First you need to select the appropriate video standard. NTSC is the video standard used in the USA, Canada, and Japan, while PAL is used in most European countries. To set the video standard, open the Setup menu, navigate to the **[Video Mode]** item, and press ▶. Highlight the required option, **[NTSC]** or **[PAL]**, and press ▶ again to confirm the selection.

Before connecting the camera to the video cord, make sure the camera power is switched off. Open the rubber cover on the left end of the camera body to reveal the video out port. Connect the narrow jack-pin of the EG-D2 cable to the A/V terminal of the camera and the other end to the TV, LCD screen, VCR, or DVD player (the yellow plug goes to the video input). Tune the TV to the video channel, then turn on the camera and press the ▶ button. The image is displayed on the television screen and can now be recorded to video or DVD. The LCD screen cannot be used to display an image or camera menus, but all other camera operations will function normally. This means that you can take pictures while the camera is connected to a TV set and use review / playback functions simply by looking at the TV monitor screen. It is probably best to use the EH-5a AC adapter and EP-5A power connector to power the camera if you intend to use the camera for image playback via a television screen for an extended period of time.

CONNECTING VIA HDMI

The D3100 can be connected to an HDMI device using a type-C mini-pin HDMI cable. Set the HDMI format options in the Setup menu under the **[HDMI]** item (see pages 189-190 for more information), then switch the camera off and connect the HDMI cable to the HDMI port (it is located immediately above the A/V connector under the large rubber cover on the left side of the camera body). Tune the device to the HDMI channel, then turn the camera on and press the ▶ button. The camera monitor will remain blank, as the display of an image or menus on the LCD monitor is not supported when the camera is connected via the HDMI output; however, all other camera operations will function normally.

CONNECTING TO A COMPUTER

The D3100 can be connected directly to a computer via the optional Nikon UC-E4 USB cable. The camera supports the high-speed USB (2.0) interface that offers a maximum transfer rate of 480 megabytes per second (Mbps). You can download images from the camera using the supplied Nikon Transfer software. Images can be viewed and organized using the supplied Nikon View NX2 software, while the optional Nikon Capture NX2 can be used to enhance images.

HINT: If you use the D3100 tethered to a computer for any function, ensure that the installed camera battery is fully charged. The preferable option is to use the EH-5a AC adapter in conjunction with the EP-5A power connector to prevent interruptions to data transfer by loss of power.

Before connecting the D3100 to a computer, check that one of the following operating systems is running:

O Windows 7 (32-bit or 64-bit versions)

O Windows Vista Service Pack 2 (32-bit or 64-bit versions)

O Windows XP Service Pack 3 – 32-bit versions (Home Edition or Professional)

O Macintosh OS X (version 10.4.11, 10.5.8, or 10.6.4)

Also make sure that the appropriate versions of Nikon software—Nikon View NX2 (2.0.3) and / or Nikon Capture NX2 (2.2.6)—are installed.

Direct USB Connection: To connect the camera to a computer, start by turning the camera off, then turn the computer on and wait for it to start up. Connect the UC-E4 USB cable to the USB port of the camera (located under the rubber cover on the left side) and to the computer, then turn the camera on. Nikon Transfer should start automatically. The first time you use the application I recommend you set the preferences by clicking on the Preferences tab before clicking on the Transfer button to initiate data transfer. The camera can be turned off as soon as the data transfer is complete.

DIGITAL WORKFLOW

281

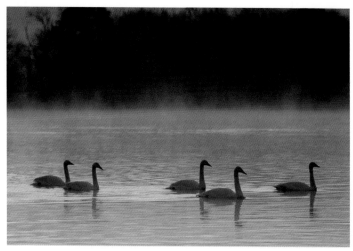

^ Once you have captured your pictures, it is advisable to download them as soon as possible and create at least one backup copy on a separate storage device.

Memory Card Readers: Although the D3100 can be tethered directly to a computer for transferring image data, there are several reasons why you should consider using a dedicated memory card reader as an alternative:

O If you use the tethered camera method, you will drain battery power and risk data being lost or corrupted if the power fails.

O Using a card reader allows you to run software to recover lost or corrupted image files as well as diagnose problems with the memory card.

O You can leave a card reader permanently attached to your computer, which further reduces the risk of losing or corrupting files as a result of a poor connection due to the wear and tear caused by constantly connecting a USB cable to the camera.

DIRECT PRINTING

As mentioned previously, the D3100 supports a standard that allows either individual or multiple pictures to be printed directly from the camera via a USB connection without a computer. This feature is only compatible with JPEG image files and a printer that supports the PictBridge standard.

NOTE: Nikon recommends that images selected for direct printing should be recorded in the sRGB color space. Use the **[Color Space]** item in the Shooting menu to select this setting.

To print pictures directly from the camera to a PictBridge compatible printer, start by turning the camera off. Then turn the printer on before connecting the printer to the camera via the optional UC-E4 USB; do not connect the camera and printer via a USB hub. Turn the camera on and a welcome message will show on the camera LCD screen, followed by the PictBridge Playback display.

NOTE: It is essential that you make sure the camera battery is fully charged, or use the EH-5a AC adapter and EP-5A power connector.

PRINTING A SINGLE PICTURE

To select a picture for printing from the PictBridge Playback display, scroll through the images saved on the memory card using ◀ and ▶; use ▲ and ▼ to display photo information. To view an enlarged section of the image, press the ९ button; press ▶ to return to the normal full-frame view. To view up to six thumbnail images at a time, press ९▦. Use the Multi Selector to highlight an individual thumbnail picture and press ९ to display the selected thumbnail image in full frame.

To print a single image selected in the PictBridge Playback display, press the ⊛ button to show the PictBridge Printing menu. Use ▲ or ▼ to select the required option and press ▶ to select it:

OPTION	DESCRIPTION
Page Size	Press ▲ and ▼ to select the appropriate paper size from the [Page Size] item; choose [Printer default], [3.5 x 5 inch], [5 x 7 inch], or [A4]. Then press ⊗ to select the option and return to the main Print menu.
Number of Copies	Press ▲ and ▼ to select the number of copies of the highlighted image to be printed (maximum 99), and then press ⊗ to select the option and return to the main Print menu.
Border	Press ▲ and ▼ to select [Printer Default] (uses default setting of current printer), [Print with Border] (white border), or [No Border]. Then press ⊗ to select the option and return to the main Print menu. Only options supported by the selected printer will be displayed.
Time Stamp	Press ▲ and ▼ to select [Printer Default] (uses default setting of current printer), [Print Time Stamp] (date and time of image exposure prints on image), or [No Time Stamp]. Use ⊗ to select the option and return to the main Print menu.
Cropping	Press ▲ and ▼ to select [Crop] (picture can be cropped in-camera) or [No Cropping] (printed full frame). Selecting [No Cropping] and pressing ⊗ returns you to the main Print menu. Selecting [Crop] and then pressing ▶ displays a dialog box; press ⊕ to increase the size of the crop, and press ⊞ to reduce the crop. Use ⊕ to position the crop frame. Press ⊗ to return to the main Print menu. Note that this item is only available if supported by the selected printer.
Start Printing	Select [Start printing] and press ⊗ to print the image highlighted in the PictBridge display. To cancel the process before all copies have been printed, press the ⊗ button.

PRINTING MULTIPLE PICTURES

Multiple pictures can be printed by connecting the camera to a compatible printer and selecting images through the PictBridge menu or by using the DPOF feature (see pages 286-288 for more on DPOF). When using the DPOF feature, either the camera or a memory card alone can be connected directly to the PictBridge printer.

To print directly from the camera, connect it to a compatible printer as described above, and make sure the PictBridge Playback display is shown on the LCD screen. Press the MENU button to display the available options (a description of these four options is set out below), highlight the required option, and press ▶.

OPTION	DESCRIPTION
Print Select	The selected images are printed.
Select date	Print one copy of all the pictures taken on the selected date.
Print (DPOF)	The current DPOF print order set is printed (DPOF date and information options are not supported).
Index Print	Creates an index print of all images saved in the JPEG format. (If the memory card contains more than 256 JPEG images, only the first 256 will be printed.)

Print Select: If the [Print select] option is chosen from the PictBridge menu and ▶ is pressed, six thumbnail images will be displayed on the LCD screen. Use the Multi Selector to scroll through the images, and press and hold ⊕ to see the highlighted image full frame. To select the image currently highlighted for printing, press ⊞ and ▲; the image is marked with the 🖶 icon and the number of copies to be printed is set to one [1]. To specify the number of copies of each image selected for printing, keep the ⊞ button pressed, then use ▲ and ▼ to increase or decrease the number respectively. Repeat this process for each image to be printed. To deselect a picture for printing, press ▼ when the number of prints is set to [1]. Press ⊛ to display the print options for multiple printing, and set [Page size], [Border type], and [Time stamp] options as required (according to the instructions above under Printing a Single Picture).

NOTE: There is no option for cropping images when printing multiple pictures, unlike when printing a single picture.

NOTE: Images saved in the NEF (RAW) format will be displayed in the [Print select] menu, but it is not possible to select them for printing. However, it is possible to create a printable JPEG copy of an NEF (RAW) file by using the [NEF (RAW) processing] item in the Retouch menu.

Select Date: To print all the pictures taken on a specific date, highlight the **[Select date]** option from the PictBridge menu and press ▶; a list of the dates for images recorded on the installed memory card will be displayed. Press ▲ or ▼ to selected the desired date, and then press ▶ to select it. To view the pictures taken on a specific date, highlight the date and press ◳; use the Multi Selector to scroll through the pictures and press and hold the ◌ button to view the highlighted picture at full screen. Once a specific date is selected, press ◉ to display the print options for multiple printing and set the **[Page size]**, **[Border type]**, and **[Time stamp]** options (as described in the instructions above under Printing a Single Picture).

Print (DPOF): The D3100 supports the Digital Print Order Format (DPOF) standard that embeds an instruction set in the appropriate EXIF data fields of an image file. This allows you to insert the memory card directly into any DPOF-compatible home printer or commercial mini-lab printer, and automatically get a set of prints of only those images you wish to print. This feature can be particularly useful if, for example, you are away from home on vacation; you can still produce prints from your digital files even if you do not have access to your own printer.

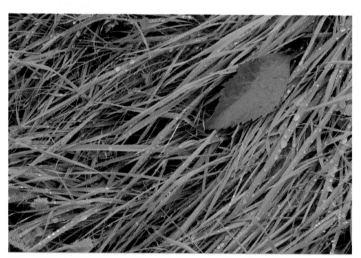

∧ The ability to print images direct from the camera obviates the need for a computer; however, the Retouch menu is no match for dedicated image-editing software if you want to make adjustments to your pictures before printing.

To print the current DPOF print set saved to the installed memory card (see below for details of how to create a DPOF print set) when the camera is connected to a compatible PictBridge printer, highlight [Print (DPOF)] from the PictBridge Playback display and press ▶ to select it. The camera will display thumbnails of all the images in the current DPOF print set in groups of up to six at a time. If desired, the current print set can be modified using the same procedure as described under the Print Multiple Pictures section above; you can change the number of copies of each picture to be printed and set [Page size], [Border type], and [Time stamp] as desired. To print the existing print set without modification, or print it once any modifications have been completed, highlight [Start printing] and press ⊛.

NOTE: If the currently saved print set is modified by deleting images using a computer or other device, the print order may not print correctly.

NOTE: There are subtle differences in the functionality between the direct printing routes. For example, direct printing of a single image with the D3100 connected to a PictBridge-compatible printer allows you to perform cropping before printing, whereas printing multiple images from the camera or memory card using a print set created using the DPOF standard can only be printed full frame.

Creating a DPOF Print Order: To select images for printing using the DPOF feature, it is necessary to create a DPOF print order. Start by highlighting [Print set (DPOF)] from the Playback menu of the D3100; the [Select/Set] option will be highlighted. Press ▶ to confirm the selection and the camera will display thumbnails of all the images stored on the inserted memory card in groups of up to six. Use the same procedure as described under the Print Select section above to select the required pictures and the number of copies to be printed. Once all images to be printed have been selected, press the ⊛ button to save the selected group of images, and display the options for data imprinting.

To imprint shooting data on the image, highlight [Data imprint] and press ▶ to switch the option on or off. To print the date / time the image was recorded on the image, highlight [Imprint date] and press ▶ to switch the option on or off. In both cases, a check mark will appear in the box to the left of the item title in the menu screen to indicate the option is turned on. To finish, save the print set order by highlighting [Done] and pressing ⊛.

NOTE: Information entered via the [Data imprint] and [Imprint date] options is not printed when the DPOF print set is printed using a direct USB connection between the camera and printer, but only when the memory card is inserted directly into a PictBridge-compatible printer.

To deselect the entire print set, highlight [Print set (DPOF)] from the Playback menu and press ▶, then highlight [Deselect all?]. Press ▶ and highlight [Yes] or [No] and press ⊛ to confirm the selection.

Making an Index Print: To make an index print (multiple images on the same page), connect the camera to a compatible printer as described above. Once the PictBridge Playback display is open on the LCD screen, it is possible to create an index print of all the JPEG files on the memory card. Start by pressing the MENU button, select the [Index print] option in the PictBridge menu, and then press ⊛.

Next, press ⊛ to display the PictBridge printing options and set [Page size], [Border type], and [Time stamp] options as required according to the instructions above under Printing a Single Picture; if the selected page size is too small, a warning will be displayed. Finally, select [Start printing] and press ⊛ to start printing. To cancel printing, press ⊛ again.

DIGITAL WORKFLOW

For many photographers who shoot with film, their direct involvement in the production of their pictures generally ends when they hand over the exposed film to be processed and printed by someone else. The digital photographer can exercise a far greater level of control over every stage of image processing, from initial capture in the camera to the output of an image as a print or for electronic display. It is essential to develop a routine to make sure you work in an efficient and effective manner. You may wish to consider the following seven-stage workflow as a starting point for establishing one of your own, built around your specific requirements.

Step 1: Prepare

O Familiarize yourself with your camera. The more intuitive you become with your equipment, the more time you are able to spend concentrating on the scene / subject being photographed.

O Make sure the camera battery is charged and always carry a spare.

O Rather than saving all your pictures to a single high-capacity memory card, reduce the risk of a catastrophic loss due to card failure / loss by spreading your images over several memory cards.

O Always clean the low-pass filter array in front of the sensor before you begin a shoot to reduce the level of post-processing work.

O Always format the memory card in the camera each time you insert it.

Step 2: Shoot

O Adjust camera settings to match the requirements of your shoot. Choose an appropriate image quality, image size, ISO, color space, and White Balance.

O Set other camera controls such as metering and autofocus according to the shooting conditions.

O Use the Image Comment feature in the Setup menu to assign a note about the authorship / copyright of the images you shoot.

O Review images and make any adjustments you deem necessary. Use the histogram display to check the exposure level and use the magnification feature to check image sharpness. However, do not rely on this display to assess color, contrast, or hue; remember, even if you shoot NEF (RAW), you only see a JPEG version of the image displayed on the camera's LCD screen.

O Do not be in too much of a hurry to delete pictures unless they are obvious failures. It is often better to edit after shooting is completed, rather than "on the fly." Memory cards are relatively cheap, so do not skimp on memory capacity.

Step 3: Transfer

O Before transferring images to your computer, designate a specific folder, or folders, in which the images will be stored so you know where to find them.

O Rather than connecting the camera directly to the computer, use a card reader. It is much faster, more reliable, and reduces the wear and tear on the camera.

O If the application used to transfer the image files from the memory card to a computer permits you to assign general information to the image files during transfer (e.g. XMP or DNPR (IPTC) metadata), make sure you at least complete the appropriate fields for image authorship and copyright.

- Consider renaming files and assigning further information and keywords to facilitate searching and retrieving images at a later date.
- Always back up your image files by copying them to at least two separate storage devices, such as the hard drive of your computer and an external hard drive.

Step 4: Edit and File

- Use a browsing application, such as the supplied copy of Nikon View NX2, to sort through your pictures. Again, do not be in too much of a hurry to erase pictures. It is often best to take a second look at images a few days, or even weeks, after they were shot; your opinions about images will often change.
- Print a contact sheet of small thumbnail images to help you decide which images to retain.

Step 5: Process

- When post-processing from RAW files, save a working copy in a file format such as TIFF (RGB) or PSD (Adobe Photoshop).
- Do not use the JPEG format for processing. Each time you modify file data and re-save it as a JPEG, compression will be applied to the altered data. The effect of such repeated compression is cumulative and will progressively reduce image quality.
- Make adjustments in an orderly and logical sequence starting with overall brightness, contrast, and color. Then make more local adjustments to correct problems or enhance the image.
- Save your adjusted file as a master copy to which you can then apply a crop, resize, unsharp mask, and any other finishing touches appropriate to your output requirements. The maxim to follow here is: process once; output many times.

Step 6: Archive

- Data can become lost or corrupted at any time for a variety of reasons—in addition to making multiple backup copies of your original files, also back up all the edited master file and working copy files.
- If you shoot in NEF (RAW) format, consider creating a copy of all your NEF (RAW) files in Adobe's open Digital Negative (DNG) format to help ensure compatibility with future iterations of software.
- CDs have a limited capacity, so consider using DVDs or an external hard disk drive. No electronic storage media is guaranteed 100% safe, nor does it have an infinite lifespan—always check your backup copies regularly and repeat the backup process as required.

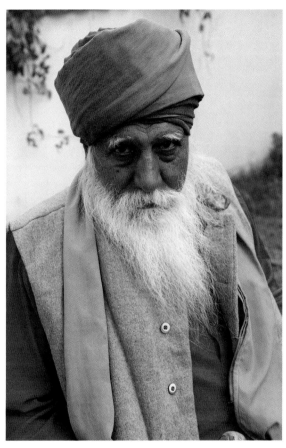

Step 7: Display

- O We all shoot pictures to share with others. Digital technology has expanded the possibilities of image display considerably: we can e-mail pictures to family, friends, colleagues, and clients; prepare digital slide shows; or post images to websites for pleasure or profit.

- O Home printing in full color is now reliable and cost effective. Spend some time to set up your system properly and work methodically: Calibrate your monitor and printer to ensure accurate display and consistent reproduction of color, use an appropriate resolution for the print size you require, and choose a paper type and finish accordingly.

- O Once you have a high-quality print, ensure you present it in a manner befitting its status; make sure to frame or mount it securely. This will also help to protect it from the effects of light and atmospheric pollutants.

Obviously, keeping your camera and lens(es) in a clean, dry environment is very important. Regardless of how scrupulous you are about doing this, dust and dirt will eventually accumulate on or inside your equipment. Since prevention is better than a cure, always keep the body and lens caps in place when not using your equipment. Always switch the D3100 off before attaching or detaching a lens to prevent particles from being attracted inside the camera by the electrical charge in its electronic components. Remember, gravity is your friend! Whenever you change lenses, get into the habit of holding the camera body with the lens mount tilted downward.

For the same reason, do not carry or store your D3100 on its back, as particles already inside the camera will settle on the optical low-pass filter. Periodically, vacuum-clean the interior of your camera bag / case; it is amazing how much debris can collect there! Sealing your camera body in a clear plastic bag, which you then keep within your camera case, will add another valuable layer of protection in very dusty or damp conditions. In the latter situation, keep some packets of silica gel inside the bag to absorb any moisture. Putting together a basic cleaning kit is straightforward. You should consider the following:

- O 1/2 inch (12 mm) artist's paintbrush made from soft sable hair for general cleaning
- O Micro-fiber lens cloth for cleaning lens elements
- O Micro-fiber towel (available from any good outdoors store) for absorbing moisture when working in damp conditions; I find these towels invaluable in all sorts of conditions, and they are soft enough to use for cleaning lenses and filters.
- O Rubber-bulb blower made for cleaning lenses and the low-pass filter

Always brush or blow as much material off your equipment as possible before wiping it with a cloth. For lens elements and filters, use a micro-fiber cloth and wipe surfaces in short, straight strokes—not long, sweeping circular movements. Turn the cloth frequently to prevent depositing the dirt you have just removed back onto the same surface! For any residue that cannot be removed with a dry cloth, you will need a lens cleaning fluid suitable for photographic lenses. Apply a small amount of fluid to the cloth—never directly to the lens, as it may seep inside and cause damage. Wipe the residue away and then buff the glass with a dry area of the cloth. Any lens cloth should be washed on a regular basis to keep it clean.

CLEANING THE LOW-PASS FILTER

Unwanted material such as dust or particles of lint can accumulate inside the D3100 and may settle on the surface of the optical low-pass filter (OLPF). This is an unfortunate problem that can afflict any digital camera, especially those with interchangeable lenses, as foreign matter can enter the camera when a lens is removed or changed. Focusing or adjusting the zoom ring of a lens causes groups of lens elements to be shifted inside the lens barrel, creating very slight changes in air pressure. This can cause dust in the atmosphere to be drawn through the lens into the camera. Furthermore, the operation of internal camera mechanisms such as the shutter and reflex mirror can generate minute particles due to the wear and tear of the moving parts. During the manufacture of the D3100, Nikon has attempted to reduce the incidence of such problems by cycling the shutter mechanism many hundreds of times before it is installed in the camera.

Any dust or other material that settles on the low-pass filter will often appear as dark spots in your pictures; they cast a shadow on the camera's sensor that is located behind this filter. The exact nature of the appearance of these shadows will depend on the size of the particle and the lens aperture you use. At very large apertures (f/1.4) it is likely that most very small dust specks will not be visible. However, at small apertures (f/22) they will probably show up with well-defined edges.

Self-Cleaning: The D3100 incorporates a self-cleaning function that vibrates OLPF at four different frequencies using a piezo-electric oscillator; this is exactly the same system used in the D300s, D700, and D5000 camera models. The cleaning process can be set to activate automatically when the camera is turned on, turned off, or both. Alternatively, it can be activated at any time the user deems it necessary.

Whenever you use the self-cleaning feature, make sure the camera is placed base down on a solid surface. There are two good reasons for this; first, the effect of vibrating the low-pass filter will be most efficient when the camera is supported firmly, and second, there is a strip of highly adhesive material located along the bottom edge of the low-pass filter that is designed to capture and retain any dislodged material.

To configure the self-cleaning feature, open the Setup menu and navigate to the [Clean image sensor] item, and press ▶ to display two options: [Clean now] and [Clean at]. [Clean now] is highlighted by default, and pressing the ⊛ button will initiate the process, during which the message "Image Sensor Cleaning" is displayed on the LCD screen. This option can be used at any time during camera operation.

> Options for the
Self-Cleaning feature
are set via the Setup
menu.

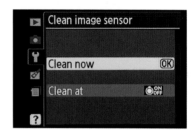

HINT: It is worth getting into the habit of checking images periodically as you shoot for any particle shadows by pressing in the ⊛ button to zoom into images during Playback.

To have the cleaning process commence automatically, open the Setup menu and navigate to the [Clean image sensor] item and press ▶, then highlight the [Clean at] option and press ▶ to display four options:

O ⊛ON [Startup]: Cleaning is only performed at startup.

O ⊛OFF [Shutdown]: Cleaning is only performed at shutdown.

O ⊛ON/OFF [Startup & shutdown] (default): Cleaning is performed at startup and shutdown.

O [Cleaning off]: Automatic cleaning function is off.

Clean at startup would appear to be the most logical selection, as it will help remove any unwanted material before you start shooting. Having the function operate at camera shut down will bring no benefit to images that have already been recorded and will have no affect on any material that settles on the low-pass filter while the camera is dormant; therefore, I can see little advantage in running the process at this point.

NOTE: Using any other camera control or function will interrupt the sensor-cleaning process. If the built-in flash is raised, the sensor-cleaning process may not operate when the camera starts up.

NOTE: If the sensor-cleaning process is repeated several times in rapid succession, the D3100 may disable the function to protect the camera's electrical circuitry. If this occurs, wait a few minutes before attempting to use the function again.

NOTE: When operating the sensor-cleaning function, a short sequence of very faint high-pitch squeaks may be heard; this is normal and not an indication of malfunction.

Airflow Control System: Nikon's innovative Airflow Control System has also been incorporated into the D3100 to supplement the self-cleaning function described in the previous section. It is designed to use changes in air pressure caused by the movement of the reflex mirror to direct air inside the mirror box toward ducts set into its base; this helps draw dust particles away from the low-pass filter located in front of the camera's CMOS sensor. Below the bottom edge of the OLPF and the ducts in the base of the mirror box are areas covered with an extremely adhesive material that is designed to capture dust and other particulate matter dislodged by the self-cleaning processes.

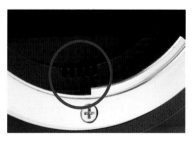

‹ The air ducts of the Airflow Control System can be seen just inside the lens mount at the base of the mirror box.

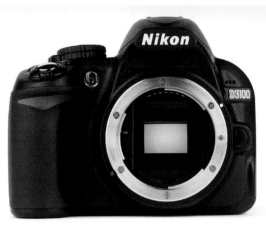

∧ Access to the OLPF for cleaning is via the lens opening. The reflex mirror must be raised and the shutter opened, using the [Mirror lock-up] item in the Setup menu, to reveal the front surface of the OLPF.

Manual Cleaning: Nikon expressly recommends that you should leave manual cleaning of the optical low-pass filter to an authorized service center. However, in recognition of the fact that this is likely to be impractical for a variety of reasons, the D3100 has a feature that enables the reflex mirror to be locked up in its raised position and the shutter opened to provide access to the front surface of the OLPF.

> **CAUTION:** Nikon states that under no circumstances should you touch or wipe the surface of the OLPF, as it is extremely delicate. Any manual cleaning process you perform is done entirely at your own risk; any damage caused to the low-pass filter or any other part of your camera as a result of manual cleaning by the user will not be covered by warranties provided by Nikon.

To inspect and / or clean the low-pass filter, you need to perform a few preparatory steps. First, ensure the camera has a fully charged battery installed or is powered by the optional EH-5a AC adapter via the optional EP-5A power connector. Second, remove the lens, or body cap, and keep the camera facing downwards. Now switch the camera on, navigate to the [Mirror lock-up] item in the Setup menu, and press ▶ to display [Start]. Press ⊛ and a dialog box will appear with the following instruction: **[When shutter button is pressed, the mirror lifts and shutter opens. To lower mirror, turn camera off]**. When the shutter release is pressed all the way down, the mirror will lift and remain in its raised position and the shutter will open, while the LCD screen and viewfinder will go blank. Keep the camera facing down so any debris falls away from the filter; look up into the lens mount to inspect the low-pass filter surface (it is probably helpful to shine a light on it).

NOTE: The **[Mirror lock-up]** item in the Setup menu is not available if the battery level is ▭ or less; it will be grayed out.

NOTE: Since the photosites on the CMOS sensor of the D3100 are approximately just 5.0 microns (μm) square (one micron = 1/1000 of a millimeter), offending particles are often very, very small, and it is unlikely you will be able to detect all of them by eye.

To clean the low-pass filter, keep the camera facing down and use a rubber bulb blower to gently puff air towards the low-pass filter surface. Take care that you do not enter any part of the blower into the camera. Never use an ordinary blower brush with bristles, which can damage the surface of the low-pass filter, or an aerosol-type blower, which might emit propellant agent or condensation that can leave a residue. Once you have finished cleaning, switch the camera off to close the shutter and return the mirror to its lowered-position. If the blower bulb method fails to remove any stubborn material, I recommend you have the sensor cleaned professionally.

CAUTION: If the power supply fails during the cleaning process, the shutter will close and the mirror will return to its down position. This has potentially dire consequences if you have any cleaning utensils in the camera at that time! Therefore, always use a fully charged EN-EL14 battery or the optional EH-5a AC adapter via the optional EP-5A power connector.

NOTE: If power from the installed battery begins to run low while the mirror is locked up for cleaning, the camera will emit an audible warning and the self-timer lamp will begin to flash, indicating the mirror will be automatically lowered in approximately two minutes.

For a user with plenty of confidence, there is a wide range of proprietary sensor-cleaning materials that can be used to clean stubborn material from the low-pass filter. These include brushes, swabs, and fluids available from a number of manufacturers (see the list of resources on page 274-275). It must be stressed that if you use any such materials or implements, it is done entirely at your own risk!

CAUTION: If you decide to clean the low-pass filter of your D3100 with a wet process, make sure you NEVER use any alcohol-based (e.g., ethanol or methanol) cleaning fluid. The low-pass filter of the D3100 has a special anti-static coating that can be damaged by such chemical compounds.

> If dark spots become apparent in your pictures, it is likely there is dust on the low-pass filter; proper storage and regular cleaning of your D3100 will help prevent this from occurring.

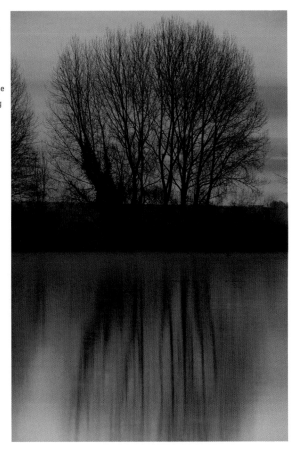

Finally, if you have Nikon Capture NX 2 software, you can use the Dust Off Reference Photo feature with NEF (RAW) files shot using the D3100 to help remove the effects of dust particles on the low-pass filter by masking their shadows electronically (see pages 194-195 for more details).

TROUBLESHOOTING

On occasion, the D3100 camera may not operate as you expect. This may be due to an alternative setting that has been made (often inadvertently) or some other reason. Many of the reasons for these problems are straightforward, and the solutions are set out in the table below:

PROBLEM	SOLUTION
Viewfinder appears out of focus	O Adjust viewfinder focus O Use diopter adjustment lens
Displays turn off unexpectedly	Set longer delay under [Auto off timers] in the Setup option of the GUIDE mode or the Setup menu in all other exposure modes
Camera does not respond to controls	See page 306 for information about electrostatic interference
Displays in LCD screen and viewfinder appear slow to react and / or are dimmed	Probably due to the affect of high or low ambient temperature
Camera takes longer than expected to turn on	Delete files / folders
Shutter release disabled	O Focus not acquired O CPU lens aperture ring not set to minimum value O Memory card not installed, locked, or full O Non-CPU lens attached but camera not in Manual exposure mode O Flash charging O ƀuℓƀ selected in M mode and then Mode dial set to S mode: choose new shutter speed
Image shows more than displayed in viewfinder	Viewfinder coverage is only 95% in both horizontal and vertical directions

PROBLEM	SOLUTION
Pictures out of focus	O AF-S or AF-I lens not attached O Camera set to manual focus O AF unable to operate; use manual focus
Focus does not lock when shutter release is depressed halfway	Camera is in AF-C Focus mode: use AF-L/AE-L button to lock focus
Cannot select focus point	O AF-A set as AF Area mode O Shutter release half depressed to turn LCD screen off, or activate exposure meter
Cannot select AF-Area mode	Manual focus selected
Image size cannot be altered	NEF (RAW) selected for image quality
Camera is slow to record photos	Turn [Noise reduction] off in Shooting menu
Randomly-spaced bright pixels appear in photos ("noise")	O Select lower ISO setting, or use [Noise reduction] O Shutter speed exceeds 8 seconds; use long exposure [Noise reduction]
Banding appears in Live View and D-Movie recording	Choose option under [Flicker reduction] that matches local AC mains power supply
Sound not recorded in D-Movie mode	[Off] selected for [Sound] in [Movie settings]
Photos are blotched or smeared	O Clean lens O Clean low-pass filter
Date is not imprinted on picture	Image quality set to NEF (RAW) or NEF + JPEG
Menu item cannot be selected	Some menu items are not available in all Exposure modes
Full range of shutter speeds is not available	Flash in use
Colors appear unnatural	O Adjust White Balance O Adjust [Set Picture Control] settings
Cannot measure Preset White Balance	Test target too dark or too bright
Image cannot be selected as source for Preset White Balance	Image not created with D3100

PROBLEM	SOLUTION
Results with Picture Control vary from image to image	Avoid A (auto) for sharpening, contrast, or saturation when shooting a sequence of pictures
Unable to adjust contrast for selected Picture Control	Switch off [Active D-Lighting]
Metering cannot be changed	Autoexposure lock is active
Exposure Compensation cannot be used	Select P, A, or S exposure modes
Only one shot taken when shutter release button is pressed in Continuous release mode	Lower built-in flash
Reddish areas and / or uneven textures appear in photos	May occur with long exposures; use [Noise reduction] when shooting with shutter speed set to ƀuㄥƀ
• Flashing areas appear in images • Shooting data appear on images • A graph appears during Playback	Press ⓘ to select photo information displayed, or change settings for [Display mode]
NEF (RAW) image is not played back	Photo taken at NEF + JPEG image quality
Some photos not displayed in Playback mode	Select [All] for [Playback folder]
"Tall" (portrait) orientation photos are displayed in "Wide" (landscape) orientation	O Select ON for [Rotate tall] O OFF selected for [Auto image rotation] O Camera orientation was altered while shooting in Continuous mode or camera was pointed up / down when shooting O Picture is already displayed in image review
Cannot delete a photo	O Photo is protected; remove protection O Memory card is locked
Cannot retouch picture	O Picture cannot be edited any further within the D3100 O Image file is a video; these cannot be retouched in camera
Cannot change print order	O Memory card is full: delete images O Memory card is locked

PROBLEM	SOLUTION
Cannot select image for direct printing	O Photo saved in NEF (RAW) format O Create JPEG copy using **[NEF Raw processing]** item O Transfer to computer and print using Nikon View NX2 or Capture NX2
Photos not displayed on TV	O Select correct Video mode O Ensure A/V or HDMI cable is connected properly
Cannot transfer photos to a computer	Computer operating system incompatible with D3100 or transfer software
NEF (RAW) photos not displayed in Capture NX2	Update software to Capture NX 2 version 2.2.6 or later
Image Dust Off option in Nikon Capture NX2 is ineffective	O Image sensor cleaning alters the position of dust and other material on the low-pass filter O The Dust Off reference data recorded before image sensor cleaning is performed cannot be used with images recorded after image sensor cleaning is performed O Dust Off reference data recorded after image sensor cleaning is performed cannot be used with photographs taken before image sensor cleaning is performed
Computer displays NEF (RAW) images differently than camera display	Off-brand software does not display effects of Picture Controls and Active D-Lighting; use Capture NX2
Date of recording is not correct	Reset camera clock
Menu item cannot be selected	Some options are not available at certain combinations of settings or when no memory card is inserted

ERROR MESSAGES AND DISPLAYS

The D3100 is a sophisticated electronic device capable of reporting a range of malfunctions and problems through indicators and error messages that appear in the displays of the viewfinder, control panel, and LCD screen. The following table will assist you in finding a solution, should one of these indicators or messages be displayed. If you see a flashing "?" in the monitor or viewfinder, it indicates that a warning or error message can be displayed by pressing the ⓆⓌ button.

INDICATOR		SOLUTION
MONITOR	VIEWFINDER	
Lock lens aperture ring at minimum aperture (largest f/number).	ғЕ Е (blinks)	Set lens aperture ring to minimum aperture (largest f-number).
Lens not attached.	F-- / ⓐ (blinks)	O Attach non-IX NIKKOR lens. O If non-CPU lens is attached, select exposure mode M.
Shutter-release disabled. Recharge battery.		O Turn camera off and recharge or replace battery.
This battery cannot be used. Choose battery designated for use in this camera.	ⓐ (blinks)	O Use Nikon-approved battery (EN-EL9a).
Initialization error. Turn camera off and then on again.		O Turn camera off, remove and replace battery, and then turn camera on again.
Battery level is low. Complete operation and turn camera off immediately.	—	O End cleaning and turn camera off and recharge or replace battery.
Clock not set.	—	O Set camera clock.
No memory card.	[-Ε-]	O Turn camera off and confirm that card is correctly inserted.
Memory card is locked. Slide lock to "write" position.	Ε d (blinks)	O Memory card is locked (write-protected). O Slide card write-protect switch to "write" position.

DIGITAL WORKFLOW

303

INDICATOR		SOLUTION
MONITOR	VIEWFINDER	
This memory card cannot be used. Card may be damaged. Insert another card.	[d / E r r (blinks)	O Use approved card. O Format card. If problem persists, card may be damaged. Contact Nikon-authorized service representative. O Error creating new folder. Delete files or insert new memory card. O Insert new memory card. O Eye-Fi card is still emitting wireless signal after Disable has been selected for Eye-Fi upload. Turn camera off and remove card.
This card is not formatted. Format card?	F o r (blinks)	O Format card or turn camera off and insert new memory card.
Card is full.	F u L (blinks)	O Reduce quality or size. O Delete photographs. O Insert new memory card.
—	● (blinks)	O Camera cannot focus using autofocus. O Change composition or focus manually.
Subject is too bright.	Η ί	O Use a lower ISO sensitivity. O Use commercial ND filter. O In mode: S – Increase shutter speed. A – Choose a smaller aperture (larger f-number).
Subject is too dark.	L o	O Use a higher ISO sensitivity. O Use flash. O In mode: S – Lower shutter speed. A – Choose a larger aperture (smaller f-number).
No Bulb in S mode.	b u L b (blinks)	O Change shutter speed or select Manual exposure mode.
—	⚡ (blinks)	O Flash has fired at full power. Check photo in monitor; if underexposed, adjust settings and try again.
Flash is in TTL mode. Choose another setting or use a CPU lens.		Change Flash mode setting on optional flash unit or use CPU lens.

INDICATOR		SOLUTION
MONITOR	**VIEWFINDER**	
—	⚡ (blinks)	O Use the flash. O Change distance to subject, aperture, flash range, or ISO sensitivity. O Optional SB-400 flash unit attached: flash is in bounce position or focus distance is very short. Continue shooting; if necessary, increase focus distance to prevent shadows from appearing in photograph.
Flash error		Error occurred updating firmware for optional flash unit. Contact Nikon-authorized service representative.
Error. Press shutter release button again.		Release shutter. If error persists or appears frequently, consult Nikon-authorized service representative.
Start-up error. Contact a Nikon-authorized service representative.	$E r r$ (blinks)	Consult Nikon-authorized service representative.
Autoexposure error. Contact a Nikon-authorized service representative.		Consult Nikon-authorized service representative.
Folder contains no images.	—	Folder selected for playback contains no images. Insert another memory card or select a different folder.
File does not contain image data.	—	File has been created or modified using a computer or different make of camera, or file is corrupt.
Cannot select this file.	—	File has been created or modified using a computer or different make of camera, or file is corrupt.
No image for retouching.	—	Memory card does not contain NEF (RAW) images for use with **[NEF (RAW) processing]**.
Check printer.	—	Check printer. To resume, select **[Continue]** (if available).
Check paper.	—	Paper is not selected size. Insert paper of correct size and select **[Continue]**.
Paper jam.	—	Clear jam and select **[Continue]**.

| INDICATOR | | SOLUTION |
MONITOR	VIEWFINDER	
Out of paper.	—	Insert paper of selected size and select [Continue].
Check ink supply.	—	Check ink. To resume, select [Continue].[1]
Out of ink.	—	Replace ink and select [Continue].

[1]See printer manual for more information.

ELECTROSTATIC INTERFERENCE

Operation of the D3100 is totally dependent on electrical power. Occasionally, the camera may stop functioning properly or display unusual characters or unexpected messages in the viewfinder and LCD displays. Such behavior is generally due to the effects of a strong external electrostatic charge. If this occurs, try switching the camera off, disconnecting it from its power supply (remove the installed EN-EL14 or unplug the EH-5a AC adapter / EP-5A power connector), and then reconnect the power and switch the camera back on. If the symptoms persist, the camera will require inspection by an authorized technician.

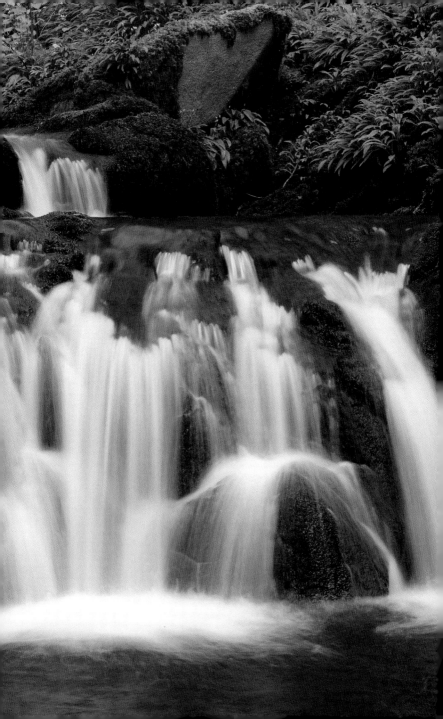

Glossary

AI
Automatic Indexing.

angle of view
The area that can be recorded by a lens, usually measured in degrees across the diagonal of the film frame. Angle of view depends on both the focal length of the lens and the size of its image area.

anti-aliasing
A technique that reduces or eliminates the jagged appearance of lines or edges in an image by filling in nearby pixels with intermediate values.

aperture
The opening in the lens that allows light to enter the camera. Aperture is usually described as an f/number. The higher the f/number, the smaller the aperture; the lower the f/number, the larger the aperture.

bit depth
The number of bits per pixel that determines the number of colors the image can display. Eight bits per pixel is the minimum requirement for a photo-quality color image.

buffer
Temporarily stores data so that other programs, on the camera or the computer, can continue to run while data is in transition. Also called a memory buffer.

card reader
A device that connects to your computer and enables the quick and easy download of images from memory card to computer.

CMOS
Complementary Metal-Oxide Semiconductor. Like CCD sensors, this sensor type converts light into an electrical impulse. Unlike CCDs, CMOS sensors allow individual processing of pixels, are less expensive to produce, and use less power. See also, CCD.

color cast
A colored hue over the image often caused by improper lighting or incorrect white balance settings. Can be produced intentionally for creative effect.

color space
A mapped relationship between colors and computer data about the colors.

compression
A method of reducing file size through removal of redundant data. Comes in two forms: lossy (i.e., JPEG) and lossless (i.e., TIFF).

contrast
The difference between two or more tones in terms of luminance, density, or darkness.

depth of field (DOF)
The image space in front of and behind the plane of focus that appears acceptably sharp in the photograph. Determined by aperture, focal length, and camera-to-subject distance.

EV
Exposure value. A number that quantifies the amount of light within a scene, allowing you to determine the relative combinations of aperture and shutter speed to accurately reproduce the light levels of that exposure.

firmware
Software that is permanently incorporated into a hardware chip. All computer-based equipment, including digital cameras, uses firmware of some kind.

focal length

When the lens is focused on infinity, it is the distance from the optical center of the lens to the film or sensor plane.

focal plane

The plane perpendicular to the axis of the lens that is the sharpest point of focus. Also, it may be the film plane or sensor plane.

FP High-Speed sync

Focal Plane high-speed sync. An FP mode in which the output of an electronic flash unit is pulsed to match the small opening of the shutter as it moves across the sensor, so that the flash unit can be used with higher shutter speeds than the normal flash sync limit of the camera. In this flash mode, the level of flash output is reduced and, consequently, the shooting range is reduced.

f/stop

The size of the aperture or diaphragm opening of a lens, also referred to as f/number or stop. The term stands for the ratio of the focal length (f) of the lens to the width of its aperture opening. (f/1.4 = wide opening, and f/22 = narrow opening.) Each stop up (lower f/number) doubles the amount of light reaching the sensitized medium. Each stop down (higher f/number) halves the amount of light reaching the sensitized medium.

gray card

A card used to take accurate exposure readings. It typically has a white side that reflects 90% of the light and a gray side that reflects 18%.

grayscale

A successive series of tones ranging between black and white, which have no color. Also, an image with purely luminance data and no chroma information.

guide number (GN)

A number used to quantify the output of a flash unit. It is derived by using this formula: GN = aperture x distance. Guide numbers are expressed for a given ISO film speed in either feet or meters.

histogram

A two-dimensional graphic representation of image tones. Histograms plot brightness along the horizontal axis and number of pixels along the vertical axis, and are useful for determining if an image will be under- or overexposed.

infinity

In photographic terms, the theoretical most distant point of focus.

ISO

From ISOS (Greek for equal), a term for industry standards from the International Organization for Standardization. When an ISO number is applied to film, it indicates the relative light sensitivity of the recording medium. Digital sensors use film ISO equivalents, which are based on enhancing the data stream or boosting the signal.

JPEG

Joint Photographic Experts Group. This is a lossy compression file format that works with any computer and photo software. JPEG examines an image for redundant information and then removes it. It is a variable compression format because the amount of leftover data depends on the detail in the photo and the amount of compression. At low compression/high quality, the loss of data has a negligible effect on the photo. However, JPEG should not be used as a working format—the file should be reopened and saved in a format such as TIFF, which does not compress the image.

latitude

The acceptable range of exposure (from under to over) determined by observed loss of image quality.

lithium-ion (Li-ion)

A popular battery technology that is not prone to the charge memory effects of nickel-cadmium (Ni-Cd) batteries, or the low temperature performance problems of alkaline batteries.

Manual exposure mode

A camera operating mode that requires the user to determine and set both the aperture and shutter speed. This is the opposite of automatic exposure.

middle grey

Halfway between black and white, it is an average gray tone with 18% reflectance. See also, gray card.

midtone

The tone that appears as medium brightness, or medium gray tone, in a photographic print.

overexposed

When too much light is recorded in the image, causing the photo to be too light in tone.

pan

Moving the camera to follow a moving subject. When a slow shutter speed is used, this creates an image in which the subject appears sharp and the background is blurred.

plugin

Third-party software created to augment an existing software program.

pre-flashes

A series of short duration, low intensity flash pulses emitted by a flash unit immediately prior to the shutter opening. These flashes help the TTL light meter assess the reflectivity of the subject. See also, TTL.

Program mode

In Program exposure mode, the camera selects a combination of shutter speed and aperture automatically.

RAW

An image file format that has little internal processing applied by the camera. It contains 12-bit color information, a wider range of data than 8-bit formats such as JPEG.

RAW+JPEG

An image file format that records two files per capture; one RAW file and one JPEG file.

rear-curtain sync

A feature that causes the flash unit to fire just prior to the shutter closing. It is used for creative effect when mixing flash and ambient light.

RGB mode

Red, Green, and Blue. This is the color model most commonly used to display color images on video systems, film recorders, and computer monitors. It displays all visible colors as combinations of red, green, and blue. RGB mode is the most common color mode for viewing and working with digital files onscreen.

S

See Shutter-priority mode.

saturation

The degree to which a color of fixed tone varies from the neutral, grey tone; low saturation produces pastel shades whereas high saturation gives pure color.

Shutter-priority mode

An automatic exposure mode in which you manually select the shutter speed and the camera automatically selects the aperture.

slow sync

A flash mode in which a slow shutter speed is used with the flash in order to allow low-level ambient light to be recorded by the sensitized medium.

synchronize

Causing a flash unit to fire simultaneously with the complete opening of the camera's shutter.

thumbnail

A small representation of an image file used principally for identification purposes.

TIFF

Tagged Image File Format. This popular digital format uses lossless compression.

TTL

Through-the-Lens, i.e., TTL metering. Any metering system – ambient exposure or flash – which works through the lens. Such systems require sensors built into the camera bodies with beam splitters to transfer incoming light to the sensor systems.

vignetting

A reduction in light at the edge of an image due to use of a filter or an inappropriate lens hood for the particular lens.

VR

Vibration Reduction. This technology is used in such photographic accessories as a VR lens and reduces camera shake and vibration.

Index

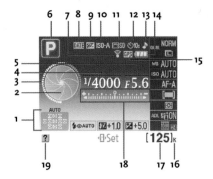

1. Auto-Area AF indicator / 3D Tracking indicator / Focus point selection
2. Aperture display
3. Shutter speed display
4. Shutter speed setting
5. Aperture setting (f/number)
6. Shooting mode
7. Eye-fi connection indicator
8. Date Imprint indicator
9. Manual flash / 🌣🖾 Flash Compensation indicator
10. Auto ISO indicator
11. Picture Control
12. Release mode
13. Beep indicator
14. Battery level indicator
15. GPS connection indicator
16. "K" indicates memory for over 1,000 exposures
17. Number of exposures remaining on card
18. Exposure / 🖾 Exposure Compensation indicator
19. Help

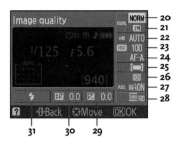

20. Image Quality
21. Image Size
22. **WB** White Balance
23. ISO setting
24. Focus mode
25. AF-Area mode
26. Metering mode
27. 🗄 Active D-Lighting
28. Movie frame size / frame rate
29. 🖾 Exposure Compensation
30. 🌣🖾 Flash Compensation
31. 🌣 Flash mode